Hiking North Carolina's
Blue Ridge Mountains

- Blue Ridge Parkway
- Grandfather Mountain
- Great
  Smoky Mountains
  National Park
- Hickory Nut Gorge
- Linville Gorge
- NC State Parks
- Pisgah National Forest

And much more

Danny Bernstein

almond, nc

Text copyright 2012 by Danny Bernstein
Maps copyright 2012 by Milestone Press, Inc.
All rights reserved
Second Printing June 2013

Milestone Press, PO Box 158, Almond, NC 28702

Book design by Denise Gibson/Design Den
www.designden.com

Front cover photo by Jim Parham; inset photo by Mary Ellen Hammond
Author photo by Lenny Bernstein
Interior photos by the author except as follows:
Bruce Bente p. 295; Ted Connors p. 289; Charles Hall p. 347; Mary Ellen
Hammond pp. 10, 20, 23, 262, 267, 346; Mack Prichard p. 169; Earl Weaver p. 142

Historical photographs appear courtesy of the following:
Chimney Rock State Park pp. 206 & 207; Cradle of Forestry p. 232; Evelyn
Underwood Collection, Southern Appalachian Archives, Mars Hill College, Mars
Hill, NC p. 161; Highlands Historical Society Archives, Highlands, NC pp. 320 & 321;
John's Market, Old Fort, NC & www.catawbafalls.com p. 197; The Loeb Family
p. 250;. Moses Cone Health System, Greensboro, NC p. 89;
NC Division of Parks and Recreation p. 50; The Woody Family p. 279

Library of Congress Cataloging-in-Publication Data

Bernstein, Danny, 1946-
  Hiking North Carolina's Blue Ridge Mountains : Blue Ridge Parkway, Great
Smoky Mountains National Park, Hickory Nut Gorge, Linville Gorge, NC
State Parks, Pisgah National forest and much more / Danny Bernstein.
     p. cm.
  Includes bibiographical references and index.
  ISBN 978-1-889596-27-3 (alk. paper)
  1. Hiking–North Carolina–Guidebooks. 2. Hiking–Blue Ridge Mountains–
Guidebooks. 3. North Carolina–Guidebooks. 4. Blue Ridge Mountains–
Guidebooks. I. Title.
  GV199.42.N662B584 2012
  917.56--dc23
                        2012003911

*This book is dedicated to the
Park Rangers and Forest Service
Rangers who walk, interpret,
and maintain our trails. Without
these devoted folks in uniform,
we'd have no place to hike.*

Acknowledgements

This book could not have been written without the help and advice of many people.

I want to express my appreciation to the following professionals who provided invaluable assistance: Lynda Doucette, Supervisory Park Ranger at Great Smoky Mountains National Park; Superintendent Edward Farr at Stone Mountain State Park; Pamela Ice-Williams, Information Receptionist at the Pisgah District of Pisgah National Forest; Tom Jackson, West District Superintendent for North Carolina State Parks; Mary Jaeger-Gale, General Manager at Chimney Rock Park; Ranger Tim Johnson at South Mountains State Park; Bob Miller, Public Affairs Officer at Great Smoky Mountains National Park; Superintendent Erik Nygard, formerly of Hanging Rock State Park and now North District Superintendent for the North Carolina Division of Parks and Recreation; Superintendent Steve Pagano at Gorges State Park; Ranger Janet Pearson at Pilot Mountain State Park; Ranger Nora McGrath at Lake James State Park; Ranger Katherine Scala, formerly of South Mountains State Park and now of Chimney Rock State Park; Ranger Debby Thomas at the Grandfather Mountain District of Pisgah National Forest; and Superintendent Randolph Thomas at Mt. Jefferson State Natural Area.

The reference librarians at Pack Memorial Library in Asheville were very generous with their time and expertise. I am grateful also to Zack Lesch-Huie and the staff of the Carolina Mountain Land Conservancy for providing guided hikes for CMLC members (of which I am one) on land not yet open to the public.

Friends and family, most of whom are members of the Carolina Mountain Club, hiked with me and provided many insights along the way. These include Bruce Bente, Lenny Bernstein, Neil Bernstein, Tom Bindrim, Ted Connors, Tish Desjardins, Stuart English, Charlie Ferguson, Jack Fitzgerald, Jean Gard, Bob Hillyer, Carroll Koepplinger, Ashok Kudva, Janet Martin, Sharon McCarthy, Jim Parham, Jim Reel, and Dave Wetmore. Without the help of the booksellers who carry my first guidebook, *Hiking the Carolina Mountains,* this book would not have been possible.

Thank you to Mary Ellen Hammond and Jim Parham, publishers at Milestone Press, whose skills, patience, warmth, and responsiveness make them a pleasure to work with.

And finally, thank you to my husband Lenny, who hiked with me, read my drafts, corrected my directions, commented on my photographs, and always encouraged me.

Contents

In Stone Mountain State Park, an old chimney still stands on Wolf Rock Loop.

Taking in a grand view from the trail on Grandfather Mountain.

Where To Find the Hikes

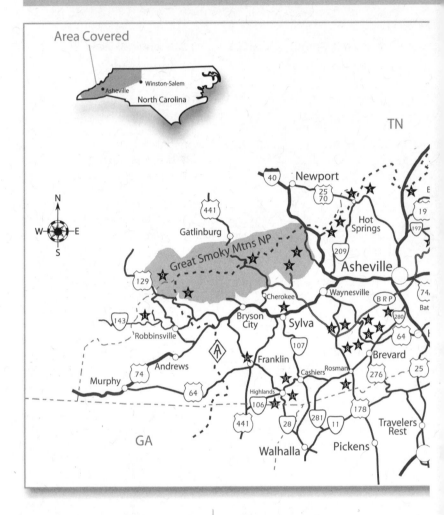

Area Covered

Winston-Salem
Asheville
North Carolina

TN

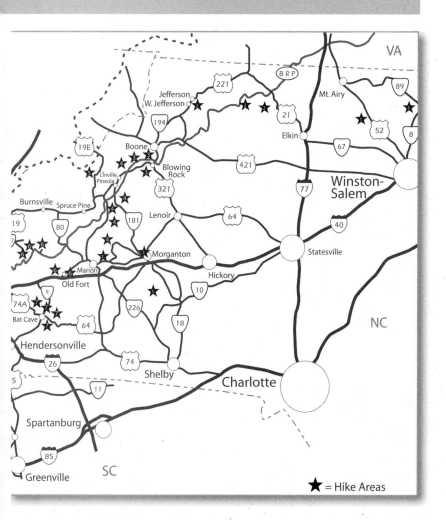

★ = Hike Areas

Introduction

Hiking alone one day in the Great Smoky Mountains National Park, I sat down on a log for lunch. I thought I saw a dog a couple of hundred feet up the trail. The animal and I stared at each other. I waited for its master to appear, but nobody came. Then it clicked. It wasn't a dog—it was a coyote! When I finished the hike, I stopped at the visitor center and confirmed the sighting with a ranger.

In western North Carolina, mountains are not only scenic; they actively shape the culture. Along with infinite opportunities to explore natural beauty and wildlife, our mountains offer historic places that few people get to see.

If you want to "get away from it all," just walk a couple of miles from your car, and you'll be on your own. On most trails you'll find solitude because few others venture beyond the main roads and visitor centers. You can take your time and stop to identify flowers or you can run through the woods—go at your own pace. You can have an adventure walking just a few miles. Even if the area isn't new to you, you'll find something different each time. I've hiked all the trails in this book several times, some many times, and each hike is a new experience because of the season, the weather, or the mood and attitude I bring to it.

Defining North Carolina's Blue Ridge

The mountains of western North Carolina are often called by

Resting on the trail.

different names: the Southern Appalachians, the Blue Ridge, or the Great Smokies. To identify them accurately, it is important to understand the geographic region in which they lie. The Appalachian Mountains run from their southern end in central Alabama northeast to Cape Breton Island in Canada. Within the Appalachians lies the Blue Ridge Province, which, according to George Ellison in his *Blue Ridge Nature Journal,* extends about 575 miles from the north Georgia hills to southwest of Harrisburg, Pennsylvania. In North Carolina, the Blue Ridge includes the Great Smokies along its western boundary and the Black Mountains on its eastern edge. The North Carolina Blue Ridge encompasses both the highest peaks and the greatest concentration of high mountains east of the Mississippi: 40 of them over 6,000 ft. The Piedmont, which means "foot of the mountain," begins at the Blue Ridge Escarpment where the mountains tumble abruptly into the lowlands.

Geology and Natural History

The Blue Ridge Mountains are among the oldest on earth. At an estimated age of 250 to 500 million years (depending on which authority you read), they're older than the Sierras and the Rockies. For millions of years, the land lifted, split, cracked, and folded to create these mountains. This gives the terrain the characteristic accordion-like parallel ridges that generally wend northeast to southwest. Over time, wind and water erosion created soft contours and rounded hills.

During the last Ice Age, which ended about 10,000 years ago, glaciers covered much of North America, but they never reached the Southern Appalachians. This has many implications for hikers. While the profile of a valley formed by a glacier is shaped like a broad U, running water cuts a V shape, which can be clearly seen in Linville Gorge and the many hollows and narrow valleys so common in the mountain landscape. Since there were no glaciers to gouge out depressions to hold standing water, we have no natural lakes in the Blue Ridge. All the lakes from Fontana

Lake to Lake James are artificial, created by impounding rivers for electricity and recreation.

Our mountains are wooded. The theoretical tree line in the Southern Appalachians is estimated at about 8,000 ft., but Mt. Mitchell, the highest mountain east of the Mississippi River, is only 6,684 ft. Though the mountains of the Blue Ridge are below timberline, they offer plenty of views from rocky outcroppings and balds.

The lack of glaciers also left us with soil, not rocks, underfoot. For hikers, this means easier trails than in the Northeast, with switchbacks instead of steep, rocky ascents. It also resulted in a diversity of plants and animals found nowhere else on earth. In the Northern Appalachians, as glacial ice advanced, it destroyed the vegetation in its way. Plants and trees that were common in those areas survived only south of the glaciers' range. Then, as temperatures rose, the range of those northern plants receded to niches in the high elevations of the Southern Appalachians. Thus the mountains became a refuge for many species of plants and animals that were dislodged from their northern homes.

More than 75 percent of all medicinal plants known to grow in the United States are found in the Southern Appalachians. Botanists call this area the seed cradle of the continent because after the last Ice Age, North America was reseeded from these plants. Above 4,000 ft., the vegetation of the northeastern and southeastern United States meet and intermingle.

As you climb in the Blue Ridge, the average annual temperature drops about one degree for every 250-ft. increase in elevation. Another way to look at it is that in terms of habitat, every 1,000 ft. of elevation is equivalent to 250 miles in latitude. So the equivalent of traveling from the Catawba River Greenway at 1,050 ft. elev. to Mt. Mitchell at 6,684 ft. elev. (the altitude range of the hikes in this book) would put you about 1,400 miles north of North Carolina—into central Quebec Province in Canada.

A Unique Heritage

North Carolina's Blue Ridge is not untouched wilderness; humans have been living here for thousands of years. When European settlers came to these mountains in the 1700s, they found Cherokees and other Indians already here. Pioneer families came from Pennsylvania on the Great Wagon Road and from the Carolina coast. They built cabins in the bottomlands close to creeks and formed small, self-sufficient communities. Poor or nonexistent roads in the mountains prevented the development of large urban centers.

Botanists and explorers were also attracted to this fascinating land. André Michaux from France; John and William Bartram from Pennsylvania; Elisha Mitchell from eastern North Carolina; and Arnold Guyot, originally from Switzerland, came to measure the mountains and catalog their diverse plants and animals.

The Chimneys is a distinctive landmark in the High Country.

Unlike those of us who hike today, early explorers did not have the network of trails and roads to get to the trailhead; many times they had to start their climbs from much lower and bushwhack up through thick vegetation. Today we're reminded of these explorers every time we look at a map or book about the area and see the names of mountains—Mt. Guyot and Mt. Mitchell are prominent peaks. William Bartram is as famous for his literary work, known today as *The Travels of William Bartram*, as he is for the botanical discoveries it catalogs. His *Travels* was one of the first in a long line of literary works inspired by this region, either by visitors from outside or those who were native to the Blue Ridge.

In the 19th century, wealthy settlers bought land from local residents to build chateaus and manor houses. They eventually sold or donated much of their holdings to the federal or state government, which turned them into parks and forests. George Vanderbilt, who in 1895 opened his Biltmore Estate, owned property from Asheville to west of present-day US Hwy. 276; this became the basis for Pisgah National Forest. Vanderbilt hired forestry pioneers Gifford Pinchot and Carl Schenck to develop and protect his forests; you can learn that history by visiting the family-friendly Cradle of Forestry. Until 2007, the Morse family, originally from St. Louis, owned and operated

A cool fern glade on Wilson Creek

the private Chimney Rock Park; the land then was bought by the state of North Carolina and turned into a state park. Farther north near Boone, properties of wealthy entrepreneur Moses Cone and insurance executive Julian Price became part of the Blue Ridge Parkway.

Grandfather Mountain had always been a privately owned commercial operation until the fall of 2008, when the State of North Carolina announced it had agreed to purchase it from the Morton family for $12 million. The 2,601-acre undeveloped portion, where the rugged and blazed trails are well-maintained, became North Carolina's 34th state park. The remaining 604 acres, including the famous Mile-

High Swinging Bridge, is now operated by a non-profit entity managed by the Morton family.

In 1904 Horace Kephart, a librarian from St. Louis, moved to the Smokies and wrote *Our Southern Highlanders* about the mountain people, and worked with George Masa, who photographed the mountains between 1918 and 1933. Both men are credited with helping to create the political climate needed to establish the Great Smoky Mountains National Park.

Today, the Blue Ridge is home to four national park units—Great Smoky Mountains National Park, Blue Ridge Parkway, Carl Sandburg Home National Historic Site, and Overmountain Victory National Historic Trail—along with Pisgah and Nantahala National Forests.

In winter, South Mountains State Park's High Shoals Falls is an icy cascade.

Several state parks also provide excellent hiking opportunities. In the Blue Ridge, the Appalachian Trail (its full name is the Appalachian National Scenic Trail) runs through the Smokies and the two national forests. The A.T. was designated as the first national scenic trail when the National Trails System Act was created in 1968. For half the population of the United States, all of these forests, parks, and trails are within a day's drive.

North Carolina has its own long-distance trail, the Mountains-to-Sea Trail (officially a state park), which runs a thousand miles from Clingmans Dome in the Great Smoky Mountains National Park to Jockey's Ridge on the Outer Banks. Today, more than 500 miles of footpath have been built, including almost all the sections in the Blue Ridge Mountains.

These mountains are steeped in fascinating history and culture. Hikes here will take you past old cabins, stone walls, chimneys, and cemeteries. Some trails follow the contour of old railroad grades that still have spikes embedded in the ground. Traveling on foot gives you a better understanding of the people who lived here before it became public land. Unlike national parks and forests in the American West, which were carved out of land already owned by the government, public land in the Southern Appalachians was bought from logging companies and families.

Many descendants of those families still live in the area.

Numerous novels about the North Carolina mountains tell the stories of families and individuals who lived here. From Wayne Caldwell's *Cataloochee,* which recounts the lives of several generations in what is now the Great Smoky Mountains National Park, to Lee Smith's *On Agate Hill,* set partly in West Jefferson, about a young, independent-minded woman growing up in the immediate aftermath of the Civil War, they all reflect the relationship between these mountains and their human inhabitants. In the back of this book you'll find a list of fiction and nonfiction works about this area, along with a list of movies filmed here.

The Blue Ridge National Heritage Area

This hiking guide covers a region that has been officially designated the Blue Ridge National Heritage Area. In North Carolina, this area is shaped like a triangle, the three points of which are Hanging Rock State Park north of Winston-Salem, Highlands in Macon County, and the Great Smoky Mountains National Park. In 2003, Congress recognized the unique character, culture, and natural beauty of western North Carolina and its significance to the history of our nation. The Blue Ridge National Heritage Area aims to "protect, preserve, interpret, and develop the unique natural, historical, and cultural resources of western North Carolina for the benefit of present and future generations, and in so doing to stimulate improved economic opportunity in the region."

There is much to see and do in the North Carolina Blue Ridge; music, crafts, cuisine, architecture, and native culture are all prominent, interconnected aspects of the area's heritage. However, visitors to this region who miss the opportunity to get outdoors and travel on a footpath through the landscape miss a critical piece of the whole picture. The mountains are literally the foundation of Blue Ridge heritage, and today we have the great good fortune to have public land and trails available that allow us to experience them firsthand.

The day hikes in this book, designed to help you enjoy these mountains, can give you a new outlook on life and a new way to think about the past. For example, after you've huffed and puffed to reach the summit of Rich Mountain in the Hot Springs area, climb the tower for an incredible 360-degree view. Walk the pristine carriage roads of Moses H. Cone Memorial Park, then visit the manor house, now a museum and part of the Blue Ridge Parkway. Hike up to Hump Mountain for outstanding views of Virginia to the north and Grandfather Mountain to the south, then walk a piece of the Overmountain Victory National Historic Trail, where Revolutionary War patriots marched on their way to the Battle of Kings Mountain.

Hiking is about adventure and discovery. It's not a competitive sport; there's no need to hike faster or longer than others. However, hiking "challenges" do encourage you to walk all the mountains or trails in a given region, and they offer the opportunity to explore that region on foot as completely as possible. Writing this book inspired me to create the Heritage Hiking Challenge: a list of 30 hikes that show off the varied outdoor history of the North Carolina Blue Ridge. You'll find the challenge list in the back of this book.

Hiking in the Blue Ridge

People often ask, "What's the best season to hike?" In the Blue Ridge, the answer is, every season. Spring brings wildflowers in great profusion and a delightful range of color. White bloodroot and star chickweed in early March signal the end of winter. Fields of trillium line the trails in midspring. You may find pink lady slippers or even a lone yellow lady slipper. Later in the season rhododendron, mountain laurel, and flame azalea, our mountain Triple Crown winners, take over.

In summer, as you climb higher, cool mountain breezes along high ridges give you that top-of-the-world feeling. Purple Catawba rhododendrons bloom at the highest altitudes. You can cool off by walking through shallow streams (keep your boots on to protect your feet) or wading in pools. Longer days allow you to hike farther. Summer's jewelweed, spiderwort, and bee balm blossoms are easy to identify.

For many hikers, autumn is the favorite hiking season, with cooler temperatures and drier days. The yellows, reds, and oranges of the changing foliage are so vibrant that it sometimes seems as if the color will come off on your hand when you touch a leaf. Fall attracts touring motorists looking at the mountains, but as a hiker, you'll be *in* the mountains. Asters, the last of the autumn flowers, hang on well after the first frost.

Mild winters in the Blue Ridge allow for comfortable hiking, particularly at lower altitudes. In winter the leaves have fallen, even fewer people are on the trails, the air is crisp and clear, and insects have long since disappeared. Winter is not the time to put away your hiking boots. Instead, pull out your fleece jacket, pull on gloves and a hat, and get outside. You will be rewarded with winter views of mountain ridges above and valleys and gorges below, scenes that in other seasons may be hidden by foliage. Snow reveals animal tracks you would never see otherwise. Rime ice coating thin branches creates a surreal wonderland of shapes.

National Parks, National Forests, Wilderness Areas, and Land Conservancies

In western North Carolina, we're blessed with an enormous amount of public land in our

Linville Gorge's Hawksbill Mountain as seen from Wiseman's View.

national and state parks and forests. And while they may all seem alike on the surface, there are vast differences in the philosophy behind each place, the way they are managed, and how that affects your hiking experience. You can't hike with your dog in the Great Smoky Mountains National Park. In Linville Gorge Wilderness, your hiking group can't be larger than 10 people. Mountain bikes whiz past you in Moses H. Cone Memorial Park. Why is each place so different, and who makes the rules, anyway?

National parks, which in this region include the Great Smoky Mountains National Park, Blue Ridge Parkway, Carl Sandburg Home National Historic Site, and Overmountain Victory National Historic Trail, were meant to preserve and restore land to wilderness and maintain historic structures and sites. The National Park System Organic Act, which created the National Park Service, cites that the "fundamental purpose of the parks is ... to provide for the enjoyment [of scenery, natural and historic objects, and wildlife]... in such manner and by such means as will leave them unimpaired for the enjoyment of future generations."

In national parks it is illegal to hunt, gather plants, or mountain bike on the trails. But beyond these rules, national parks focus on recreation. They have more extensive facilities, better maintained trails, and generally are more user-friendly than national forests. Their backcountry campsites even have bear poles to hang packs on, so bears can't get to your food.

National forests, operated by the Forest Service under the Department of Agriculture, stress conservation, the careful utilization of a natural resource to prevent depletion. In practice, that means hunting is allowed, along with logging by timber companies, road building, plant-gathering by permit, mountain biking, and even all-terrain vehicles. Recreation is only one of several missions.

And then there are wilderness areas. The very word "wilderness" evokes awe and perhaps even a bit of fear, since venturing into wilderness means encountering the unknown. Our wilderness areas, ravaged over the centuries by logging, fire, and exotic insects, are among the favorite hiking areas in the Southeast. Each wilderness area is created by an act of Congress and comes with its own set of rules. Old roads are now gated. Logging is not permitted, and only hand tools can be used to maintain trails. Because it's more difficult to saw a large blowdown with a handsaw than with a chainsaw, you may have to go around a downed tree. Trails aren't blazed, which leads to a maze of "social trails" pounded bare by hikers trying to find the real trail.

North Carolina's state parks and forests are both overseen by the North Carolina Department of Environmental and Natural Resources, but the parks are quite distinct from the forests. For example, Mt. Mitchell State Park is surrounded by Pisgah National Forest land. In Mt. Mitchell State Park, you can buy a snack or a book and even sit down for a restaurant meal, and trails are manicured and well-marked. As you follow the trails into Pisgah National Forest, they become rugged, with few blazes.

Most state parks have operating hours and shut their gates after hours. Because Mt. Mitchell State Park is surrounded by a national forest, it's an exception to that rule. Like Mt. Mitchell, most state parks are very well maintained. They don't allow hunting, and they emphasize "soft" recreation like swimming and car camping. And unlike our neighboring states, most of North Carolina's state parks don't charge an entrance fee.

Land conservancies are nonprofit, private organizations which protect land from further development. The Nature Conservancy may be the best known, but in western North Carolina there are several other active local conservancies. Some conservancy lands are open to the hiking public; to visit others you must go on a guided hike led by conservancy members. Consider becoming a member of a land conservancy when you go on their hikes.

How to Use This Guide

The Appalachian Mountains run northeast to southwest. In this book the hikes are organized by area in the same direction, from Stokes County north of Winston-Salem to the southwestern corner of North Carolina. All the hikes within a geographical entity, such the Great Smoky Mountains National Park, are listed together.

Information at the beginning of each group of hikes includes:

Rules/Fees/Facilities: Pets on the trail, wilderness area rules, entrance fees, visitor centers, if any.

Closest town: Helpful if you are looking for a meal or lodging after the hike.

Website: Official website, if one exists.

Books and movies about the area: Novels and movies set in the area. Also movies filmed in the area, even if the story is set in a different place.

Hike Details at a Glance

Type of hike:

Loop – A closed figure that is walked without retracing your steps.

Out and back – Walking to a certain point and returning the same way.

Shuttle – A one-way hike starting and ending at different places. To organize a shuttle hike, drive all the cars to the end point and leave half the cars there. All hikers then get in the remaining vehicles and drive to the starting point to begin the hike.

Distance: The hike distance is the total distance of the hike as described, including any side

A good trail map is an essential piece of equipment for any hike.

trips. This distance was measured with a GPS. In determining overall hike difficulty, many hikers look at distance first.

Total ascent/descent: Total vertical rise and descent, over the whole day, whether in one uphill stretch or over many ups and downs, measured with a GPS. Except for shuttle hikes, the total descent is the same as the ascent. When hikers label a hike "easy," "moderate," or "strenuous," they are referring to their perception of total ascent. This book provides an actual number, rounded to the nearest 50 ft.

Starting elevation: Elevation at the trailhead helps you decide if the hike is right for the weather. Hike from Mt. Mitchell (6,684 ft. elev.) in the winter only if you are prepared for a full winter experience—if you can even get to the trailhead. Conversely, you might want to skip Morganton's Catawba River Greenway (1,050 ft. elev.) on a hot summer day.

Highlights: What you can expect to experience on the hike, for example views, waterfall, cabin, artifacts, rock formations, wildflowers.

Topographic map: The 7.5-minute quadrangle topographic ("topo") map on which the hike can be found. Topo maps are often available at local outfitter stores, and can be ordered from the U.S. Geological Survey (www.store.usgs.gov).

Returning to Black Balsam on Little Sam Trail in Pisgah National Forest.

Trail map: The official trail map for each hike. You can buy most trail maps in outdoor stores or on the web, but some are only available at the visitor center. Trail numbers in this guide correspond to those on trail maps, if available.

Land managed by: For example, Great Smoky Mountains National Park, Grandfather Mountain, Pisgah National Forest.

Getting to the trailhead: Directions to the trailhead are described from a North Carolina road map.

Maps

Each hike entry has two maps. The small map shows you the roads that will get you to the trailhead; you may not always find these roads on a state road map. The larger map shows the hiking route. Although you may want to look at the official trail map as well, this one should be sufficient.

Rating Hike Difficulty

The hikes are not rated by difficulty because such rating is so subjective. Instead, I've listed distance, total ascent, and a description of the terrain. Considered as a whole, these indicate the difficulty of the hike. Within a hike description, steep sections are noted.

Trail Directions

Directions on the Appalachian Trail (A.T.) always go trail north toward Maine or trail south toward Georgia, independent of compass directions in any one spot. Similarly, the Mountains-to-Sea Trail (MST) is an east-west trail which starts at Clingmans Dome on the Tennessee border and proceeds east to the North Carolina coast.

The Blue Ridge Parkway is a north-south road, from Shenandoah National Park in Virginia to the entrance of the Great Smoky Mountains National Park at Oconaluftee.

There's No Time Like the Present

If you've always thought you'd like to try hiking, don't wait until the weather gets better, you finish school, you lose 10 pounds, your kids are older, or you retire. We're not talking about climbing Mt. Everest. Though you'll exert some effort and may break a sweat

as you climb those hills, it's not all that difficult; you just need perseverance. In the words of Grandma Gatewood, who at age 67 became the first woman to hike the whole A.T., "It takes more heart than heel." A healthy person can walk six to eight miles a day and enjoy it. The reward is feeling good, feeling confident, feeling powerful, and having a sense of self-actualization that you can't get in town. So get out and hike—there's no better place than the North Carolina Blue Ridge.

Your Comments Requested

After my first guidebook *Hiking the Carolina Mountains* was published, I received many comments on what I had left out and should include in my next book. Meeting readers and fellow hikers, whether on the trail or via email, is one of the joys of writing a hiking guide. If you have questions, corrections, or just want to give me your reaction to this book, I want to hear from you; please visit me at www.hikertohiker.com.

1

Before the Blue Ridge

I propose to create a Civilian Conservation Corps to be used in simple work, not interfering with normal employment, and confining itself to forestry, the prevention of soil erosion, flood control, and similar projects.

— Franklin D. Roosevelt, in a message to Congress, 1933

Hanging Rock State Park

Essential Facts

Rules/Facilities:
Pets must be leashed.
Visitor center, camping,
cabins, lake.
Closest town:
Winston-Salem
Website:
www.ncparks.gov

Pilot Mountain State Park

Essential Facts

Rules/Facilities:
Pets must be leashed.
Information center,
camping, picnic area.

Closest town:
Winston-Salem
Website:
www.ncparks.gov

Hanging Rock State Park and Pilot Mountain State Park are in the Sauratown Mountains, the easternmost mountain range in North Carolina. Because these mountains are surrounded by valleys 800 ft. in elevation, they're not considered part of the Blue Ridge and are sometimes referred to as "the mountains away from the mountains." The two parks are connected by the Sauratown Trail, a 35-mile section of the Mountains-to-Sea Trail. Their exposed cliffs and rocky knobs rise 1,500 ft. out of the valley and can be seen for miles around.

The Sauratown Mountains were named for the Saura Indians who settled along the Dan River, near the northern section of Hanging Rock State Park. By the late 18th century, long after the Saura Indians disappeared, the area developed a small iron industry. But it was a sparsely populated area because the land was not suitable for farming.

A 1930 map shows that the park area still didn't have any roads. In 1936, the philanthropic

Pilot Mountain State Park   Hanging Rock State Park

★★ Winston-Salem

Asheville

North Carolina

Hanging out on Hanging Rock.

Winston-Salem Foundation sold property to the State of North Carolina for $10 with the stipulation that it become a park. The Civilian Conservation Corps (CCC) then essentially created the park as we know it today. They built the access road, dammed Cascade Creek to form the lake, and constructed the parking lots and the stone bathhouse. Hanging Rock State Park was formally opened in 1944 and the CCC camp was converted into a group camping area.

As in all state parks, trails in Hanging Rock State Park are meticulously maintained. Each trail blaze has not only a color but also an individual number for emergency purposes. It's a popular park with good facilities, close to the Winston-Salem, Greensboro, and High Point Triad. Besides a well-appointed campground, it offers vacation cabins which outrank many private cabins in their amenities. The cabins were designed for families who spend their vacations there. Even today, in the summer you can rent these cabins only by the week. Bring your own food, linens, and dishwashing soap. With a living room, furnished kitchen, bathroom, and screened-in porch, you may want to move in. There's a lake with a sand beach where you can swim, fish, or rent a boat—the park is almost a resort.

Hanging Rock Trail is the most popular trail in the park because the short walk leads to outstanding views. After enjoying the panorama, leave the crowds and continue to Wolf Rock and Cook's Wall, where you'll discover new views of Sauratown Valley and majestic Big Pinnacle in Pilot Mountain State Park.

Type of hike: Loop

Distance: 7.5 miles

Total ascent: 1,500 ft.

Starting elevation: 1,750 ft.

Highlights: Views, rock formations

USGS map: Hanging Rock

Trail map: Available at the visitor center

Land managed by: Hanging Rock State Park

Getting to the trailhead: From Winston-Salem, take US 52N to exit 114/NC 8 north. After 23.5 miles, turn left on Hanging Rock Rd. (SR 2015). Drive 1.7 miles to the park entrance. Once in the park, make a left at the four-way intersection toward the visitor center and Hanging Rock Trail.

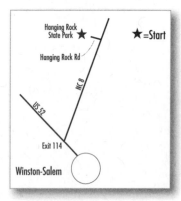

Trailhead GPS Coordinates: N 36° 23.71 W 80° 15.91

The Hike

The trailhead for Hanging Rock Trail [red circle blazes] is in the first parking area on the right before you reach the visitor center building. Follow a paved path in a forest of pine, oak, and maple with benches along the trail. The pavement soon ends; continue on a wide unpaved road. Pass the intersection with Wolf Rock Loop Trail on your right at 0.5 mile; you'll come back here after going up Hanging Rock. The trail soon ascends on solid wooden steps. You'll reach the first view of the rock overhead as the trail goes down and right. Don't climb the rocks; you'll be on top soon. The trail goes under a rocky overhang and starts a serious climb through mountain laurel, white pine, and American holly.

At 1.2 miles, you'll reach the top of Hanging Rock but not yet the views. The trail turns left and climbs gently for another 0.1 mile to a bifurcated rock at 2,150 ft. elev. Each end of the forked rock, peppered with table mountain pine (these are small trees, shaped by the wind, with spiny cones), sticks out into space and offers tremendous views of the valleys below. Looking west, you'll see Moore's Knob and may be able to make out the observation tower on top. In the distance to the northwest, the chain of mountains you see is the Blue Ridge. Retrace your steps and at 2.0 miles make a left on Wolf Rock Loop Trail [blue triangle blazes].

The trail switchbacks gently upward through mountain laurel in an oak and maple forest and soon flattens out. You will have left the crowds behind, except for a few mountain joggers. To your left will be obstructed southeastern views. As the trail turns to the right, continue straight on to Wolf Rock at 2,000 ft. with great southern views into the valley, including the Winston-Salem skyline.

Return to Wolf Rock Loop Trail as it turns right, keeping the views to your left. At 3.1 miles, continue straight on Cook's Wall Trail [white diamond blazes]. Wolf Rock Loop Trail turns right; you'll come back to this point after you visit House Rock and Cook's Wall. Here, the signpost says "House Rock 0.7, Cook's Wall 1.5."

Continue on the ridge and you'll soon reach an intersection with a connecting trail on the right, leading to Moore's Wall (see Moore's Wall Loop hike, p. 29). Stay straight and turn left at 3.8 miles to House Rock, a group of huge topsy-turvy boulders with a flat top, again with tremendous southern views. Looking north, you can see Moore's

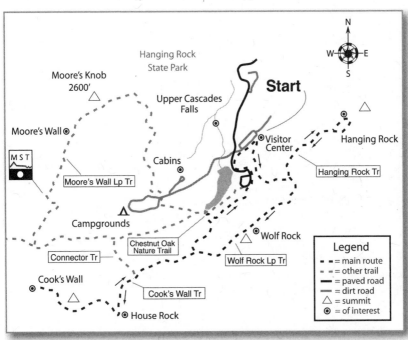

Knob. Turn back to the main trail and continue left toward Cook's Wall. At 4.0 miles, the rocky trail starts climbing more steeply through the woods. Come around a boulder on your right as the trail flattens. You may feel as if you somehow missed the top because you're still in the woods as the trail descends. In a half-mile, the trail opens up into a field where you may see tiny lizards scampering under rocks.

At a rocky outcropping with a 180-degree panorama, you're very close to the end of the trail, but this point has better views and a wider area to sit down for a snack break, so now is the time for that. Down below to

Seen from below, Hanging Rock appears to be a giant tower of stone.

your right is the wedding-cake top of Big Pinnacle, the high peak in neighboring Pilot Mountain State Park.

You'll reach the end of the trail at 4.7 miles (2,400 ft. elev.) on a rock outcropping where turkey vultures glide past. Return on Cook's Wall Trail to the intersection with Wolf Rock Loop Trail. Take time now to stop at any rock you want to look at more closely, because soon you'll be leaving the ridge.

At 6.2 miles (2,000 ft. elev.), turn left on Wolf Rock Loop Trail, which descends gently and then steeply on red clay through the woods. (Some hikers climb up from the lake, a difficult ascent.) At the intersection with Cook's Wall Trail on the left, stay right on Wolf Rock Loop Trail, which here runs concurrently with Chestnut Oak Nature Trail, marked by numbers on wooden posts. The trail descends gently, reaches the back of the bathhouse at 6.8 miles, and makes a right to go up a gravel road. At the covered picnic shelter and restrooms, turn left in the parking lot and walk the road. Beyond the lake, take the footpath on your right. The path ends at the edge of the visitor center parking area and so does the hike.

Variation: To Hanging Rock Trail and back—2.6 miles with 700 ft. ascent.

Moore's Wall Loop

2

Moore's Wall Loop, taken counterclockwise, goes from Cascade Lake at the base of the wall to the observation tower on top of Moore's Knob. The Mountains-to-Sea Trail uses part of Moore's Wall Loop Trail as it goes from the Sauratown Trail and traverses the park. The views from the top of the observation tower are outstanding, encompassing Winston-Salem skyscrapers, Pilot Mountain, and the Blue Ridge. You may see geese by the lake or an occasional deer on the trail.

Type of hike: Loop

Distance: 4.8 miles

Total ascent: 1,900 ft.

Starting elevation: 1,800 ft.

Highlights: Views, rock formations, lake

USGS map: Hanging Rock

Trail map: Available at the visitor center

Land managed by:
Hanging Rock State Park

Getting to the trailhead:
From Winston-Salem, take US 52N to exit 114/NC 8 north. After 23.5 miles, turn left on Hanging Rock Rd. (SR 2015). The entrance to the park is in 1.7 miles. In the park, follow signs to the lake and bathhouse.

Trailhead GPS Coordinates:
N 36° 23.44 W 80° 16.02

The trail starts at the far corner of the lake parking area.

The Hike
Moore's Wall Loop Trail [red circle blazes] starts at the corner of the parking area closest to the bathhouse and picnic area. Follow signs for Moore's Knob and Cook's Wall Trails. At the edge of the bathhouse, make a left at an information board. The trail takes you to the back of the bathhouse. At the fork, make a right which is also Chestnut Oak Nature Trail, heading to the southwestern edge of the lake. Some of this stretch is a boardwalk, to keep you out of the mud and protect the trail.

When Moore's Wall Loop Trail leaves the lake and the Nature Trail, it climbs gently, turns right, and crosses a creek on a bridge flowing into the lake. At 0.4 mile you'll pass a sign listing several trails including Moore's Wall Loop Trail. You may be surprised to learn that the park considers these trails "long distance," since one is less than two miles. Stay left; this is where you'll come back to close the loop.

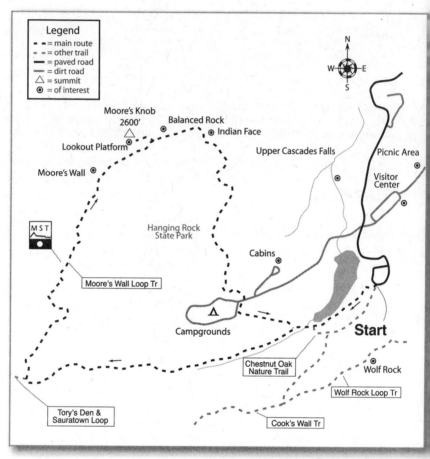

The flat trail leads through mountain laurel and rhododendron under a canopy of maple and oak. At 1.0 mile, where the trail splits, make a right where the sign says "Moore's Knob 1.7 miles." The trail starts climbing and passes turtleback-shaped boulders. Take another right at the intersection with Tory's Den and Sauratown Loop where the trail joins the MST (though you may have been seeing its white circle blazes for a while).

The trail climbs steadily on a rocky path through the forest with sassafras, oak, maple, and straight pitch pines—medium-sized trees with thick, deeply furrowed bark.

At 2.2 miles (2,400 ft. elev.) you'll reach the ridge where the trail is flat but rocky, with obstructed views out to the left. When the trail starts down, you may feel as if you've missed something until you look up through the woods to see the knob and the observation tower ahead. The trail climbs up to the ridge and wiggles between two huge boulders. You'll arrive at a massive rock wall with an outcropping that looks like a finger pointing out in space. The trail makes a sharp right at a sign reading "Moore's Wall Trail. Follow red markers."

At the intersection with the side trail to the observation tower, make a left on solid rock steps. At 3.0 miles (2,600 ft. elev.) you'll reach the tower. Stairs take you up to 360-degree views from the observation platform at the top; this was formerly a fire tower, and has a room below the observation deck. Looking southeast, you'll see the Winston-Salem skyline in a sea of flat, green land. To the northwest is the prominent top of Pilot Mountain. Way out west is the Blue Ridge. Most of the land in the valley is forested with only a few houses in sight.

Go back to the intersection with the Moore's Wall Loop Trail

Rock steps climb the trail to the observation tower and 360-degree views.

and continue straight on wide rock steps. The new trail work, done by a professional trail-building company, cost $80,000. Gravel and pebbles have been placed on flatter sections of trail to prevent erosion; it's a beautiful piece of trail. Cross a creek on boulders at 4.0 miles. Go up the steps where the trail turns sharply left and passes behind the campground amphitheater; you'll see tents and trailers to your right. Cross the campground road, make a right, and walk the road following red circle blazes on the trees. The trail turns left between campsites 39 and 40 with a sign for "Moore's Wall Loop Trailhead Lake Access." The trail descends steeply on a set of steps and turns right. Follow the circles and you've closed the loop. Make a left to retrace your steps to the bathhouse and then a right to your car to end the hike.

This hike proves that it's not just absolute altitude that counts; it's the difference in altitude between the mountain and the valley floor. The hike loops the park counterclockwise and goes up to Little Pinnacle and Big Pinnacle, both with outstanding views. Big Pinnacle is the highest point of Pilot Mountain; its wedding-cake top can be seen for miles, including from Hanging Rock State Park. Though you can't walk to the top of Big Pinnacle, you can encircle it. As you traverse Little Pinnacle, you're practically within kissing distance of the rock formations. After this hike, you'll understand why Pilot Mountain was named a Registered Natural Landmark in 1975. If you have a second car, leave it at the visitor center to save yourself almost a mile of road walking.

Rules/Facilities: Pets must be leashed. Information center, camping, picnic area.

Closest town: Winston-Salem

Website: www.ncparks.gov

Type of hike: Loop

Distance: 8.5 miles

Total ascent: 2,000 ft.

Starting elevation: 1,450 ft.

Highlights: Rock formations, views

USGS map: Pinnacle

Trail map: Available at the visitor center

Land managed by: Pilot Mountain State Park

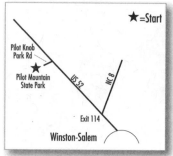

★=Start

Pilot Knob Park Rd

Pilot Mountain State Park

US 52

NC 8

Exit 114

Winston-Salem

Trailhead GPS Coordinates: N 36° 20.88 W 80° 28.39

Getting to the trailhead: From Winston-Salem, take US 52 for 24.0 miles north to the Pilot Mountain State Park exit. Make a left off the exit ramp on Pilot Knob Park Rd. (SR 2053) and after 0.3 mile, a left at the park sign. After 0.5 mile, turn right toward the campground; it's another 0.7 mile to the trailhead. The trailhead is between campsites 16 and 17. You can park on the grass, making sure that you don't block any campsites. When the campground area is closed, park at the rock building (the old information center and ranger station) on the left of the main park road just before turning onto the campground road.

The Hike

Grindstone Trail [blue circle blazes], which starts on your left between campsites 16 and 17, climbs and turns right almost immediately. It's a well-maintained gentle trail through maple and oak trees with winter views north into the valley toward Mt. Airy. Cross a dirt road where an arrow points up to keep you on the trail. The trail has been well placed between interesting boulders where you'll cross several old roads. At 0.8 mile, the trail makes a right on a road. At the Y intersection, stay left. Here the trail is marked with blue and yellow circles. Toward the top, you'll pass a sign on the right for Three Bears Gully, three rock formations which you'll access more easily on Ledge Spring Trail. At 1.6 miles (2,100 ft. elev.), at the end of Grindstone Trail, turn left on Ledge Spring Trail [yellow circle blazes] and go

up a wide, smooth path with a wooden fence on your right. Signs urge you to stay on the trail. Pass the picnic area with a group picnic shelter on your left, continuing to the upper parking lot with bathrooms and water. Most visitors park here to walk several short trails leading to the views.

Stay right toward the fence to catch all the outstanding viewpoints and don't get distracted by the parking area. The first overlook, at the extreme south point of the parking lot and well appointed with two stone

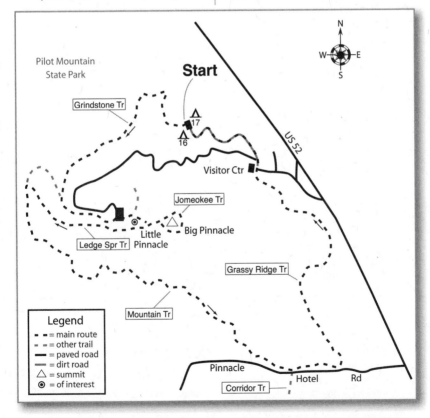

The 200-ft. flat knob of Big Pinnacle gives it a wedding-cake shaped top.

benches, looks south into the Yadkin Valley. Continue on the paved path hugging the fence on your right. You won't come back to the parking area, so take it all in now.

Make the first right away from the parking lot where there are several more lookouts. Continuing counterclockwise, go right on a side trail to Little Pinnacle Overlook for the best view of Big Pinnacle. To the left of Big Pinnacle in the distance are the cliffs of Hanging Rock. You're at 2,300 ft. elev., the highest point on the trail.

Return and continue right to take Jomeokee Trail, a 0.8-mile loop, which circles Big Pinnacle. Go down stone steps and on your right pass the junction to Ledge Spring Trail, which you'll pick up after you've made the circuit. Stay left and go up stone steps to take the loop clockwise. Fractured rocky columns are fringed with table mountain pine at every level. You'll go under ledges where water constantly drips from higher up. In the winter, sounds of civilization in the valley to the northwest drift up from below. During the school year, this short loop is a favorite for school groups.

At the end of the loop, make a left and very soon a second left on Ledge Spring Trail at 2.7 miles (2,200 ft. elev.). This puts you under Little Pinnacle Overlook. The trail climbs on good stone steps to hug Little Pinnacle, with marvelous views to the right (southwest) down the valley. This rocky trail then descends more steeply, moving away from Little Pinnacle.

Going west on Ledge Spring Trail, you'll pass overhead ledges forming open caves. The trail continues to hug boulders as you descend on good rock steps. At 3.3 miles, the trail turns sharply left and down. At the bottom of Ledge Spring Trail, where a spring comes out of a sidehill, you'll leave Little Pinnacle.

When Ledge Spring Trail turns into a wide road and heads right to loop back toward the parking lot, turn left on Mountain Trail [red circle blazes] at 3.5 miles (1,650 ft. elev.) and descend rock steps into an oak and maple forest. The trail has some interesting boulders but after what you've already seen on this hike, you may not be impressed. It also has plenty of short uphill stretches, curving around coves, and dips, but overall the direction is down.

In a half-mile, you'll leave most of the rocks and drips to walk on a dry hillside frequented by white-tailed deer. At 4.3 miles, you'll pass a sign pointing up to "summit" and down to "corridor"; continue down. If the weather is wet, you may see toads and even a turtle. The first sign of civilization toward the bottom of Mountain Trail is a treehouse on the right. The trail zigzags sharply down to the right then follows along the backs of several houses.

You'll come out on Pinnacle Hotel Rd. (SR 2061) at 5.9 miles (1,100 ft. elev.) and make a left. Across the road on Culler Rd. (SR 2063), the 6.6-mile Corridor Trail leads to the river section of the park. After a few hundred feet, turn left off the road and head back into the woods on Grassy Ridge Trail [white blazes], also a horse trail. The trail parallels the road at the perimeter of the park but soon

High rock walls fringed with table mountain pine on the Jomeokee Trail.

enters the woods. You'll see an old abandoned car and other evidence of former homesites.

As you turn left, following Grassy Ridge Trail, Big Pinnacle comes into view again, like a standing sentinel. The trail is lined with holly, yucca, Christmas fern, and club moss. On the right is a field of juniper. You'll cross two tributaries of Grassy Creek and pass an old barn with a metal overhang on your right. It's falling apart so stay clear of it. Tobacco was cured there; note the new bricks at the bottom in a semicircle, providing air circulation.

Stay left when the horse trail goes right. At 7.5 miles, cross the park road, go up steps, and turn left toward the visitor center where Grassy Ridge Trail ends. If you don't have a car here, you'll need to walk along the side of the road back to the campground, about 0.9 mile, to end the hike.

Variation: For a quick look at the rock formations, drive to the top parking lot and walk the Jomeokee Trail, which encircles Big Pinnacle in 0.8 mile.

Heritage

Mount Pilot: Jomeokee the Guide

Weathering and erosion produced the two prominent pinnacles of Pilot Mountain, a monadnock that has survived for millions of years while the surrounding peaks have eroded down to a rolling plain. Along with the rocky escarpments of Hanging Rock, Big Pinnacle and Little Pinnacle are all that remains of the ancient Sauratown Mountains. Big Pinnacle, with its bare rock walls and rounded, vegetation-covered top, rises 1,400 ft. above the valley floor. A saddle connects Big Pinnacle with Little Pinnacle.

Pilot Mountain was called *Jomeokee* by the Saura Indians, which means "great guide" or "pilot." The mountain guided Native Americans and early European hunters along a north-south path. It will also guide you when you see it first appearing ahead of you on US 52. It was first commercialized by W.L. Spoon, who built a wooden stairway to the top of Big Pinnacle in 1929, charging an entrance fee of 25 cents for pedestrians and 50 cents for motorists. He sold the park to the Beasley family when he felt he was too old to maintain it properly. J.W. Beasley put in a swimming pool, improved the road, and kept it a going concern until 1965. When J.W. Beasley died, his widow sold the land to the State, and it became a state park in 1968. The State removed the ladders from Big Pinnacle and today you can walk around it on the Jomeokee Trail or admire its top from Little Pinnacle. A Yadkin River section of Pilot Mountain State Park, added in 1970, connects to the mountain section by the 6.6-mile Corridor Trail, mostly used by horseback riders.

This crumbling barn on the Grassy Ridge Trail was once used to cure tobacco.

South Mountains State Park

Essential Facts

Rules/Facilities:
Pets must be leashed.
Visitor center, camping.
Closest town:
Morganton
Website:
www.ncparks.gov

The South Mountains lie at the boundary between the Blue Ridge and the Piedmont, sheltering a mountain habitat in the foothills. South Mountains State Park is a prime year-round destination, except perhaps at the height of summer, when it can be too hot for some. On the other hand, because of its low altitude, winter hiking is very comfortable. Though the highest point is about 3,000 ft., when you're looking down into a valley 2,000 ft. below, you can feel on top of the "local" world. Wind whistling through the pines, ridge vistas, and tumbling water give you the same rush as at higher altitudes. The state park has cut trees to open up views and even arranged logs to sit on. White-tailed deer, not usually seen at higher elevations, are abundant here.

The park now conducts prescribed-burns to encourage table mountain pine and pitch pine to reseed. These pines need fire for their seeds to open. Fire clears the forest floor so seeds quickly reach the soil. It also

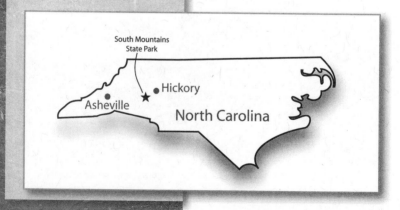

South Mountains State Park

Hickory

Asheville

North Carolina

thins the overhead canopy, allowing more sunlight to penetrate. Serotinous pine cones may persist unopened on the tree for years and burst open only during a forest fire. Fire also keeps the mountain laurel in check; it would otherwise overtake the area and crowd out other plants. The park only burns areas that were burned in the past.

Geology

Walking alongside High Shoals Waterfall can stir any hiker's interest in geology. Rock slabs have moved down the slope and piled up at the base. Water winds through the park toward the Catawba River and cuts deep into the land, forming steep slopes. Rock has broken off through the process of exfoliation, a type of continual weathering that occurs in rocks with uniform texture. Think of peeling off the layers of an onion: The top layer is worn away and the underlying rock expands upward. Then cracks form parallel to the surface of the rock which in turn create another layer which breaks off and falls away.

Coming down the High Shoals Waterfall stairway, you'll see large slabs of rocks with vertical fractures called joints. The joints expand when water seeps in and freezes. Flowing water also widens the joints, along with plant roots that work their way into cracks. Every once in a while, a block of rock separates from the cliff along one of the joints and tumbles down the slope. In 1989, Hurricane Hugo dumped a great deal of rain in the South Mountains. Many loose rocks slid off at once, resulting in the Hugo landslide. Such geologic processes have been going on for millions of years.

Human History

The South Mountains were the buffer between the Cherokee and Catawba Indians. Permanent white settlers arrived in the area as early as 1752. Revolutionary soldiers also passed through the region on their way to the Battle of Kings Mountain. When gold was discovered in 1828, population in the area exploded and boom towns flourished. The gold rush didn't last long, though some gold was mined until the early 20th century.

In the 1930s, the Civilian Conservation Corps, stationed close by at Camp Dryer in Enola north of the park, built roads through the woods and an observation tower on Horseridge Trail. The tower is no longer on that trail but the upper and lower CCC roads can still be hiked. The park, now 18,000 acres, was established in 1975. A beautiful new visitor center offers maps, advice, exhibits, and a movie.

This counterclockwise loop encompasses the northeastern half of the park. It climbs to Jacob Fork River Gorge Overlook, where you'll see High Shoals Waterfall across the gorge. Continue to Chestnut Knob Overlook, a rocky outcropping with outstanding views toward the Kings Mountain Range and on a clear day Charlotte's city skyline. Later, after a climb, you'll reach the top of High Shoals Waterfall—truly awesome. Also impressive is the wooden stairway and platform, which allows you a good close look at the falls and the jumble of rocks in Jacob Fork.

Type of hike: Loop

Distance: 9.3 miles

Total ascent: 2,350 ft.

Starting elevation: 1,350 ft.

Highlights: Views, waterfall, spectacular wooden stairway

USGS map: Benn Knob

Trail map: Available at the visitor center

Land managed by:
South Mountains State Park

Getting to the trailhead: From I-40 exit 105 near Morganton, turn south on NC 18. Travel 11.1 miles and make a right turn on Sugarloaf Rd. (SR 1913). Follow it for 4.3 miles to Old NC 18 and turn left. Travel 2.7 miles and make a right turn on

Trailhead GPS Coordinates:
N 35° 36.14 W 81° 37.75

Ward's Gap Rd. (SR 1901). After 1.4 miles, bear right on South Mountains State Park Ave. (SR 1904). In 1.1 miles, enter the park and pass the visitor center. Drive 2.5 miles to the end of the road. There's one trailhead for all trails in the park.

The Hike
From the trailhead, walk through the picnic area and past the restrooms to H.Q. Trail. Within a quarter-mile, turn right on Chestnut Knob Trail. The trail climbs north through hemlocks, holly, doghobble, and Christmas fern. While the ascent is moderate to steep, the trail is of such good quality, with steps where needed, that you may not notice the climb. The Little River is below on your right. It only takes 300 to 400 ft. of climbing to get outstanding winter views of the western ridge. At 0.8 mile, turn right at Jacob Fork Ridge Gorge Overlook and walk about a hundred yards. A couple of logs have been placed in a cleared area for the best views. It may look as if the trail continues from here but it peters out quickly. Across the gorge, in the middle of a heavily forested

slope, you'll see High Shoals Waterfall, your destination near the end of the hike.

Return to Chestnut Knob Trail where the climb is gentler than at the start of the trail. You'll enter a pine forest with an understory of blueberry bushes. At 1.7 miles (2,300 ft. elev.), make a left to Chestnut Knob Overlook. You'll come back here to get on Sawtooth Trail. At the horse tie-up, you'll have good winter ridge views. Follow the "Hiker" sign on the left and go down a narrow trail a couple of hundred yards to a large rock. Looking southeast, you can see the Kings Mountain range and even the Charlotte skyline on a cloudless day. Retrace your steps to the intersection and continue straight. Turn left on Sawtooth Trail, going toward Horseridge Trail.

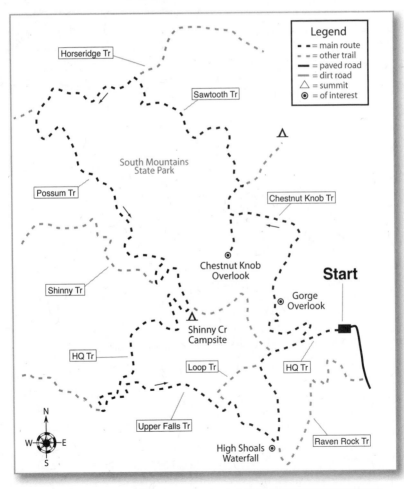

At this intersection, you've done about half the major climbing for the day, the steepest part at the beginning of Chestnut Knob Trail. Later in the day there'll be another stiff uphill to the top of the waterfall. You'll head into the woods, temporarily losing the views. In April, mountain laurel blossoms create a pink wonderland. Sawtooth Trail is a broad horse trail; there are no stairs to moderate the steep parts for those of us with only two legs. It's exceptionally quiet here except for the occasional sound of an airplane. From the viewpoint on your left (complete with a log seat), look southwest toward Benn Knob at the park boundary. Benn Knob is the highest point in the park, although it has no views.

At 3.4 miles (2,250 ft. elev.), make a left on Horseridge Trail on the northern park boundary. At this intersection, a prescribed burn has left an open field now filling in with pines. Make a left on Possum Trail and continue downhill on a wooded trail with distant views of mountain ranges on both sides. On a rise to your right, look for a signal tree with a horizontal bend in the trunk. Native Americans made signal trees by bending a sapling and rigging it in place until the first curve was fixed by growth; the trees were used as trail markers. Possum Trail turns left, and after passing a large semicircular clearing, narrows and continues

A viewing platform offers the best vantage point for photographing High Shoals Waterfall.

downward. Mica, a silicate mineral which looks like shiny, paper-thin layers of glass, sparkles on the ground.

The trail crosses over to the left side of the ridge and suddenly you're deep in the forest descending uneven stone steps with the sound of Shinny Creek (pronounced *shiny*) below and to your right. Ignore the intersection with Shinny Trail on the right and continue on Possum Trail through a large stand of rhododendron. Cross Shinny Creek on a split-log bridge and farther down on low, flat rocks. The trail parallels the creek downstream. You'll reach Shinny Creek campsites at 5.8 miles (1,600 ft. elev.).

By backpacking standards, these are luxurious sites, with picnic tables, an outhouse, and even a garbage can. If you took a left here, you'd be back at your car in 1.2 miles, but you'd miss the waterfall. Take a right on H.Q. Trail to start High Shoals Waterfall Loop counterclockwise; from here, it's not a complete loop.

This wide, steep road seems to go on forever, moderating as it turns south. You'll reach an open view where the wind whistles through pine trees; looking southwest you'll see Benn Knob to the right. At 7.0 miles, at a major intersection, make a left on Upper Falls Trail; the sign indicates 1.3 miles to the falls. After another climb, looking far into the distance on your left, you'll see the beginning of the Blue Ridge Mountains, including Table Rock and Hawksbill in Linville Gorge.

At the intersection, make a right to stay on the Upper Falls Trail. A left would take you directly to the parking lot, missing the falls. There is no separate Upper Falls. The name of the trail means it comes out above High Shoals Waterfall instead of below it.

At 8.1 miles, make a sharp left at High Shoals Falls Loop. From this point you can see Jacob Fork above the falls. Pass a wooden fence between the trail and the falls and cross Jacob Fork on a bridge. You'll be at the top of an elaborate wooden stairway paralleling the falls, with occasional viewpoints and benches. Pass huge, fissured rock walls with trees growing out of the cracks and information boards explaining the geology of the

Time for a snack at Chestnut Knob Overlook.

area. A side path to your left leads to a platform with the best view of the waterfall. This is the best vantage point for photographing the falls. In winter they are framed by icicles, and springtime brings a carpet of wake robin trillium and hepatica.

As you descend, you'll follow a jumble of car-sized rocks all the way down to the river, with rhododendron filling the spaces between boulders. Rock steps now replace the wooden stairway, paralleling a series of small cascades.

At 8.9 miles, pass Hugo Rock, a rock slide caused by Hurricane Hugo in 1989. At the bottom, continue straight down toward a picnic table, pass an information board, and make a right on H.Q. Trail. You'll be 75 ft. upstream of the confluence of Shinny Creek and Jacob Fork, where you'll cross Shinny Creek. You'll pass a trail down to the stream, several information boards, and then the Chestnut Knob Trail intersection on the left. This closes the loop a quarter-mile from your car, where you'll end the hike.

Variation: Chestnut Knob Loop without High Shoals Waterfall— 7.0 miles with 1,550 ft. ascent.

Walking sticks and hiking poles are helpful when descending stairs.

Jacob Fork Watershed

The South Mountains are a mountain range, not a single peak. Once you climb up to the ridge, the trails undulate gently. You'll hike the whole Shinny Trail (pronounced **shiny**), following the creek. After that, much of this hike is on old roads built by the Civilian Conservation Corps (CCC). On the ridge, you'll see Table Rock and Hawksbill in Linville Gorge, Grandfather Mountain, and other smaller peaks in Burke County. These outstanding views are not confined to winter because the park has cut trees to maintain views all year long.

Type of hike: Loop

Distance: 11.6 miles

Total ascent: 2,150 ft.

Starting elevation: 1,350 ft.

Highlights: Views

USGS map: Benn Knob

Trail map: Available at the visitor center

Land managed by:
South Mountains State Park

Getting to the trailhead:
From I-40 exit 105 near Morganton, turn south on NC 18. Travel 11.1 miles and make a right turn on Sugarloaf Rd. (SR 1913). Follow it for 4.3 miles to Old NC 18 and turn left. Travel 2.7 miles and make a right turn on Ward's Gap Rd. (SR 1901). After 1.4 miles,

Trailhead GPS Coordinates:
N 35° 36.14 W 81° 37.75

bear right on South Mountains State Park Ave. (SR 1904). In 1.1 miles, enter the park and pass the visitor center. Drive 2.5 miles to the end of the road. There's one trailhead for all trails in the park.

The Hike
From the trailhead, walk through the picnic area and go past the restrooms to the wide, manicured H.Q. Trail. On the left, steps lead down to Jacob Fork. Within a quarter-mile, Chestnut Knob Trail takes off on the right (see Chestnut Knob/ Waterfall hike, p. 40). You'll soon cross the creek and pass Shinny Creek Picnic Area. At 0.5 mile, in the middle of the picnic area, make a right on Shinny Trail where a wooden sign says "To Shinny Creek Campsites, 0.75 mi." Follow a wide jeep trail where, on some stretches, Shinny Creek is far below you on the right, cascading over and around boulders. The trail comes down to cross Shinny Creek on a wooden bridge.

Pass the Shinny Creek campsites on your left and turn right at 1.2 miles to stay

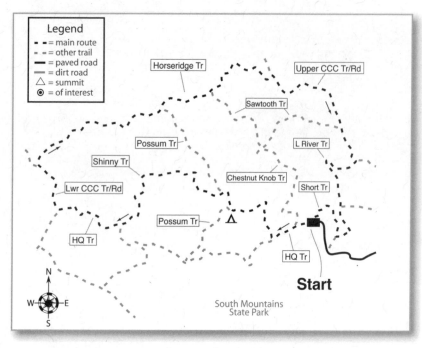

Legend
- **– –** = main route
- **– –** = other trail
- **—** = paved road
- **—** = dirt road
- △ = summit
- ◉ = of interest

Horseridge Tr

Upper CCC Tr/Rd

Sawtooth Tr

Possum Tr

L River Tr

Shinny Tr

Chestnut Knob Tr

Lwr CCC Tr/Rd

Short Tr

Possum Tr △

HQ Tr

HQ Tr

Start

N
W—◉—E
S

South Mountains
State Park

on Shinny Trail. Going straight would take you on Possum Trail toward High Shoals Waterfall. Shinny Trail is now a narrow "hiking only" trail running next to the creek. Cross the creek on flat rocks, go through a narrow rhododendron tunnel, and cross the creek again on a wooden bridge. When Possum Trail takes off right, continue straight on and descend on stone steps for another creek crossing.

You'll follow the creek upstream on a gentle ascent. A few trees are marked with red circles but the trails in South Mountains State Park are not generally blazed. This beautiful woods trail, now lined with galax, leads farther away from the river. After a sharp left turn,

the trail starts up steeply; it's a good heart pumper as you hike through holly and white pine, several times reaching a local top and then going down again.

Suddenly the trail turns flat at 2.8 miles (2,300 ft. elev.). Turn right on H.Q. Trail, a wide jeep trail. A sign says "0.8 To Lower CCC." You'll climb to your first good views looking north (right). At 4.0 miles (2,550 ft. elev.) turn right on Lower CCC Trail/Rd. and in another half-mile, right again on Horseridge Trail. If you'd continued straight on CCC Trail/ Rd., you'd be heading toward the Enola community, where the CCC boys lived in the 1930s.

Horseridge Trail is the gateway to several trails which could be used to shorten this hike. You'll pass gate posts that have fallen down and also a prescribed-burn unit, used to encourage propagation of pitch pines and table mountain pines. Keep looking left (northwest) for outstanding views of rock formations in Linville Gorge: Table Rock, which at this angle doesn't look flat, and Hawksbill farther back on the right. You'll move on to new views, looking north. In the distance Grandfather Mountain follows you as you walk the ridge. Morganton is below with I-40 running between two water towers to the right.

You'll pass another prescribed-burn spot where mountain laurel has been kept down by fire, to prevent it from covering the whole area. You'll pass Possum Trail on your right at 6.2 miles (2,250 ft. elev.). Continue on Horseridge Trail, passing Sawtooth Trail at 7.0 miles. Another view reveals an old lookout tower on Walker Top Mountain and to its right Burkemont Mountain. Farther on, High Peak Mountain is topped with antennas.

Pass another prescribed-burn area and bear right on Upper CCC Trail/Rd. at 7.9 miles (2,100 ft. elev.). A left would lead to Simms Hill, where a stand of bear oak remains. Bear oak is rare in North Carolina and needs an open canopy to survive. Fire clears out the mid-story canopy, opening the lower growth to sunlight. You'll see old fence posts at 8.5 miles (2,000 ft. elev.) and

a horse tie-up. Look right for a stand of loblolly pines, planted by Champion International, a timber company, before the area became a park. The tree's straight trunk makes it major commercial southern pine; it is not naturally found at this elevation. Pass the intersection to Sawtooth Trail, leading to the Sawtooth Trail campsites on the right, and continue left through pitch pines where the trail is flat.

At 9.5 miles (1,850 ft), turn right on Little River Trail, which descends gently. The trail crosses the creek on a wooden plank bridge and finally descends to pass Turkey Ridge Trail on your left. Continue straight where the sign says "Raven Rock Trail," but turn off on Little River Trail before Raven Rock Trail. At 10.9 miles, turn right on Short Trail, a hiking-only trail, which leads back to the parking area in another 0.7 mile to end the hike.

A dry ford at Shinny Creek.

If you want to encourage young children to hike, the trip must have a destination; just walking through the woods is less likely to excite them. At Lake James State Park you'll find two of the few flat hikes available in western North Carolina: Two Overlooks and Fox Den Loop. The Two Overlooks hike is the perfect one to start with; it's short and flat, and when you get to the lake, it's a wow! On the Fox Den Loop Trail, you'll see fox dens and since foxes sometimes walk the trail, there's a small chance you may see a gray or red fox. These two short hikes can easily be done in one visit, either as one extended hike or two separate half-day hikes. Their combined total distance is listed below; see individual hike descriptions for the length of each one. The swimming area past the visitor center is the only legal place to swim.

Rules/Facilities:
Pets must be leashed. Visitor center, camping, lake.

Closest towns:
Marion, Morganton

Website: www.ncparks.gov

Related movies: *The Last of the Mohicans* (1992) with Daniel Day-Lewis and *The Hunt for Red October* (1990) with Sean Connery

Type of hike:
Out and back and loop

Distance (total for both hikes): 4.9 miles

Total ascent: 500 ft.

Starting elevation: 1,250 ft.

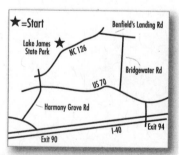

Trailhead GPS Coordinates:
N 35° 43.94 W 81° 54.22

Highlights: Lake views, fox dens, views of Shortoff Mountain

USGS map: Marion East

Trail map: Available at the visitor center

Land managed by:
Lake James State Park

Getting to the trailhead:
From I-40, take exit 90 to Nebo/Lake James and head north. After 0.5 mile, turn right on Harmony Grove Rd. and follow it for 2.0 miles to a stoplight. Proceed straight across the intersection past Nebo Elementary School to a stop sign. Turn right on NC 126 and follow signs to the Lake James State Park entrance, 2.3 miles on the left.

The Overlooks Hike

Distance: 2.7 miles with 250 ft. ascent

Walk southeast in the upper parking lot and turn left at the "Trail" sign with white circle and red diamond blazes. At the trail split, stay straight following white circles toward Sandy Cliff Overlook. The lake becomes visible through white pine on your right. The trail ascends gently north through oak and rhododendron.

At 0.3 mile, you'll reach a wooden platform and bench at Sandy Cliff Overlook. The cliff across the lake is Shortoff Mountain on the east side of Linville Gorge (see Shortoff Mountain hike, p. 140). The obvious cut is where the Linville River bisects Linville Gorge Wilderness and eventually flows into Lake James. Table Rock is a little farther back. Dobson Knob is the first top you'll see, to the left of the cut. The lake has many coves and sandy beaches, most of them not in the park.

Retrace your steps and stay left. Turn left at 0.6 mile at the sign "Lake Channel

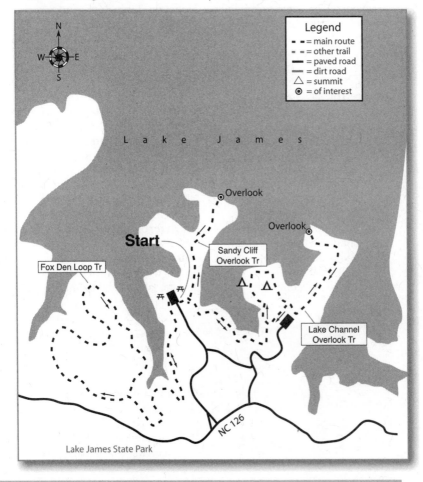

Overlook," following red diamond blazes; this is the Lake Channel Overlook Trail. The trail above the lake skirts the shore, where you may hear squawking Canada geese, and turns gently right and left to follow an inlet where you get another wonderful view of Shortoff Mountain. You'll pass a stand of rhododendron and hemlock and go down a wooden stairway and across a small wooden bridge. At the T-junction, take a left to follow the lake toward the campground, passing a wooden and metal pier. At this point the trail parallels the lake and goes up a flight of wooden stairs between picnic tables. At the top of the stairs, pass a brown carsonite sign reading "15 16 17," which refers to campsites, and make a left turn. Stay on the gravel path; stairs take off left and right to various campsites. Make a left at the sign which says "Campsite Parking/Campsite Washhouse/Lake Channel Overlook" and go up a wooden stairway.

You'll reach the washhouse, available only when the campground is open, and make a left toward the overlook. Now you're above the lake walking on a finger of land, heading north. You'll pass an amphitheater on the left. Through trees you'll see a bridge across the lake on NC 126 and a spillway. The trail continues down gently; at 1.6 miles, you'll reach the platform at Lake Channel Overlook. Looking northeast, there are fine views of Shortoff Mountain, Table Rock, and Linville Gorge. Palatial private homes sit on the shoreline.

Retrace your steps to the washhouse on the Lake Channel Overlook Trail and make a sharp right turn to go down the stairs. At the bottom of the stairs, on a jeep road, make a sharp left and aim for a sign reading "Trail Site 18," where you'll take a right on the trail down toward the lake. Near the bottom, go left across the bridge, at the sign which reads in part "Sandy Cliff Overlook." Go up wooden stairs to retrace your steps and turn left to return to the parking lot and end the hike.

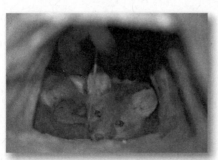
You may see foxes on the Fox Den Loop Trail.

The Fox Den Loop Hike

Distance: 2.2 miles with 250 ft. ascent

From the parking area, go down past a large group picnic shelter to a sign reading "Trail," following blue square and orange triangle blazes. The trail follows a small segment of the Overmountain Victory Trail (see Hump Mountain hike, p. 172). The first section of the trail, down to a large wooden fishing pier, is paved and wheelchair accessible. Past the pier, the dirt trail continues around an arm of the lake, following orange triangles.

The trail is lined with rhododendron, Christmas fern, and club moss as it leaves the lake and climbs on an elaborate wooden stairway. At a T-junction, it makes a right at the arrow; this is not yet the beginning of the loop. You'll see the lake below on your right and private houses in various stages of construction; go under the power lines where NC 126 is above you.

You'll reach the loop at 0.5 mile; take it clockwise by making a left at the double orange triangles and head uphill. Here the pine and oak forest is regenerating and blowdowns and "hazard" trees have been cut, leaving a mess of tree trunks on the trail sides. You'll see the same private houses again from a different angle on your left. Across the water, the swimming beach and visitor center are visible

Start looking on your right for fox dens—large, deep holes close to the trail which may be covered up with leaves. Please look with your eyes only and don't disturb them. At 1.6 miles, you've closed the loop. Retrace your steps past the pier and back to the parking area to end your hike.

─Heritage─

Lake James

Located between Marion and Morganton, Lake James was created in the 1920s by damming the Catawba River. It's one of nine artificial lakes created by Duke Power Company to generate hydroelectric power. Named for the company's founder James B. Duke, Lake James is a paradise for water sports, including sail and power boaters, skiers, and wind surfers. With its 150 miles of shoreline, fishing on the lake is excellent. The lake is located at the base of Linville Gorge, with outstanding vistas of peaks in the Linville Gorge wilderness. Lake James State Park, which opened in 1989, is on the south edge of the lake.

In 2004, North Carolina Governor Mike Easley authorized the purchase of nearly 3,000 additional acres for Lake James State Park, increasing nearly sixfold its former size of 605 acres. The new area is on the lake's north side where the Linville River enters it; 30 additional miles of hiking trails are promised.

This is a very popular park, with most visitors coming from Asheville and Charlotte. On busy summer weekends the entrance to the park is sometimes closed by 11 am, because all the parking spaces have been taken.

Catawba River Greenway

The Catawba River Greenway system in Morganton offers an easy stroll along the Catawba River, with a diversion to Freedom Park. You'll walk on a wooded, paved path past benches, restaurants, and other amenities and meet a lot of friendly people. You can enter and leave the Greenway at one of five access points, making the hike any length you want. The hike described here starts at Greenlee Ford Access and goes to Rocky Ford Access with a side trip to Freedom Park.

Rules/Facilities: Bathrooms, snack bar, restaurant, and parking at various points on the Greenway

Closest town: Morganton

Website: www.ci.morganton. nc.us/html/greenwaytrails.html

Related book: *The Ballad of Frankie Silver* by Sharyn McCrumb

Type of hike: Out and back

Distance: 9.6 miles

Total ascent: 300 ft.

Starting elevation: 1,050 ft.

Highlights: River, birds, early spring flowers, flat walking

USGS map: Morganton North, Morganton South

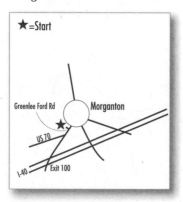

★=Start

Greenlee Ford Rd   Morganton
US 70
I-40   Exit 100

Trailhead GPS Coordinates: N 35° 44.42 W 81° 43.08

Trail map: On the web at www.ci.morganton.nc.us/ prgw-greenwaymaps.pdf

Land managed by: The City of Morganton

Getting to the trailhead: From I-40, take exit 100/ Jamestown Rd. and turn left. Go 2.0 miles on Jamestown Rd., then turn right on Carbon City Rd./US 70 east. After 0.6 mile, turn left on Greenlee Ford Rd. Drive 0.3 mile to the Catawba River Greenway entrance on the right.

The Hike

Greenlee Ford Access, at the start of the Greenway, is a small park with a picnic area, playground, information board, and restrooms. Pick up a booklet on tree identification in the black mailbox. Turn right to start on the Greenway; a left takes you down to the Catawba River. You'll pass a wooden stairway leading to another spot on the river and then a fishing pier. Continue on the paved path with numbered posts, which should correspond to the numbers in the booklet.

The Greenway heads northeast, following the

Catawba River downstream. At 0.3 mile, make a left on an attractive pedestrian bridge over the Catawba River. The bridge, with its new wooden walkway under an old arched steel frame, connects the north and south sides of Morganton.

You're now on the Freedom Trail Greenway, heading north away from the river. You'll follow first a quiet road and then a line of Virginia pines and scrub, a haven for songbirds. The greenway attracts walkers, joggers, bikers, parents pushing

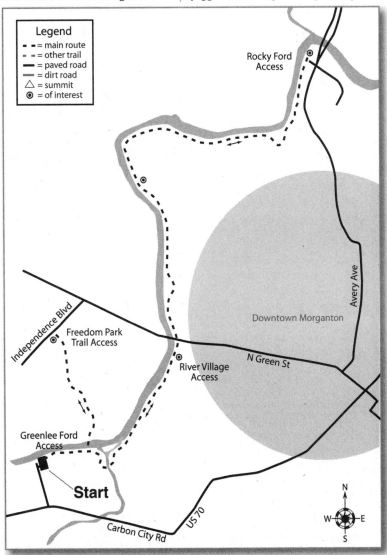

Legend
- ▪ ▪ = main route
- ▪ ▪ = other trail
- ▬ = paved road
- ▬ = dirt road
- △ = summit
- ◉ = of interest

Rocky Ford Access

Freedom Park Trail Access

Independence Blvd

River Village Access

Downtown Morganton

N Green St

Avery Ave

Greenlee Ford Access

Start

Carbon City Rd

US 70

N
W E
S

strollers, and folks going on their exercise walks.

In 1.0 mile you'll reach Freedom Park with a walking track, tennis courts, picnic shelters, and restrooms. After you've checked out the park, return to the Catawba River Greenway and make a left after crossing the bridge.

Turn right to go over a wooded ravine on a bridge and continue above the river. Hemlock trees, open to the light, flourish along with mockingbirds, sparrows, and other songbirds you don't usually see deep in a forest. Ducks swim in the quiet Catawba River. In early spring, maroon sessile-flowered trillium and star chickweed are plentiful. As the greenway parallels US 64 toward Lenoir, you'll hear highway noises, birds, dogs, and sometimes the rustle of squirrels and even deer in the bushes.

At 2.6 miles, you'll reach the information board for River Village Access. The trail goes between the river on the left and a restaurant on the right. You'll pass behind a strip mall on a boardwalk where you can buy a snack and sit on a bench overlooking the river. The metal markers placed in the middle of the Greenway are safety markers that pinpoint your location in case of an emergency.

The trail goes under NC 181 on a wooden walkway and reaches a meadow of Virginia pines and posts demarcating

There are five different access points along the Catawba River Greenway.

the 250-ft. riparian buffer line. These white-topped posts outline the area meant to preserve the river's natural characteristics, protect water quality, and improve habitat for plants and animals on land and in the water. Here you'll cross a minor tributary of the Catawba River and enter a flat field of white pines where purple martin nesting boxes have been erected.

At 3.7 miles, Catawba Meadow Park spreads out on your right. It's a huge city park with softball fields, restrooms, and a river overlook. The city has big plans for this land, including a museum, several softball fields, tennis courts, and mountain bike trails. From here, Rocky Ford Access is about 1.7 miles. This section has a wilder feeling, with more songbirds and a greater variety of spring flowers including violets, bloodroot, trillium, bluets, chickweed, and cut-leaf toothwort. Once across the river, you'll pass a few large and interesting houses on a hill with good river views.

Cross a tiny tributary on a small bridge and you're above the river where there is a fishing platform. Rocky Ford Access, at 5.5 miles, has no facilities other than a parking area. If you don't have a car waiting for you, retrace your steps to return to Greenlee Ford Access and end your hike.

Heritage

Burke County and Morganton: Civil War Raids and Murder

Burke County and Morganton have featured in several important historical episodes. The greenway follows the route of the Overmountain Victory Trail and has markers commemorating the march to Kings Mountain, SC, during the Revolutionary War. See Hump Mountain hike (p. 172) for more details.

Morganton is also listed on the North Carolina Civil War Trails Map. Toward the end of the Civil War, Stoneman's Raiders passed through Morganton and fought Confederate soldiers. This was part of a large raid, from Tennessee across the Blue Ridge Mountains

Walking on the Greenway's Freedom Bridge.

into western North Carolina, mounted by the Union cavalry under Major General George Stoneman. Stoneman's men moved back and forth across the North Carolina and Virginia borders, targeting railroads, industries, and warehouses for destruction. The mission was to "destroy and not fight battles" to speed up the end of the war.

In the 19th century, Morganton was the big city for settlers living and farming in the mountains. It was also the town where, in 1833, Frankie Silver was tried and hung for the ax murder and dismembering of the body of her husband Charlie; both were still teenagers. She was popularly thought of as the first white woman to be hanged in North Carolina, though historians have now disproved this. The details of how Charlie died and exactly why he was killed remain a secret. Some say Frankie suspected her husband of infidelity; others believe she killed him in self-defense as a reaction to spousal abuse. Charlie, who was drunk, had threatened to kill her and her baby. In her novel, *The Ballad of Frankie Silver,* Sharyn McCrumb writes that a large crowd heard Frankie's father yell out, "Die with it in ye, Frankie." Frankie is buried about 8 miles outside Morganton. Frankie and Charlie lived in what is now Mitchell County but at the time was a part of Old Burke County. The story continues to inspire writers and storytellers.

The Catawba River Greenway follows the route of the Overmountain Victory Trail.

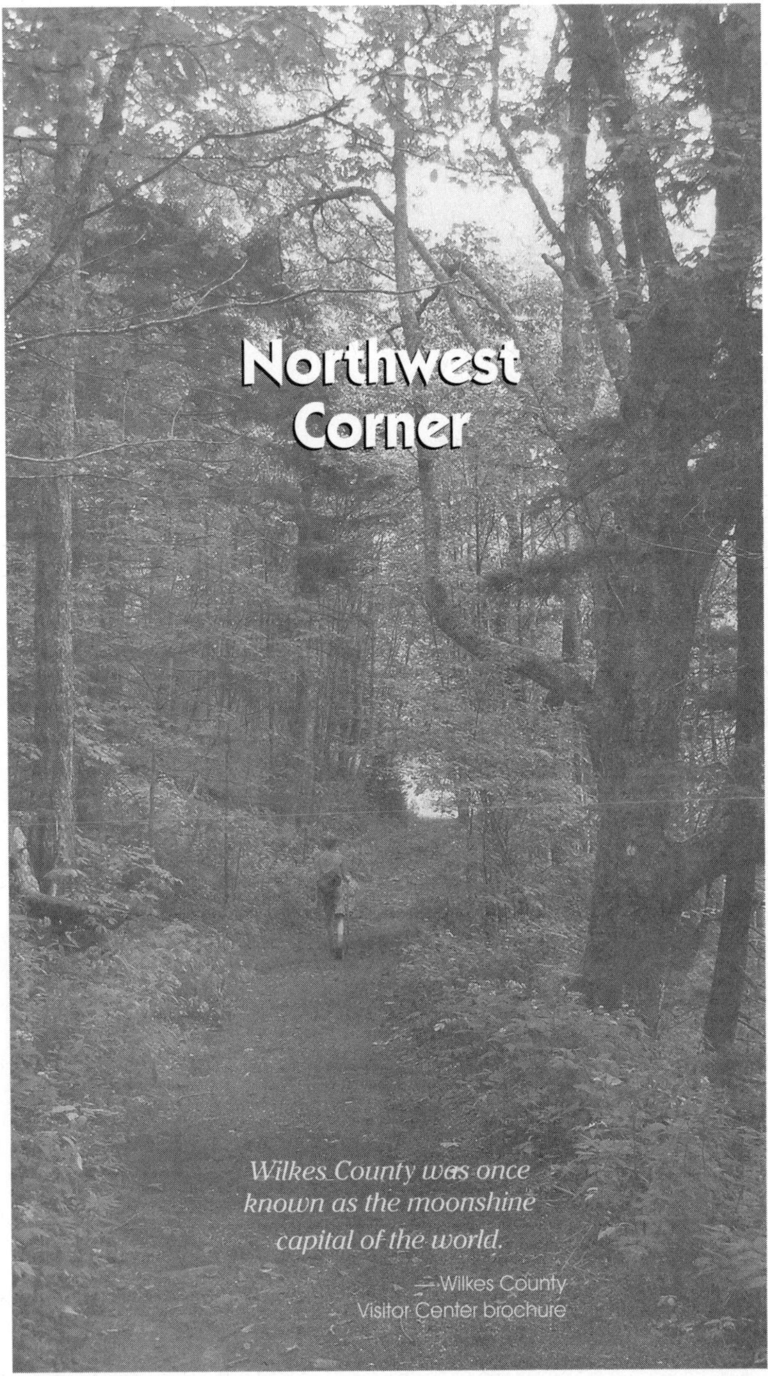

Northwest Corner

*Wilkes County was once
known as the moonshine
capital of the world.*

—Wilkes County
Visitor Center brochure

Stone Mountain State Park

Essential Facts

Rules/Facilities:
Pets must be leashed.
Visitor center, restrooms
at the trailhead.

Closest town:
Elkin

Website:
www.ncparks.gov

Related book and movie:
*Driving with the Devil:
Southern Moonshine,
Detroit Wheels, and the
Birth of NASCAR* by Neal
Thompson; *Thunder Road*
(1957) with Robert Mitchum

Heritage

Granite, Waterfalls, and Moonshine

Stone Mountain (not to be confused with Stone Mountain in Georgia) rises 700 ft. out of the surrounding valley. The signature feature of Stone Mountain State Park, north of Statesville, is this spectacular granite rock dome, which you could drive to until the early 1970s. Depressions in the rock, called weathering pits, pockmark the dome's surface, as if a giant's feet had left huge impressions on the ground. This mountain is a granite pluton, an igneous rock formed beneath the earth's surface by molten lava about 300 million years ago. The granite is peeling away as a result of exfoliation, like dead skin cells on a living body. Wet-weather springs continue to carve grooves in the granite. Until the 1960s, Stone Mountain was home to a herd of feral goats.

Most people just climb to the top of Stone Mountain and back

Stone Mountain
State Park

★

● Winston-Salem

●Asheville

North Carolina

down. If you continue past the top and follow Stone Mountain Loop, you'll leave most tourists behind and see three waterfalls. The elaborate stairway paralleling Stone Mountain Falls, the main waterfall, is almost as impressive as the falls itself.

Northeast of the state park, the North Carolina Granite Corporation in Mt. Airy operates the largest granite quarry in the world. North Carolina Granite Corporation donated the first tract for the park, which included Stone Mountain itself. Mt. Airy is better known as the model for the fictional home of Sheriff Andy Taylor on the television show starring Andy Griffith, who was born there.

Moonshine and NASCAR

Bootleg liquor is part of Stone Mountain's history, and the state park is loaded with artifacts of its moonshine past. "Moonshine used to be hush-hush," local hiker Bob Hillyer explained, "but now they're proud of it."

Just a couple of hundred feet off the trail to Lower Falls, you'll come down to a field where you'll see the remnants of stills. On large steel drums whose tops were blown off by dynamite, the metal has peeled and curls in beautiful spirals, like some high-priced garden sculpture. The pipes, which fed the gas to cook the mash, are still visible. Rubber tubes and jerry cans lie helter-skelter on

Stone Mountain is a granite pluton formed by molten lava beneath the earth's surface approximately 300 million years ago.

the ground. Around several stills, you'll see a pile of old Coca-Cola bottles—heavy, 12-ounce bottles made of dark green glass. These bottles prove the old saying, "Whisky was for selling, not for drinking;" the workers making moonshine drank Coke! These artifacts, including the Coke bottles, are all protected by law.

Tax on liquor was not really enforced until 1877 when Rutherford B. Hayes became president. Reconstruction was ending, Federal troops had been pulled out of the South, and President Hayes had to show that the Federal Government was in control of the whole country, including the southern states. Moreover, he was a supporter of the temperance movement. There was nothing illegal about making whiskey as long as you paid taxes on it; the revenue agents, known colloquially as revenuers, were looking for whiskey made illegally.

Moonshine is associated with many stories, myths, and jokes—and the start of NASCAR. The first race car drivers had learned their skills on backcountry roads, souping up their vehicles and driving fast to make quick getaways from revenuers. Junior Johnson, a Wilkes County native, became NASCAR's most famous moonshine hauler.

Stone Mountain State Park is full of old roads; only some have become official trails. According to the Park Superintendent, the trail up from Lower and Middle Falls was a route moonshiners took to bring their liquor to Sparta without having to use a major road. The heyday of the moonshine business—and it *was* a business—ran from the 1920s to the 1960s. North Carolina instituted prohibition before the Federal Government did. When the 18th amendment was passed in 1919, whiskey prices jumped up and moonshiners flourished. As the park visitor center exhibit proudly explains, the area has swift-flowing creeks of mineral-free water, hardwood trees for fuel, and fertile bottom lands for corn, all of which are needed for profitable whiskey making.

So what happened to bring the moonshining industry to an end? Mostly, it was jobs. With better employment opportunities, moonshiners turned to less risky ways to make a living.

You'll see remnants of moonshine stills just off the trail to Lower Falls.

Stone Mountain Loop

8

Stone Mountain, a granite dome which rises 700 ft. from the valley floor, is particularly spectacular because the isolated rock is not connected to a mountain range. Circling the rock clockwise, you'll reach the bottom of Stone Mountain Falls via a long stairway. On a side trail, Middle and Lower Falls are quieter versions of the main waterfall, where you'll find remnants of the area's moonshine past.

Type of hike: Loop

Distance: 6.4 miles

Total ascent: 1,350 ft.

Starting elevation: 1,550 ft.

Highlights: Views, waterfalls, homestead , field of old moonshine equipment

USGS map: Glade Valley

Trail map: Available at the visitor center

Land managed by:
Stone Mountain State Park

Getting to the trailhead:
From N. Wilkesboro on NC 18, turn east on Mountain View Rd. and drive for 5.4 miles. Turn left on Traphill Rd. (SR 1002). After 10.1 miles, turn left on John P. Frank Parkway, which leads into the park after 2.6 miles.

From I-77 north of Statesville, take exit 83/US 21N Bypass.

Trailhead GPS Coordinates:
N 36° 23.87 W 81° 03.09

Drive for 11.0 miles and turn left on Traphill Rd. (SR 1002) for 4.4 miles. Turn right on John P. Frank Parkway, which leads into the park after 2.6 miles.

Once in the park, go past the visitor center and drive 2.4 miles, then turn left into the parking area at the "Hiking—Lower Lot" sign.

The Hike
From the trailhead, make a left on the well-signposted Stone Mountain Loop Trail [orange circle blazes] and follow a stream on your right. At the intersection, stay left and continue uphill, following the signs to Stone Mountain. Cross a road and continue toward the summit of Stone Mountain on well-manicured steps. You'll walk under rhododendron, mountain laurel, oak, maple, and white pine. At 0.6 mile (1,850 ft. elev.), you'll start seeing a section of Stone Mountain on your right. Here the rock is not completely bare but has fringes of trees. The black streaks on the rock are water courses which have cut through granite and continue to eat away at the rock.

Beautiful wooden steps and cable railings have been placed so you'll know you're

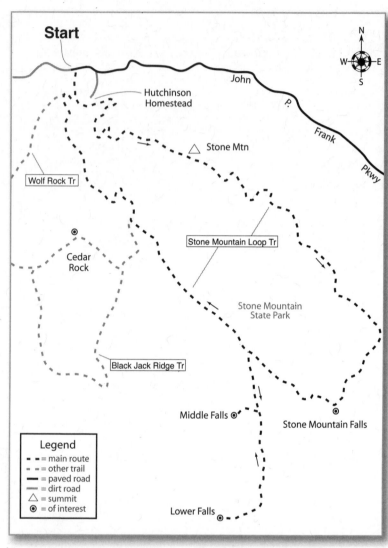

Start

Hutchinson Homestead

John

Frank Pkwy

P.

△ Stone Mtn

Wolf Rock Tr

Stone Mountain Loop Tr

Cedar Rock

Stone Mountain State Park

Black Jack Ridge Tr

Middle Falls ◉

Stone Mountain Falls ◉

Legend
- ▪ ▪ = main route
- ▪ ▪ = other trail
- ▬ = paved road
- ▬ = dirt road
- △ = summit
- ◉ = of interest

Lower Falls ◉

going the right way, which is up. As you climb farther, you'll see a sprinkling of table mountain pine. When the trail turns rocky, you can follow gold or pink circles painted on the rocks, as there are few trees on which to nail the orange circles. Before you reach the top, the 180-degree panorama opens up due west: hills and mountains beyond with almost no signs of civilization.

After the first panoramic *wow* view, make a left and then a quick right to continue up on the rocks, going generally east. Reach the top at 1.0 mile (2,300 ft. elev.). It's dotted with table mountain pine, small trees with irregular crowns and horizontal branches, weathered by the wind. You will have lost the crowds and, temporarily, the views. The rock is pockmarked with weathering pits, surface depressions that begin as small cracks and are enlarged by erosion. When you leave the bare rock, you'll walk on a wide gravel trail flanked by wooden boards, a gentle downhill through maple and oak trees. You'll pass a flat rock seat at 1.8 miles. At a couple of points, the trail is on bare rock again where you can enjoy the last of the outlying views to the southwest, spotting the Blue Ridge Mountains in the distance.

At 2.3 miles, ignore an unnamed trail coming from the left, which leads to another parking lot used by hikers who've come to see the waterfall. Continue straight and pass a chimney on the left and signs to a picnic area. Soon you'll reach the top of Stone Mountain Falls on Big Sandy Creek, gathering momentum for its 200-ft. slide. Descend a long and elaborate wooden stairway, enhanced with several flat decks and benches to allow you to get a better look at the waterfall. When the stairway splits, take the left branch to the base of the waterfall where water slides over sloped rock into a small pool. Come back up and continue down the right-hand

set of stairs on the main trail. You'll follow the stream on your left as it spills over moss-covered rocks and roots.

At 3.1 miles, make a left on a side trail to Middle and Lower Falls [turquoise blazes]. Cross the creek and turn right at the "Middle Falls" sign. It's a short distance to the top of the waterfall. Then the narrow trail takes you down steeply toward the base of Middle Falls, a smaller version of Stone Mountain Falls, but without the people. Water slides into a big pool surrounded by a thick stand of rhododendron. Return to the main side trail to continue to Lower Falls. The trail crosses a creek and starts climbing. When you reach the top of this saddle,

At Stone Mountain Falls, water slides over 200 ft. of smooth rock.

scramble up on the right bank for a view of the moonshine paraphernalia left here: barrels, jerry cans, and hoses.

The trail descends and crosses the creek again. You'll walk on a wide road which, according to park staff, was a back road used by moonshiners to transport liquor. As the trail goes down, water cascades to a sliding rock and into a pool more impressive than the one at Middle Falls. The trail ends at a sign reading "Falls trail ends;" you're now at the edge of the park, though the dirt road continues. There are several places to scramble down to the water and enjoy a quiet picnic on flat rocks.

Retrace your steps to Stone Mountain Loop Trail at 4.8 miles, where there's a bench on the right side of the trail. Cross the creek on a new wooden slat bridge. The creek is now a trickle as you walk on a wide road at the base of the rock, though you can't see it here because of all the vegetation. Cross the creek three more times on similar bridges. After the fourth bridge, the trail opens to reveal Stone Mountain with its dark, wet, downward streaks. Pass the junction to Cedar Rock and Wolf Rock Trails at 5.4 miles on your left. On your right, an idyllic meadow lies between the trail and the base of the rock, with a short path to the best views. Here you may see climbers rappelling down Stone Mountain.

When you reach the Hutchinson Homestead at

The Hutchinson Homestead is representative of the life and times of Stone Mountain settlers.

5.7 miles, take the time to explore its many buildings, including a barn, corn crib, meat and tobacco houses, and blacksmith shop. The enclosed garden has been overtaken by weeds. The house was built by the Hutchinsons in 1855 and expanded through the years to accommodate their growing family. This restored farmstead is representative of the life and times of Stone Mountain settlers; four generations lived and worked here. Imagine living at the base of such a rock!

From the homestead, cross the bridge and go up the steps. Turn right to continue down the road. On the left you'll pass a trail to Wolf Rock and soon you'll complete the circle. Turn left to get back to your car and end the hike.

Variation: To the top of Stone Mountain and back—2.0 miles, 750 ft. ascent.

Wolf Rock Loop

9

A *good way to appreciate the impact of Stone Mountain on the surrounding landscape is to be on another rock and get a different perspective. This counterclockwise loop to Wolf Rock and Cedar Rock gives you great views of Stone Mountain and a spectacular panorama of the mountain ranges beyond. You'll also pass an old homesite with an outbuilding, chimney, and other artifacts. On summer weekends, when everyone seems to be heading up Stone Mountain, you'll appreciate the relative solitude of this loop.*

Type of hike: Loop

Distance: 3.2 miles

Total ascent: 950 ft.

Starting elevation: 1,550 ft.

Highlights: Amazing views, old homesites with artifacts

USGS map: Glade Valley

Trail map: Available at the visitor center

Land managed by: Stone Mountain State Park

Getting to the trailhead: *From N. Wilkesboro on NC 18,* turn east on Mountain View Rd. and drive for 5.4 miles. Turn left on Traphill Rd. (SR 1002). Drive 10.1 miles and turn left on John P. Frank Parkway, which reaches the park at 2.6 miles.

Trailhead GPS Coordinates: N 36° 23.87 W 81° 03.09

From I-77 north of Statesville, take exit 83/ US 21N Bypass. Drive for 11.0 miles, turn left, and follow Traphill Rd. (SR 1002) for 4.4 miles. Turn right on John P. Frank Parkway, which reaches the park entrance at 2.6 miles.

Once in the park, drive past the visitor center and at 2.4 miles, turn left into the parking area at the "Hiking–Lower Lot" sign.

The Hike

From the trailhead, make a left on the well-signposted Stone Mountain Loop Trail [orange circle blazes] and follow a stream on your right. At the first intersection, make a right, as a sign indicates, toward Hutchinson Homestead and "view of Stone Mountain," then another right at 0.2 mile toward Wolf Rock on Wolf Rock Trail.

The well-manicured trail, with a few red circle blazes, leads through tuliptrees and hemlock. As you climb steeply on wooden steps, Stone Mountain comes in and out of view on your left. When the trail switchbacks right, you lose the view. The trail curves left at the Wolf Rock sign. At 1.1 miles, the trail parallels a rock wall which outlines an old homestead on your left. The wall now seems to be held together by moss. Follow the trail through a field of pine and eastern red cedar, a type of juniper.

At 1.7 miles (2,000 ft. elev.), turn right off Wolf Rock Trail to Wolf Rock, a wide, flat expanse with clumps of table mountain pine. From Wolf Rock, you're looking north-northwest into a remote part of the park. The Blue Ridge Parkway snakes along the ridge in the vicinity of Devils Garden Overlook at milepost 235.7 and Stone Mountain Overlook at milepost 232.5. The highest point on the right is Green Mountain; looking

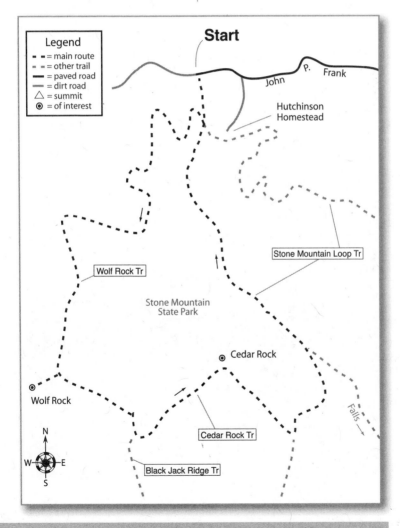

down on your left, the smooth rock is Little Stone Mountain.

Back on the main trail, make a right to continue the loop through a stand of cedar. The trail goes from bare rock back to soil. On your right, you'll pass a homestead site. The wooden building falling apart may have been a chicken coop. It has a solid stone foundation, but who knows how long the wooden parts will last? Farther along at the site stands a dry stack chimney and old stove parts lie on the ground, along with a metal headboard in the flat field. Please remember to take only pictures; all artifacts are protected by law.

Continue on Wolf Rock Trail. On the left, the bare rock is your first look at Cedar Rock. Make a left on Cedar Rock Trail, following signs to Cedar Rock, and start a gentle climb on rock. A right would take you on Black Jack Ridge Trail. Once on Cedar Rock, follow gold circles on the rocky ground. There are wonderful views of Stone Mountain to your right (east) as you keep going up. The trail leaves the rock and turns right through table mountain pine.

The trail splits. The left leg takes you to Cedar Rock, a rocky shelf with spectacular views of Stone Mountain, at 2.0 miles (1,950 ft. elev.). Cedar and pine tree roots clutch the rock. You'll feel you can almost touch Stone Mountain; note its many cracks and dark streaks. On a busy summer weekend, you can watch rock climbers following the curve of vertical fissures in the rock.

Taking in the view from Wolf Rock.

A dry stack chimney is the main artifact at an old homestead site.

At the intersection, turn left to go down to the parking area and end your hike.

The hike continues down the right leg, first on rocks, then back on soil, through pine and oak trees. Black Jack Ridge Trail comes in from the right. Continue left and down on a wide jeep road.

At 2.4 miles (1,650 ft. elev.), make a left on Stone Mountain Loop Trail toward the Hutchinson Homestead site. A right would take you to Stone Mountain Falls. The Homestead started with a modest cabin in 1855 and expanded to become the home and workplace for several generations of occupants. After exploring the garden and outbuildings, continue on the trail which now parallels a road (used for handicapped access only) to the homestead.

Doughton Park

Essential Facts

Rules/Facilities:
Pets must be on a leash.
Bluffs Coffee and Gift Shop,
service station, picnic area,
campground, Bluffs Lodge.
Closest town:
Sparta
Website:
www.nps.gov/blri

Doughton Park: Stepping Back in Time

Doughton Park, located on the Blue Ridge Parkway near its halfway point, offers 30 miles of trail, all well-marked, connected, and very diverse. The park was originally known as The Bluff—for the cliffs that tower over Basin Cove—but was renamed in 1961 for Robert Doughton, a Congressman from Sparta for 42 years (1911-1953). As chairman of the powerful House Ways and Means Committee, Doughton (nicknamed "Muley Bob") was influential in promoting the building of the Parkway. Doughton Park offers a step back in time and a window into the lives of settlers along the Blue Ridge.

At milepost 238.5, you can visit Brinegar Cabin, the home of Martin and Caroline Jones Brinegar. At the overlook, there's a picture of the old couple looking straight into the camera. Follow steps down to the springhouse where you can still hear the

Doughton Park
Blue Ridge Parkway
● Winston-Salem
●Asheville
North Carolina

water bubbling. This tiny cabin was built by Martin Brinegar around 1880 and occupied until the 1930s when the homestead was purchased from his widow to make way for the Parkway.

To understand how isolated people were in this area of the Blue Ridge, hike Basin Creek Trail to the Caudill Cabin. The Caudill were a prolific family. James Harrison Caudill was 16 years old when he left Elkin in 1855 and settled in Basin Cove about a mile down from the current cabin. With Mary, his first wife, he had six children. After Mary died in childbirth, he married her teenaged sister and had 16 more children. Martin, one of the sons, built the cabin at the end of the cove and raised 14 children.

By 1916, over 50 families lived in the cove. The community had a Baptist Church, schoolhouse, gristmill, and blacksmith shop. Rich farmland produced a variety of grain including corn, rye, wheat, and barley. Honey, vegetables, and farm animals added variety to the diet. But no community is entirely self-sufficient; farmers took their excess produce to markets in Mt. Airy and Winston-Salem where they bought goods not available in the cove.

In July 1916, a flood that devastated many mountain communities in western North Carolina washed away almost everything in Basin Cove. Chunks of earth broke loose from the steep

Brinegar Cabin is located at Blue Ridge Parkway milepost 238.5.

slopes and huge trees were ripped from mountainsides, crashing into whatever lay downstream. Cabin logs and furniture flowed down through the cove, but somehow the Caudill Cabin was spared.

The cabin was restored in 2001 by the National Park Service and descendants of Mark Alfred Caudill. The cabin was then over a hundred years old; the logs were falling apart and the chimney was leaning. If the chimney had fallen, the cabin would have been destroyed. The restoration used traditional materials and original tools, all of which were flown in by helicopter to the cabin site. The large extended Caudill family still holds regular reunions, though not at the cabin.

To get another perspective on Basin Cove, look down from Basin Cove Overlook on the Parkway at milepost 244.7. To see the cabin from above, go to Wildcat Rocks, which begins at the far end of Bluffs Lodge at milepost 241. From the left side of the overlook, you can see the cabin down in the clearing.

Basin Creek

10

Doughton Park's Basin Creek Cove was once home to over 50 families. On this solitary walk, you'll discover few people but many artifacts. You'll ford Basin Creek up to 16 times, passing elaborate rock formations, cascades, and several waterfalls. The trail leads you deep into the cove and ends at the Caudill Cabin, the only remaining structure. Bring a small flashlight to peruse the books in the cabin.

Type of hike: Out and back

Distance: 10.2 miles

Total ascent: 1,500 ft.

Starting elevation: 1,450 ft.

Highlights: Cabin, creek and crossings, artifacts

USGS map: Whitehead

Trail map: Available at the Blue Ridge Parkway District Ranger Office at milepost 245.5 or the gift shop at milepost 241

Land managed by: Blue Ridge Parkway

Getting to the trailhead: The hike starts on Grassy Gap Fire Rd., off Longbottom Rd. From Blue Ridge Parkway milepost 248, take NC 18 east (toward N. Wilkesboro) for 6.0 miles. Make a left on Longbottom

Trailhead GPS Coordinates:
N 36° 22.50 W 81° 08.66

Rd. and drive for 6.6 miles. Watch for a small parking area on the right side of the road after a bridged stream; a metal sign on the bridge reads "269." The trailhead is on the left side of the road. The Doughton Park sign is visible only after you get on the trail.

The Hike

Almost as soon as you leave the trailhead on Grassy Gap Fire Rd., you'll see signs for the Brinegar Cabin pointing right and Basin Cove Overlook pointing left. Stay straight on Grassy Gap Fire Rd., following the creek to your left, and pass a small dam. The slow-moving creek goes in and out of sight. You'll be in a hemlock, maple, and oak forest with semi-cleared flat areas that indicate old homesites. On the left, three huge pines are stuck together like triplets. Rosebay rhododendron blooms here in July. Huge boulders look as if they were sawed off on top.

After crossing Basin Creek, you'll reach a primitive campsite on your left at 1.8 miles (1,600 ft. elev.). The large, flat campground is shaded by tall maple and oak trees.

Several campfire rings are provided and an information board explains the heritage of the area. To camp here, you'll need a permit from the District Ranger Office.

Leaving the campsite, cross Basin Creek and continue straight on Basin Creek Trail [blue blazes], which narrows from a road to a trail. You will have left Grassy Gap Fire Rd., which makes a left turn; from that point, Bluff Ridge Primitive Trail makes a right to climb steeply to the Parkway.

On your left, you'll pass a huge boulder leaning diagonally. Beside the trail, in Basin Creek, water moves swiftly over rocks. The trail starts uphill—no more easy

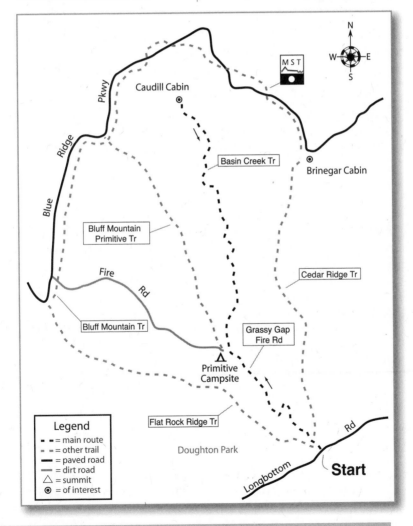

MST

Caudill Cabin

Basin Creek Tr

Brinegar Cabin

Pkwy

Blue Ridge

Bluff Mountain Primitive Tr

Cedar Ridge Tr

Fire Rd

Bluff Mountain Tr

Grassy Gap Fire Rd

Primitive Campsite

Flat Rock Ridge Tr

Doughton Park

Longbottom Rd

Start

Legend
- ▪ ▪ = main route
- ▪ ▪ ▪ = other trail
- ▬ = paved road
- ─ = dirt road
- △ = summit
- ◉ = of interest

meandering. You'll be walking in a fecund forest, with fern, rhododendron, and jungle-like vines—a rainforest

raining, the logs will be more slippery than the trail.

The blue circle blazes marking the trail are

On Basin Creek Trail, water cascades between two mossy boulders.

habitat that may remind you of Tarzan territory.

At 2.6 miles on the left, a chimney is all that remains of a cabin. A little later on the right, a round millstone from a grist mill lies on the creek's banks, a reminder of how self-sufficient residents were.

From the start of Basin Creek Trail you'll cross the creek 14 to 16 times, depending on how you count a couple of minor tributaries. At some point, you'll get your feet wet. You'll pass an enchanting cascade with water flowing between two moss-covered boulders into a pool that feeds a larger pool. Logs have been placed to keep you out of the muck but if it's been

intermittent and most frequent on either side of the creek crossings, but the trail is wide and obvious. The trail goes up and becomes dark and enclosed by dense vegetation. In the distance to your right at 3.2 miles, there's a high waterfall guarded by two huge boulders.

Periodically you'll see mileage posts with numbers—take the distances as estimates only. After passing another old chimney facing the creek, the trail runs between two creeks and becomes rougher and steeper. The foliage opens up, allowing sunlight to filter through. Water flows forcefully from every side of every rock, carving out caves and potholes as it surges down.

At 3.9 miles (2,350 ft. elev.), on the left, a waterfall flows into a small pool, which cascades into a large bowl surrounded by rocks. After passing a stump marked "1.0 mile," you'll find the land clearer with fewer ferns and more flowers: bee balm, rue-anemone, Indian cucumber, and Dutchman's-pipe.

Climbing the last stretch, you can spot the cabin through the trees, and get a sense of its remoteness. You'll reach Caudill Cabin at 5.1 miles (2,900 ft. elev.)—a 14 ft. by 16 ft. room with two doors but no window, supported in the front by columns of flat stones. The cabin was restored in 2001 by the National Park Service and the descendants of the Caudill family. An enigmatic wooden sign reading "100" hangs over the door, perhaps put up as an inside joke by Park staff when the cabin was restored.

Unlatch the cabin door and walk inside. Two books on the mantelpiece explain the Caudill genealogy and include photographs of the cabin restoration. Unfortunately, the book with most of the photos is nailed to the wall. You'll be able to read it only if you remembered to bring a flashlight.

When you sign in, note the date of the people who visited before you and you'll realize how obscure this trail is. The land around the cabin looks as if it's kept as pasture land. When you reach the cabin, it is literally the end of the line. Look up and you'll see the Parkway; however, the trail doesn't connect to the Parkway, so you'll need to go back the way you came to end the hike.

Caudill Cabin is the only surviving structure in Basin Cove.

Bluff Mountain Trail is part of the Mountains-to-Sea Trail and parallels the Blue Ridge Parkway. It offers cool, outstanding alpine views alternating with gentle, shaded woods paths and a coffee shop on the way. Since it passes several overlooks, any one of which could be a destination, you can make this hike as short as you want. The hike ends at the Brinegar Cabin. Though you can take this hike in the opposite direction and save yourself 100 ft. of ascent, it's nice to explore the cabin after the hike.

Type of hike: Shuttle

Distance: 7.9 miles

Total ascent/descent: 1,050 ft./950 ft.

Starting elevation: 3,300 ft.

Highlights: Outstanding open views, farm scenes, cabin

USGS map: Whitehead

Trail map: Available at the Blue Ridge Parkway District Ranger Office at milepost 245.5 or the gift shop at milepost 241

Land managed by: Blue Ridge Parkway

Getting to the trailhead: Leave a car at Brinegar Cabin Overlook (the end of the hike) on the Blue Ridge Parkway at milepost 238.5. Drive to Basin Cove Overlook (Blue

★=Start
★=Finish

Sparta
US 21
Doughton Park
Basin Cove Overlook
Parkway
Ridge
Brinegar Cabin Overlook
Blue
NC 18
North Wilkesboro

Trailhead GPS Coordinates: N 36° 23.45 W 81° 11.99

Ridge Parkway milepost 244.7) to begin your hike.

The Hike

Go down the steps behind the information board, turn left, and go through a stile. The access trail descends steeply to the Mountains-to-Sea Trail [white circle blazes], which here follows Bluff Mountain Trail. Go left toward Brinegar Cabin, heading MST-east. A right turn would take you on Flat Rock Ridge Trail, which descends through Basin Cove to Grassy Gap Fire Rd.

Follow this good, wide trail under a canopy of white pine, tuliptree, and maple, with the Parkway above you on the left. The trail, covered with pine needles, is soft underfoot. You'll pass old and newer farming artifacts such as stiles, barbed wire, and posts signifying old property boundaries and grazing land. Just as you're settling into a forest walk, you come out into the open—a pattern you'll follow for most of the hike—and go through a stile.

Grassy Gap Fire Rd., a gated jeep road, comes in

from the right and heads gently down to Longbottom Rd. There are few MST signs here and none when you're in the woods. You can see evidence of cows on the ground and a herd may be grazing in the fields above you.

Make a sharp right at the "Trail" sign. Straight ahead is the access trail for Bluff Mountain Overlook at milepost 243.4. You'll pass a watering trough, farm implements, and mucky stretches.

Note the split-log fences above you on the Parkway. Go through a stile and come out into the open at 1.6 miles,

below Bluff Mountain Overlook. This opening is filled with sunny yellow tickseed, Turks-cap lily, and spiderwort. The trail plunges back into the forest in a rosebay rhododendron tunnel with a few boulders.

Close to the Parkway, you'll hear the occasional motorcycle or see bicyclists slowly pumping uphill as the trail shoots up to the right at the "Overlook Ahead" sign. You'll reach Alligator Overlook at milepost 242.4, with a sign reading "Elev. 3,385 / 20 min. to Bluff Overlook 3,745" at 2.8 miles. The "alligator back" refers to not the shape of the

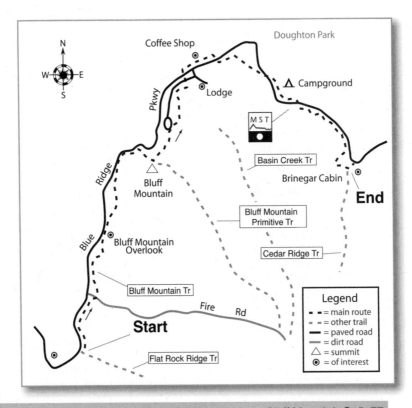

mountains but to the pinstripe formation on the rock, which you can only see close up; the pattern resembles an alligator's skin. Continue to the right of the overlook and pass a viewpoint enclosed by stones and an information board about the importance of predators.

Continue on the trail which here is paved as it heads back into the woods

The paved section doesn't last too long; the trail climbs up on its way to Bluff Mountain, the first real climb on this hike, switchbacking high above the Parkway through a dark tunnel of rhododendron and mountain laurel. As you climb, you'll reach a wooden stairway and elaborate stonework built by Friends of the MST, a volunteer group committed to building and improving the MST.

Take in a breathtaking view on rocks, looking northwest at 3.3 miles (3,700 ft.)— ridge upon ridge of mountains in the distance with charming farm scenes below. The rocky trail continues upward past more views, with table mountain pines holding precariously to the side of the rocky outcropping. Hobblebush and milkweed stick out between rocks. Continue through a former orchard with old posts. When you reach an open field, go left toward the Parkway; a right would take you down on the Bluff Ridge Primitive Trail.

Pass a picnic area and walk on a paved road for a short while. After going

through a stile, make a sharp right and follow the paved path around the parking area. Look for an MST sign pointing to a stile and into a field. Here you'll enjoy open alpine views with windswept trees and almost no sign of civilization. Stone markers lead you across the meadow with only the occasional tree or rock to provide a little shade. You may meet a few people strolling in from the parking area. In the distance, you'll see the back of Bluffs Lodge, with cows in the field.

Continue between the lodge on your right and the road through the picnic area on your left. Look for the trail leading back into the woods. Go through a stile and turn left. After a short distance in the woods, you'll come out into the open with views on both sides. Juncos flit through fields of spiderwort, gayfeathers, Queen Anne's lace, and milkweed. Pass a side trail to comfort stations on your left. The trail avoids the lodge and makes a left at the "Coffee Shop 0.4 mile" sign. Cross the access road to the restrooms and picnic area and continue following MST signs. The trail crosses the Parkway and turns right.

At 5.0 miles (3,700 ft. elev.), at milepost 241, you can get a map of Doughton Park at the Parkway Information and Gift Shop. The coffee shop next door, which offers breakfast and lunch, is where hikers are more likely to spend money than the Lodge. Cross the parking area and follow an MST sign at the far end.

The MST soon turns right, crosses the Parkway, and heads uphill on a mowed path. Cross a stile at an unnamed Parkway overlook and descend into an active grazing field. The trail goes east into the woods, passing through another stile. Cross the Parkway at 5.9 miles and go back into the woods as the trail climbs up.

You're at the edge of the campground where you'll turn right, walking below the campground road. A sign points you to Brinegar Cabin. You'll come out at an information board and a sign saying "Cabin 1.2 miles."

At 6.4 miles, the trail goes into the woods, paralleling the Parkway, and leaves the campground briefly. Cross the Parkway and reenter the campground in the RV section. Follow white circle blazes on the pavement into cool woods, going through a cathedral-like grove of white pines with soft needles underfoot. After 0.5 mile, go through a stile into an open field paralleling the Parkway.

You'll see a sign on the Parkway which says "Brinegar Cabin Turn Ahead." Back in the woods following the MST, at 7.7 miles, turn left at the Brinegar Cabin sign. Cedar Ridge Trail goes straight ahead and leads down into Basin Cove. You'll emerge from the woods at the far end of the parking area for the cabin to end the hike. It's well worth taking the time to explore the site.

Stone markers lead across a windswept meadow on the Mountains-to-Sea Trail.

Mount Jefferson

Mt. Jefferson State Natural Area lies along the drainage divide between the North and South Fork of the New River, one of the oldest rivers on the continent. It's a small park, but the mountain rises more than 1,600 ft. above the surrounding valley, dominating the landscape. This hike takes you to the top of Mt. Jefferson and on a clockwise loop through the forest where a wide array of plants blooms from March to November. Though it's a short hike, the trail is rocky in places. Sturdy, closed-toe footwear is a good idea.

Rules/Facilities: Pets must be leashed. Picnic shelter and tables at the summit.

Closest town: West Jefferson

Website: www.ncparks.gov

Related book:
On Agate Hill by Lee Smith

Type of hike: Loop

Distance: 1.3 miles

Total ascent: 300 ft.

Starting elevation: 4,500 ft.

Highlights: Views, Catawba rhododendron, aspens

USGS map: Jefferson

Trail map: Available at the park office

Land managed by:
Mt. Jefferson State Natural Area

Getting to the trailhead: The park is located on US 221

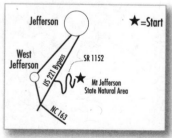

Trailhead GPS Coordinates:
N 36° 24.28 W 81° 27.92

Bypass between the towns of Jefferson and West Jefferson in Ashe County. Traveling north on US 221 Bypass, cross the intersection with NC 163. Turn right on SR 1152, which leads into the park.

The Hike
Drive through the park, passing two overlooks. The trailhead is at the end of the road, where there are picnic tables and restrooms.

Walk past the picnic shelter and swing right. Wild raspberry, mayapple, and trillium are just a few of the spring flowers you'll see here. Summer brings Turk's-cap lily, yarrow, and bee balm. Ignore the trail coming from the right (that's the way you'll come back) and continue on the jeep road. Turn left at the signboard, heading to the highest point in the park.

At 0.3 mile, you'll reach the top of Mt. Jefferson at 4,650 ft. elev. For a better view, go under the transmission tower, looking north at panoramic vistas in the distance. Return to the signboard and continue straight into the woods on Rhododendron Trail, dominated by chestnut oak.

At 0.7 mile, turn left to Luther Rock. From Luther Rock, looking left, you'll see the summit of Mt. Jefferson and the tower. Red-tailed hawks often soar overhead. Below Luther Rock, large-toothed aspens grow along with red maple. Aspen is considered a northern tree and in North Carolina is found only in Ashe and Haywood Counties. Amphibolite stone, the major rock in the park, gives the mountain its dark color and weathers into soil which supports rare plant species.

Backtrack to Rhododendron Trail where, in early June, Catawba rhododendron blooms spectacularly purple. Frequent natural history signboards explain what you're seeing. The trail descends in an oak forest. At 1.2 miles, you're back on the wide main trail. Make a left to go back to the picnic and parking area to end the hike.

Note: If you want to see Mt. Jefferson from a distance, go to Mt. Jefferson Overlook on the Blue Ridge Parkway at milepost 266.8 for a northern view. To the south, you'll see Grandfather Mountain's distinctive outline.

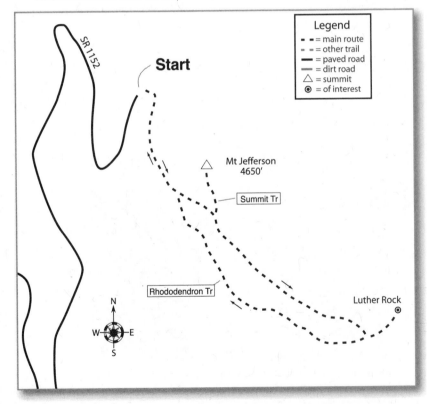

Legend
- = main route
- = other trail
— = paved road
— = dirt road
△ = summit
◉ = of interest

SR 1152

Start

△ Mt Jefferson 4650'

Summit Tr

Rhododendron Tr

Luther Rock ◉

N
W E
S

Mt. Jefferson and its Botanical Diversity

Mt. Jefferson was named for Thomas Jefferson and his father, Peter Jefferson, who owned land in the area and surveyed the nearby North Carolina-Virginia border in 1749. Legend holds that caves beneath Mt. Jefferson's ledges served as hideouts for escaped slaves traveling to freedom on the Underground Railroad.

Explorer and scientist Elisha Mitchell visited Mt. Jefferson in 1827. He climbed to the top and in his diary recorded that he had never seen anything more beautiful than the view from the big rock near the summit. That was more than a century before the mountain became accessible; the road up was not built until the Great Depression, using WPA funds and a donation of land to the town of West Jefferson. Later, the town deeded its land to the State of North Carolina and the park became a recreation area. When it became a state park in 1956, both the name of the mountain and the park were changed to Mt. Jefferson. No one wanted to retain the old name, "Negro Mountain." Because of its botanical diversity, the area was designated a national natural landmark by the National Park Service in 1975.

Recently, a student working on his masters degree at nearby Appalachian State University identified and documented over 702 vascular plants in Mt. Jefferson State Natural Area. The North Carolina Heritage Program classified 16 of these plants as "significantly rare." The research helped to substantiate previous assertions that plants growing in this amphibolite-dominated area are unique and diverse.

Mt. Jefferson was designated a national natural landmark in 1975.

Blowing Rock

*Blowing Rock at times lies
above the clouds, with all the
world blotted out excepting
the Grandfather's summit
rising out of the white mists.*

— Margaret W. Morley,
The Carolina Mountains, 1913

Blowing Rock Drive

This auto tour will take you to several natural attractions in Boone and Blowing Rock and on the Blue Ridge Parkway. You'll start in Boone at the well-tended Daniel Boone Native Gardens and drive up to Blowing Rock, a pretty mountain town with good restaurants and shops. Once there, you can hike down to Glen Burney Falls and then walk around The Blowing Rock (the attraction from which the town takes its name) to take in its dramatic views. On the Parkway, you can visit popular Bass Lake and quiet Price Lake, ending with great views on Beacon Heights.

Related book: *At Home in Mitford* by Jan Karon; *Boone: A Biography* by Robert Morgan

The Drive

Starting in Boone at the intersection of US 321, US 221, and NC 105, set your trip meter to zero.

Take US 321 north toward downtown Boone for 0.4 mile. Turn right on Horn in the West Dr. and right again at the top of the hill. Parking for Daniel Boone Native Gardens is on the right in the same parking lot as Horn in the West.

0.5 mile on the right—**Daniel Boone Native Gardens** (www.danielboonegardens.org)

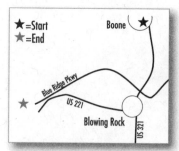

Drive Start GPS Coordinates: N 36° 12.99 W 81° 40.13

Here you can stroll through three acres of Southern Appalachian wildflowers. The gardens concentrate on native plants, and as the seasons change, so do the gardens. It's like a different garden every week. You could easily be overwhelmed by azaleas and rhododendron when they're in bloom, but you will be richly rewarded by taking time to look at the wealth of less showy plant life. The garden makes good use of limited space with benches, walkways, and a historic cabin.

The gardens, owned by the Town of Boone and managed by a nonprofit garden club, are open daily May through October. It's well worth the $2 admission.

Return to US 321 and turn left. Drive 7.2 miles and turn right on Business 321S toward Blowing Rock. Pass the intersection with US 221, then turn right in 0.2 mile onto Laurel Lane; this shady street looks like a boulevard with trees in the median. After another 0.2 mile, turn left into Cannon Memorial Garden.

It's not well signed; the turn is the first left after the median.

9.2 miles on the left—
Glen Burney Trailhead

The Glen Burney parking area has an information board with a map. Starting at 3,350 ft. elev., the trail descends gently at first, then sharply into the Johns River Gorge. Though the hike to Glen Burney Falls is only 2.4 miles round trip, it's a steep 700-ft. climb and you'll do most of it on the return.

The trail crosses New Years Creek and passes the remains of an abandoned wastewater treatment plant. Cross the creek a second time on a wooden bridge as the trail zigzags downhill. At 0.9 mile (3,050 ft. elev.), at a trail split, take a right to pass a picnic table and reach a fenced-in overlook at the top of Glen Burney Falls. The thin waterfall is bisected by a log.

Go back up to the split and take the left fork to continue down. At the next split, stay right to the bottom of Glen Burney Falls; there's occasional pink flagging tape on trees. At 1.2 miles (2,800 ft.

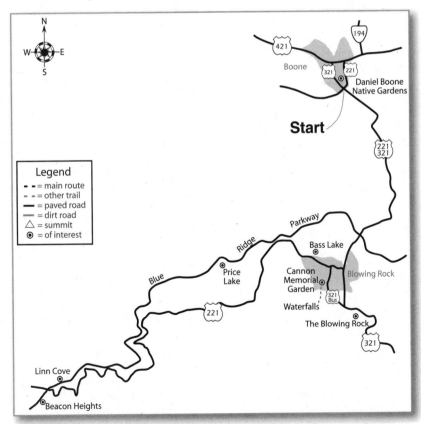

elev.), the trail turns right and descends on rock steps to the bottom of Glen Marie Falls, a beautiful triple falls. Return to your car the way you came.

Drive to Main St./Business US 321S and turn right. After 1.8 miles, turn right on The Rock Dr. and drive another 0.4 mile to the parking area.

11.8 miles—The Blowing Rock

(www.theblowingrock.com)

The Blowing Rock is a commercial attraction ($6 for adults) which offers tremendous views over the Johns River Gorge. Walkways and overlooks with an observation tower give you a panorama of Grandfather Mountain, Hawksbill, and Table Rock, all the mountain icons seemingly in a row. The Blowing Rock itself is a large slanted rock with mysterious winds which flow upward. The attraction has a gift shop and snack bar and is open year-round, weather permitting.

Return to Blowing Rock and make a left on US 221S. Drive 0.6 mile and turn right at the Bass Lake parking area sign then continue 0.2 mile to park in front of the lake.

15 miles—Bass Lake in Moses H. Cone Memorial Park.

Here you can walk around Bass Lake, a pleasant, flat 0.8-mile loop.

Continue on US 221S for 1.0 mile and turn right at the Parkway sign. Head south. (If

The Blowing Rock

you haven't seen Flat Top Manor in Moses H. Cone Memorial Park. (see p. 88), head north for a short distance.) Turn left at the boat rental amphitheater sign for Price Lake. Park at Boone Fork Overlook.

19.4 miles on the left—
Price Lake, milepost 296.9

This 2.5-mile loop around Price Lake has good views of the lake and the stark mountains above. From the information board, start by turning right onto a wheelchair- accessible boardwalk and take a second right onto the trail. There's a snack bar on the left. You'll cross several creeks feeding into Price Lake. At the beginning, the path is mostly flat with a couple of benches by the lake.

Once you're on the other side of the lake from the

Parkway, the trail goes into the woods and becomes swampy. Turn left to go over a plank bridge through a muddy beaver area with gnawed tree stumps. There are good views across the lake.

Back on the Parkway at Price Lake Overlook, make a left to stay on the paved path hugging the lake. The trail then turns to dirt and comes out at a campground. Go straight and cut across a field through a picnic area. Follow a narrow paved path through the campground with signs to an amphitheater. When the trail comes out on the road, turn left to return to your car.

27.7 miles on the left— **Linn Cove Information Center,** milepost 304.4

The information center explains how the viaduct on the Parkway was built.

29.1 miles on left— **Beacon Heights Trail,** milepost 305.2

This leg-stretcher is less than a mile round trip with two major rock outcroppings and grand views of Grandfather Mountain. From the Beacon Heights parking area (4,200 ft. elev.), cross an access road and go up Beacon Heights Trail. Continue right as you pass the start of the Tanawha Trail on the left. The MST takes off to the right as you go left.

You'll reach a T-intersection toward the top. Make a left and go up stone steps to a large rock outcropping, looking east toward Grandfather Mountain. Return to the split and take the right fork with more excellent views to the south. Return the same way back to your car.

Retrace your route or go north on the Parkway for 0.1 mile, turn on US 221 north, and then take NC 105 back to Boone to end the tour.

A 2.5-mile loop encircles Price Lake, with views of mountains all around.

Moses H. Cone Memorial Park

Essential Facts

Rules/Facilities:
Flat Top Manor has become the Blue Ridge Parkway Craft Center and a National Park Service information desk, where you can get a trail map of the park. Restrooms are in a separate building. Pets must be on a leash.

Closest town:
Blowing Rock

Website:
www.nps.gov/blri

Related books and movie:
A Mansion in the Mountains: The Story of Moses and Bertha Cone and Their Blowing Rock Manor by Philip T. Noblitt; *At Home in Mitford* by Janet Karon; *The Green Mile* (1999) with Tom Hanks

Heritage

The Legacy of Moses H. Cone

Tourists and summer residents in mountain communities were part of Blue Ridge culture for over a century before the Blue Ridge Parkway was built. Blowing Rock in particular was an established resort town which tripled its population in the summer.

Moses Cone was one such summer resident who built a mansion outside Blowing Rock, now at milepost 294. Cone was born in 1857 in Jonesboro, TN, the son of Jewish-German immigrants. Like many first-generation Americans, Cone went into his father's business, which was groceries. Little by little, he moved into textiles and built a mill in Greensboro. Over time, one mill became 30 mills and Cone became known as "the Denim King."

Having made his money, Cone and his wife Bertha bought over 3,500 acres adjacent to Blowing

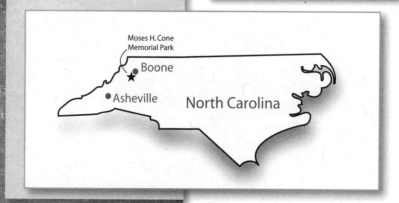

Moses H. Cone
Memorial Park

Boone

Asheville

North Carolina

Rock and began building their dream house and estate, including two lakes stocked with trout and bass.

The Cones created a life of the landed gentry, a kind of modest Biltmore Estate. Cone looked up to the Vanderbilts, his social betters, and modeled the design of his property on the Biltmore Estate, just as Vanderbilt had patterned his mansion on French chateaus. The Cones' 20-room house, Flat Top Manor, was in the Colonial Revival Style with large white columns, elegant leaded glass windows, and dormers set high. Like George Vanderbilt, Cone hired Gifford Pinchot to help him landscape the property with fruit trees, sugar maple, and rhododendron. Several horse carriages are still stored in the original carriage house, which now also contains the park restrooms.

Moses H. Cone

The Cones' dream house was finished in 1901, but Moses Cone did not enjoy it for long; he died in 1908 in his early fifties. Moses and Bertha had no children and when Bertha died 39 years later, she bequeathed her entire estate to build, as a memorial to her husband, the most modern hospital in the South: Moses H. Cone Memorial Hospital in Greensboro. The land and house were subsequently donated to the Parkway, which turned it into the lovely park it is today.

Bertha wanted her home closed permanently to the public after her death because it had been her private haven. In his biography of Moses Cone, Philip T. Noblitt explains that the National Park Service did not quite know what to do with the estate. Up to that point, the Blue Ridge Parkway had emphasized the life of settlers living in remote log cabins. After much consideration by Parkway administrators, in 1951 all the outlying buildings on the Cone estate were torn down and the manor house was turned into the Parkway Craft Center. The craft store fit with the story the Parkway was trying to tell—that of mountaineers engaged in work like sewing quilts and whittling native wood. The Craft Center now sells high-quality pottery, jewelry, and decorative wood products made in Appalachia. On selected occasions, you can tour the whole mansion.

Moses Cone passed on the textile company to his brothers. The company went bankrupt in 2003 and was bought out by a large conglomerate; the textile magnate of the 19th century had become a victim of the global economy.

The Parkway weaves its way for 2.5 miles through the estate. Moses H. Cone Memorial Park is not a wild, natural place but an elegant landscaped estate with 25 miles of gentle carriage roads. You'll share the trails with horse riders, joggers, and in the winter cross-country skiers.

This hike will make you feel as if you're walking through the hills and dales of northern England, even if you've never been to England. You'll walk partway around peaceful Trout Lake and climb gently through forest and pasture, winding your way through a cove. The top of Rich Mountain offers 360-degree views of nearby Grandfather Mountain and Beech Mountain. The hike makes a figure-eight with a short tail. Like all Moses Cone carriage roads, this walk is gentle and takes much less effort than its 9.5-mile length would imply.

Type of hike: Loop

Distance: 9.5 miles

Total ascent: 800 ft.

Starting elevation: 4,050 ft.

Highlights: Open views, lake, gentle carriage roads

USGS map: Boone

Trail map: Available at Flat Top Manor House

Land managed by: Blue Ridge Parkway

Getting to the trailhead: Moses H. Cone Memorial Park is on the Blue Ridge Parkway at milepost 294.

★ =Start

Boone

Moses H. Cone Memorial Park

US 321

Blue Ridge Pkwy

US 221

Blowing Rock

Trailhead GPS Coordinates: N 36° 08.97 W 81° 41.58

The Hike

Walk down to the Manor House to pick up a free trail map, turn left, and go past the restrooms. The trail continues uphill and goes under the Parkway. Turn left at the sign reading "Trout Lake 1.0 mi."; the other fork goes to Flat Top Tower.

The trail passes through gently rolling hills but soon heads into the woods where it's lined with rhododendrons. You'll zigzag down, passing a small wooden corral to a three-way intersection. Cross Flannery Fork Rd., which has car traffic, and go straight at the sign that reads "Trout Lake 0.25 mi. Rich Mtn 5.2 mi." You'll also be following the Mountains-to-Sea Trail, heading trail west.

At a T-intersection (1.4 miles), go right and walk partway around Trout Lake, one of two lakes that Moses Cone created and stocked with fish. Hemlocks reflect in the water and geese and mallards wade and swim—what an idyllic scene! Trout Lake is smaller than Bass Lake and attracts fewer joggers.

The trail turns right toward the spillway and goes up gently. You'll reach an intersection at a sign which says "4.0 mi." pointing right and "2.6 mi." pointing left. Turn right, following the MST.

You'll come back to this point toward the end of the hike.

The trail zigzags north with magnificent hill views on your right. Imagine the Cones living here and taking guests on a carriage ride up Rich Mountain through the forest of rhododendrons and pines. You'll cross several creeks with spillways under the road lined with impressive stonework. Moses Cone loved to build stone walls.

This quiet horse trail climbs up a cove, different from the rolling agricultural land lower down. Go through a metal gate designed to keep animals out. At 3.5 miles (4,100 ft. elev.), you'll reach a broad pasture at an intersection; make a right to continue up into the hills. This is beautiful open grazing land with a small corral. The next intersection starts the upper loop on Rich Mountain Rd. Make a left,

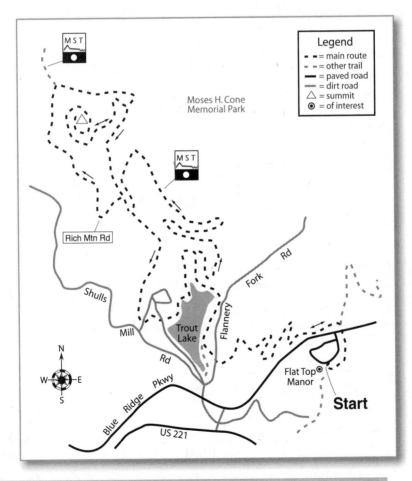

following the MST at a sign reading "Rich Mtn 1.9 mi." You'll come back down on the right.

Rich Mountain Rd. ascends moderately, winding in and out of open land and giving you spectacular views of rocky Grandfather Mountain to the left (southwest). At 4.1 miles, the MST turns left over a stile, leaving the carriage road to head west toward Julian Price Memorial Park. The carriage road continues climbing the western flanks of Rich Mountain. As you reach a split in the trail in another half-mile, go right toward the "Rich Mtn 0.8 mi." sign. The left-hand trail is the way you'll go back. The trail zigzags up the mountain through open land with western views following you. The ski runs on Beech Mountain are most prominent when there's still snow on the ground; at over 5,500 ft., there's snow up there long after it's balmy lower down. The trail encircles Rich Mountain in tight turns; the carriage road was designed to go around the top of Rich Mountain and show off views on all sides.

At 5.5 miles (4,400 ft. elev.), the top of Rich Mountain, with 360-degree views, is marked by—you guessed it—a low stone wall. Retrace your steps down to the intersection with a sign "Rich Mtn 0.8 mi." Turn right, descending through the grass which soon leads to a gravel trail, to close the upper loop at 6.8 miles.

Continue straight past the corral at the right fork signposted Shulls Mills Rd. On this section of trail, you'll see people coming up from Shulls Mill Rd. parking lot for their daily constitutional. At the bottom, go through a chain-link fence; Shulls Mills Rd. is on your right. Make a left toward the parking lot. If you leave a second car here, you can make this a shuttle hike and shorten it to 7.2 miles.

Cross the parking access road and turn left on a trail leading to Trout Lake.

Turn right, away from the parking lot, and stay on the carriage road; Trout Lake is visible through the trees. Cross another parking access road and continue toward the lake. After going partway around Trout Lake, you'll be back at the "Rich Mtn 4.0 mi." sign, having closed the lower loop at 7.7 miles. Make a right turn; the left is the way you went up to Rich Mountain. You'll be retracing your steps. Leave the lake area by following the MST on your left and going uphill to finish the hike.

Variation: Leave a car at Shulls Mill Rd. parking area—7.2 miles with 500 ft. ascent.

Bass Lake/The Maze

15

On this loop you'll see how the upper middle class lived at the beginning of the 20th century. Bass Lake is where Moses and Bertha Cone walked every day. Then you'll take The Maze, a trail with a tight set of switchbacks, up to the apple barn. Toward the end of the loop, you'll approach the Manor House from below and see how well it sits on the land. The Cones could look out from the manor porch, which now has rocking chairs, onto Bass Lake and to a ridge of hills beyond.

Type of hike: Loop

Distance: 7.5 miles

Total ascent: 400 ft.

Starting elevation: 4,050 ft.

Highlights: Bass Lake, apple barn, carriage trails, wildflowers

USGS map: Boone

Trail map: Available at Flat Top Manor

Land managed by: Blue Ridge Parkway

Getting to the trailhead: Moses H. Cone Memorial Park is on the Blue Ridge Parkway at milepost 294.

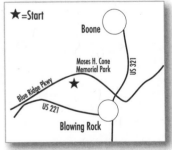

Trailhead GPS Coordinates: N 36° 08.97 W 81° 41.58

The Hike

From the parking lot, walk down to Flat Top Manor.

Descend the manor steps and turn left on the Mountains-to-Sea Trail [white circle blazes], heading downhill. Make a sharp right at the first junction, leaving the MST. You're now directly below the house.

Walking through open fields of grasses, wildflowers, and thistles with an old orchard on the right, you can see Bass Lake below. At 0.5 mile, stay left as the trail, unnamed on the map, goes into a maple and oak forest with an undergrowth of ferns, filmy angelica, and jewelweed. This is also a horse trail.

Continue left to Bass Lake at 0.8 mile where a sign says "Bass Lake 1.4 mi." A right would lead to the horse stables. You'll be on Duncan Rd., heading toward Bass Lake as you come out into the open again. Duncan Rd. switchbacks gently into the woods, through ironweed, white snakeroot, mountain laurel, and several types of fern.

As you descend, look at the quality of the road, the stonework, and the drainage pipes. One of Moses Cone's hobbies was road building, and

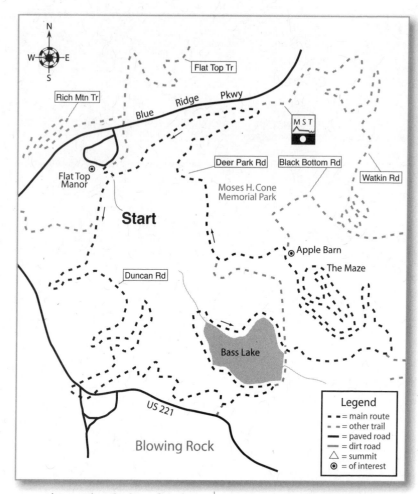

we're reaping the benefits of his pastime. Though the scene is idyllic, all the shrubbery, foliage, and trees don't mask the sounds of trucks going up the nearby highway. Yonahlossee Turnpike, now US 221, predates the Cone estate.

At 2.4 miles, cross US 221 carefully. Duncan Rd. continues straight and a little left toward Bass Lake. You'll meet many more people around the lake, running and walking with or without dogs. Make a left to take the loop clockwise and look up to the commanding position of the Manor House. Cone planted hydrangeas on the hills encircling Bass Lake and stocked it with black bass. Benches placed around the lake offer pleasant places to sit and fishing is allowed here.

About half-way around the lake, pass the parking lot

on the left. Two small stone-walled ponds on the left were stock ponds for Bass Lake.

At 3.5 miles, make a left turn toward The Maze before you complete the loop; a sign says "The Maze 2 mi." The trail to The Maze switchbacks gently uphill in a northerly direction. Pass several houses built right next to Cone Park and parallel a road to your right that leads to a housing community. You will have left most of the running, jogging, and dog-walking crowd and soon you'll leave the road.

The Maze is a set of tight switchbacks going up toward the apple barn under a maple canopy (such switchbacks made it possible for Moses Cone to squeeze in 25 miles of carriage trails on his property). Then the trail switchbacks downhill on its way to the apple barn. If you feel as if you're going up and down and back and forth without a way of getting out, that's a maze.

At 5.8 miles, at the three-way intersection, continue straight to the apple barn. The right turn on Blackbottom Rd. leads to the top part of the property. A sign reads "Cone Manor—3.5 miles." Cone planted more than 30,000 apple trees in four orchards and built an apple house close to each orchard. The apple barn is a two-part building: a big apple house where apples were sorted and stored, connected at an angle to a horse barn with an overhang—a good place to find shade on a sunny day.

At the next intersection, the trail to Bass Lake goes left. Take a right on Deer Park Rd. toward the Cone manor, signposted "1.3 mi." The carriage road switchbacks through thick woods. Barbed wire fencing on the left remains from when cattle grazed there. At 6.9 miles, make a left to return to Flat Top Manor (straight ahead is Watkin Rd., on the MST). You'll be paralleling the Parkway, high above you. The trail, lined by a stone wall on the right, climbs gently back to Flat Top Manor to end the hike.

Moses and Bertha Cone walked at Bass Lake every day.

Flat Top Tower

16

The highlight of this gentle hike is the excellent view from the tower on top of Flat Top Mountain. On the way, a wide variety of wildflowers line the trail, an old carriage road which takes you deep in the woods and through open pasture land, giving the area the feel of pastoral Europe. You'll also take a short detour to the Cone cemetery.

Type of hike: Out and back

Distance: 5.6 miles

Total ascent: 500 ft.

Starting elevation: 4,050 ft.

Highlights: Open views, Flat Top Tower, wildflowers, cemetery

USGS map: Boone

Trail map: Available at Flat Top Manor

Land managed by: Blue Ridge Parkway

Getting to the trailhead: Moses H. Cone Memorial Park is on the Blue Ridge Parkway at milepost 294.

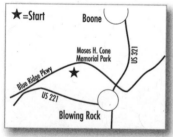

Trailhead GPS Coordinates: N 36° 08.97 W 81° 41.58

The Hike

Walk down to Flat Top Manor to pick up a free trail map. Descend the steps, turn left, and go past the restrooms. The trail then continues uphill and goes under the Blue Ridge Parkway. At the trail intersection, go up and straight, following the sign to Flat Top Tower and the Cone graves. A left turn would take you to Rich Mountain.

A full array of spring flowers, including spring beauty, blood root, and star chickweed, line the carriage road, with open fields on the left. Summer brings bee balm, foamflower, jewelweed, spiderwort, and starry campion. At 0.9 mile, the road bisects fields filled with tall grasses, black-eyed Susan, and New York ironweed. A little farther on, make a left turn toward the Cone graves.

The grassy Cone cemetery is dominated by a huge headstone for Moses and Bertha Cone, with no religious symbols. Sophie Lindau and Clementine Lindau, Bertha Cone's two spinster sisters, lie to the left with smaller grave markers. The graves are enclosed by a green fence.

Return to the main trail and make a left to continue up to the tower. Erosion of the hillside was caused by hikers who cut their own trail to the tower. Please stay on the beautifully maintained carriage trails. The trail switchbacks into the woods through a forest of oak and maple. At 2.1 miles, on the right, a rocky outcropping gives you a preview of what you'll see on top. Under rhododendron and red oak, you'll look south into the valley. In the summer, larkspur, Solomon's plume, and Turks-cap lilies bloom profusely. A deer might cross your path.

You'll reach Flat Top Tower at 2.9 miles (4,550 ft. elev.). If you climb the tower, you'll note that trees have grown up around it, but you can still enjoy the views of ridge after mountain ridge. Return the same way you came to end the hike.

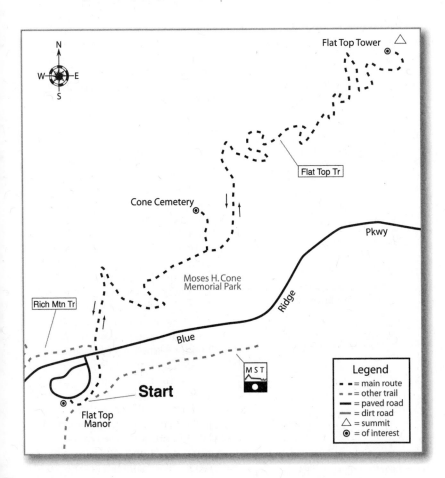

Boone Fork Trail crisscrosses several tributaries of Boone Fork through quiet woods filled with rhododendron, which explode with color in midsummer. Taking this trail clockwise lets you walk the challenging section through huge boulders and cascades first and arrive at Boone Fork itself toward the end of the hike. The trail takes you into the backwoods, away from the Blue Ridge Parkway, while remaining on Parkway land. This gives you the excellent and unusual combination of a backcountry trail (no road noise) that's well-signed. The mileage is posted every half-mile, going the opposite way from this hike description.

Rules/Facilities: Pets must be on a leash. Picnic tables and restrooms.

Closest town: Blowing Rock

Website: www.nps.gov/blri

Related book: *Boone: A Biography* by Robert Morgan

Type of hike: Loop

Distance: 5.0 miles

Total ascent: 650 ft.

Starting elevation: 3,350 ft

Highlights: Water, cascades, pasture

USGS map: Boone

Trail map: Available on an information board at the start of the hike

Land managed by: Blue Ridge Parkway

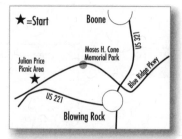

Trailhead GPS Coordinates: N 36° 08.35 W 81° 43.63

Getting to the trailhead:
The trail starts at the Julian Price Picnic Area on the Blue Ridge Parkway at milepost 296.5.

The Hike
Boone Fork Trail [red diamond blazes] starts to the right of the restrooms in the picnic area and crosses a creek on a wooden bridge. Go across the field and head west through rhododendron and the constant sound of water. Early in the morning, you might see a great blue heron take off from the river banks. Soon you leave the babble of the creek behind, heading into a silent forest with Price Lake to your left, on the other side of the Parkway. Ignore a side trail to your left, pass a couple of picnic tables to your right, and go between two buildings toward a campground section for travel trailers.

At 1.1 miles (3,500 ft. elev.), the Tanawha Trail (see Tanawha Trail hike, p. 102) joins Boone Fork Trail from the left and quickly leaves in the same direction. Continue right where the Mountains-to-Sea

Trail, heading trail east, now joins Boone Fork Trail. You're climbing out of the forest into open grazing land as the trail ascends. There's a good view of Grandfather Mountain on your left, looking southwest.

The trail turns sharply right, leaving the pasture, and heads downhill, becoming rough and eroded. You'll be close to water for the rest of the hike. Pass huge slanted limestone boulders fringed by hemlocks and cross Bee Tree Creek, a tributary of Boone Fork, while passing another huge limestone slab. You'll cross the creek several times—on a metal bridge, on flat rocks, on a split-log wooden bridge, and sometimes through the water. You'll be deep in a fresh green forest filled with rhododendron and hemlock. The remnants of a stone bridge lie in the water as you rock hop on flat rocks on the side of the creek and sometimes in the creek itself.

At 2.1 miles, cross a small metal bridge over the creek. The creek widens, gathers strength, and forms cascades and small waterfalls as you follow it downstream on rocky steps.

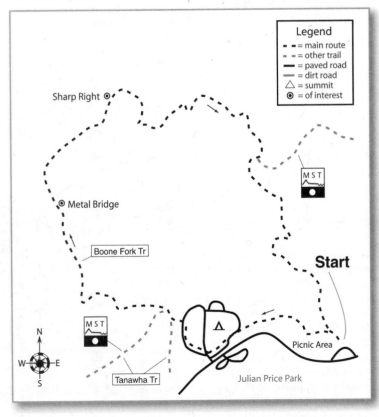

Julian Price, Insurance Magnate

Julian Price Memorial Park lies between the cultivated Moses H. Cone Memorial Park and wild Grandfather Mountain. Julian Price, head of the Jefferson Standard Life Insurance Company in Greensboro for over 30 years, bought this land in the late 1930s as a recreational retreat for his employees. When he died in a car accident in 1946, the firm donated the land to the Parkway. Price didn't found Jefferson Standard, but he expanded it into a national insurance company. In the 1920s, he built a skyscraper in downtown Greensboro for its headquarters, a bold move at the time. Jefferson-Pilot, as it was later known, is no more; it was bought out by another insurance company, Lincoln Financial.

The park has a picnic area, campground, and Price Lake, created in Julian Price's honor. (See Blowing Rock Drive, p. 84.)

there are a couple of rock slabs to help you get across.

Soon you'll leave the creek as it bubbles below you on the left. Follow the flat road for a short while, then work your way through rocks above the rushing Boone Fork and climb up with a help of a wooden banister on a wide trail. Then go down again on stone steps.

At this point Boone Fork is a wide stream, split by an island of roots and rock jumble. Go up a stone stairway with an old wooden banister. After crossing several tiny tributaries, you'll head northeast on a wide, drier trail. Below, Boone Fork crashes through massive rocks, creating cascades below.

At 3.3 miles, make a right past several boulders and ascend on stone steps

Evidence of beaver work on the trail.

At 2.5 miles, the half-way point, cross the creek on flat stones and quickly cross it again, passing a large stone cavern. In the spring when the water is high, you'll get your feet wet. In another 0.2 mile, watch for a sharp right turn where you'll cross the creek again. This may be a challenging crossing when the water is high, but

Crossing Boone Fork.

through a tight squeeze between rocks. The trail turns left and passes an open cave formation. Go down a wooden ladder. At this point, there are few boulders and you enter an idyllic rhododendron forest.

Up to this point, you'll probably have the loop to yourself. But soon you'll see more casual hikers coming toward you from the other direction, because the trail is good and they haven't had to cross the creek yet. You'll come out into the open with the slow-moving stream and grassy bank below. But the water isn't slow moving for long—it forms a waterfall just before the trail goes back into the woods.

The MST leaves Boone Fork Trail on the left at 3.9 miles and crosses Boone Fork, now a wide river, heading toward Moses H. Cone Memorial Park. Continue straight on, where beavers have been busy at the edge of the slow-moving water. Go up and around a set of boulders once more. Toward the end of the hike, the area is flat and the river languid. A signboard about beaver work is askew, almost falling into the stream; the beavers have changed the course of the water.

The trail follows the grassy banks of Boone Fork. The hike ends in a flat area, through scrub and plenty of beaver activity. Close the loop at the Julian Price information board and make a left across the bridge back to your car.

The Tanawha Trail goes from Beacon Heights parking area north to Price Park campground for 13.5 miles. In the winter, the large wooden signs on the Parkway are removed so they can be refurbished, but there's always a small metal plaque letting you know the name of the parking area.

Tanawha, a Cherokee word for hawk or eagle, was also the original name for Grandfather Mountain. The trail itself was built in 1987 at a cost of almost three-quarters of a million dollars. This hike takes in a spectacular section from Stack Rock parking area to Raven Rocks Overlook, where you'll go past gigantic boulders, climb up and down steps, and enjoy 360-degree views, including Grandfather Mountain, within a fragile ecosystem. You'll pass the Linn Cove Information Station and walk beneath the famous and controversial Linn Cove Viaduct (see discussion on p. 105). With all the rocks and steps, you'll probably go a lot slower than the average hiking speed of two miles per hour.

Rules/Facilities: Pets must be on a leash and are not allowed at all between Wilson Creek Overlook and Rough Ridge parking area. Linn Cove Information Station with restrooms open in season.

Closest town: Blowing Rock

Website: www.nps.gov/blri

Related book: *Super-Scenic Motorway: A Blue Ridge Parkway History* by Anne Mitchell Whisnant

Type of hike: Shuttle

Distance: 4.0 miles

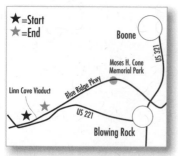

Trailhead GPS Coordinates:
N 36° 05.34 W 81° 49.32

Total ascent/descent:
1,150 ft./1,050 ft.

Starting elevation: 4,300 ft.

Highlights: Amazing views, boardwalk, viaduct

USGS map:
Grandfather Mountain

Trail map:
Available at Linn Cove Information Station

Land managed by:
Blue Ridge Parkway

Getting to the trailhead:
The hike starts at Stack Rock parking area on the Blue Ridge Parkway at milepost 304.8 and ends at milepost 302.4, Raven Rocks Overlook.

The Hike
From Stack Rock parking area, looking up across the Parkway, you can see the swinging bridge on Grandfather Mountain. The trail starts toward the south side of the parking area. Within 90 ft.,

you'll see a white Tanawha feather blaze and a Mountains-to-Sea Trail white circle blaze. Turn left to go trail east on the MST. The trail descends gently and then comes back up among boulders. The voices you may hear can be confusing: they can come from the Parkway above you or from the trail below. Sound travels far in the mountains. The trail goes up a wooden stairway and down again around a huge boulder, taking you under the Parkway.

Cross Stack Rock Creek with its waterfalls. Then cross another wooden bridge where the Parkway loops above you on the left and below on the right. The trail continues down and up, down and up, then goes through a rocky slit on wooden walkways.

In 0.5 mile, you will leave the rocks behind and proceed on a flat dirt trail paralleling the Parkway on your left. When you reach a gravel path heading toward the outer buildings of the Linn Cove Information Station (closed in winter), stop in to learn about the Linn Cove Viaduct, which was built so the Parkway could traverse the boulder fields of Grandfather Mountain without cutting into the mountain itself. Outside a plaque honors Steven T. Mather, the first director of the National Park Service, with these words: "There will never come an end to the good that he has done."

The trail goes under a breezeway through the building and continues on a wheelchair-accessible paved path bordered by a rock wall. Go up steps

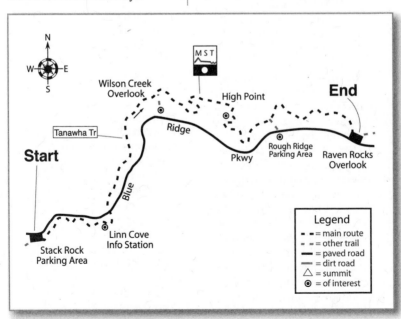

and under the viaduct; you can hear the roar of cars above you. In a short time you will again encounter challenging rock steps and pass under a granite slab leaning against another boulder to form an arch.

Cross Linn Cove Branch on a wooden bridge close to the Parkway and ignore a trail coming from the right. Another wooden bridge goes over a jumble of rocks—lots of ups and down as you pick your way through rocks. It's slow going, but spectacular.

At 1.8 miles (4,350 ft. elev.), a right would take you to the Wilson Creek Overlook on the Parkway. Instead, stay left and cross Wilson Creek on a footbridge to begin a famous and spectacular stretch of the Tanawha Trail.

Pets are not allowed on this section because the terrain is so fragile and people need to stay on the trail. This segment starts off wooded but soon switchbacks around boulders on rock steps. Beyond a rock tower with huge ledges you'll reach a 360-degree view, but continue to greater heights where Grandfather Mountain looms above. The stunted spruce trees and sand myrtle growing here are more typical of the White Mountains of New Hampshire than North Carolina. Cable fencing keeps people on the trail and channels them to an even better view where mountain laurel, rhododendron, and turkey beard bloom in midsummer.

A giant slab leaning against a boulder forms an arch on Tanawha Trail.

You'll reach the highest point on this hike at 4,750 ft. elev. On a sunny afternoon, many people come up from Rough Ridge parking area just to take in this panorama, including the Piedmont, Linn Cove Viaduct, Hawksbill, Table Rock, and Grandfather Mountain. A boardwalk loops below and so does the Parkway. The trail descends through windblown rhododendrons on rocky steps. It's slow going and you may feel as if you're in a maze as the trail zigzags downhill. The tops of the heads of people below you are barely visible. The boardwalk section with a couple of benches is the most popular part of the Tanawha Trail; the boardwalk protects the vulnerable alpine vegetation from human feet. The trail keeps going down. At the end of Rough Ridge, cross Little Wilson Creek on an arched wooden bridge.

At 3.2 miles, the access trail to Rough Ridge parking area is to your right. Continue left up the steps. You'll leave the fragile area and enter a hemlock forest where pets are allowed on a leash. You'll go up log steps, working your way around boulders, and cross a long, thin waterfall on a wooden footbridge. Directionally, this section is down, a good leg stretcher after having to watch your step for a long time. At the next signpost, make a right turn toward Raven Rocks Overlook and your car to end the hike.

Heritage

Linn Cove Viaduct: Engineering Marvel and Environmental Solution

The Linn Cove Viaduct, considered an engineering marvel, is remarkable even to those not easily impressed by manmade wonders. A viaduct is a bridge over land, and here it became the solution to building a road at an elevation above 4,000 ft. without defacing Grandfather Mountain.

In 1967, the Blue Ridge Parkway was almost finished—all but 7.5 miles around Grandfather Mountain and Linn Cove. The State of North Carolina was reluctant to take the land by eminent domain. Since the area skirted private land and was environmentally sensitive and filled with boulders to boot, it took over 12 years of negotiations, compromise, and planning to start building that last section—the "missing link" in the Parkway.

The viaduct was built from the top down to eliminate the need for an access road and earth-moving equipment on the ground. Each pre-cast section of the road was placed in position and the next section attached to it; the concrete was painted to match the color of Grandfather Mountain. The Linn Cove Information Station shows the construction steps in great detail. No names of engineers or designers are associated with the viaduct, even though it was the first bridge of this type to be built in the United States. Work began in June 1979 and was completed in November 1982 at a cost of almost 10 million dollars. The final link of the Parkway opened in 1987, 52 years after construction began.

The project was not without controversy. For a lively discussion of the history of Linn Cove Viaduct, see *Super-Scenic Motorway: A Blue Ridge Parkway History* by Anne Mitchell Whisnant.

The High Country

We ascended the Grandfather, the
highest as well as the most rugged
and savage mountain we had yet
attempted, although by no means
the most elevated in North Carolina,
as has generally been supposed...

— Asa Gray, Harvard botanist
Scientific Papers of Asa Gray, 1841

Grandfather Mountain

Essential Facts

Rules/fees/Facilities:
Restaurant, museum, picnic tables, fudge shop. The fee for adults is currently $14.

The attractions on Grandfather Mountain are operated by a non-profit managed by the family that owned it for more than a century.

In 2008, the State of North Carolina purchased the mountain's 2600 undeveloped acres, which are now a state park.

Closest town:
Linville

Website:
www.grandfather.com

Related book:
Super-Scenic Motorway: A Blue Ridge Parkway History by Anne Mitchell Whisnant

With several thousand miles of hiking trails in the Blue Ridge, you might wonder why anyone would pay to hike. About 250,000 people a year visit Grandfather Mountain, mostly to walk across the Mile High Swinging Bridge. On a good day, you can see the Charlotte skyline a hundred miles away from the bridge.

Climbing to the top of Calloway Peak on the Grandfather Trail takes a lot more effort; an estimated 1,200 people climb to Calloway Peak each year.

Grandfather Mountain became a state park in 2008. But in the 1920s, before the Great Smoky Mountains National Park was formed, it was a serious contender for national park status. The mountain is less than 6,000 ft. high, but today it has the distinction of being the first privately owned park to be designated an International Biosphere Reserve, an area of ecological significance, by the United Nations. Grandfather Mountain supports 16 distinct

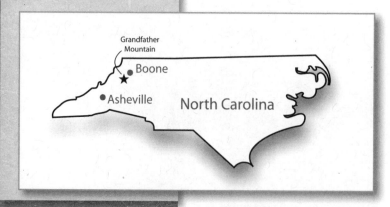

Taking in the grand view from Grandfather Trail.

ecological communities; its abrupt rise above the valley floor creates the climatic conditions to support such a diversity of life. To see the same range of habitats, you'd have to drive from Georgia to southern Canada. The 12 miles of trails, though rugged, are flawlessly maintained.

The mountain is called "an island of the North in the South," partly because of the heath bald at its summit. Sand myrtle bushes with their little white and light pink flowers, small stunted trees, house-sized boulders, and the trail, boggy in places, may remind you of hiking in the White Mountains of New Hampshire.

In 1794, when André Michaux, a French explorer and botanist, climbed Grandfather Mountain, he sang *La Marseillaise* with joy because he thought he had reached the highest point in North America. By the time Asa Gray came to the area in 1841, the mountain was no longer thought to be the tallest, even in North Carolina. However, Gray was right—it might be the most rugged mountain in Southern Appalachia. How did Michaux and Gray climb Grandfather Mountain before trails, ladders, and ropes?

In 1849, Charles Lanman, in his *Letters from the Alleghany Mountains*, wrote that the Grandfather "is said to be altogether the wildest and most fantastic mountain in the whole Alleghany range." Lanman traveled through the Southern Appalachians, then referred to as the Alleghany (as it was spelled then) Mountains, staying with local people. He recorded this story:

A man Jim Riddle and his loving spouse lived in a cabin near the summit of Grandfather Mountain. A more successful hunter than Jim never scaled a precipice. To the comprehension of Jim Riddle, the Grandfather Mountain was the highest mountain in the world. He used to say that he had read of the Andes, but did not believe that they were half as high as the mountain on which he lived. His reason for this opinion was that when a man stood on the top of the Grandfather, it was perfectly obvious that "all the other mountains in the world lay rolling from it..."

In 1888, Hugh MacRae bought a tract of land which included Grandfather Mountain from W.W. Lenoir, son of the Revolutionary War soldier and politician. The mountain has been in the family ever since, but it was Hugh Morton, MacRae's grandson, who made Grandfather Mountain a commercial success. Morton, a World War II photographer, built the swinging bridge and the Nature Museum and improved the hiking trails. He created special events to keep visitors coming back, the most famous being the Scottish Highland Games. Morton was also instrumental in creating a series of conservation easements that forever protect the Grandfather Mountain backcountry from development. When Hugh Morton died in June 2006, his heirs vowed to continue his mission of keeping Grandfather Mountain in its natural state.

Calloway Peak, named for the family that owned the farm below Grandfather Mountain, is Grandfather's highest point at 5,950 ft. It's also the highest point in the Blue Ridge, which extends from Pennsylvania to north Georgia. According to Catherine Morton, the peak represents the crown of the Grandfather's head, as the grandfather lies down on a slant. However, the mountain's elevation makes it look as high as peaks farther west because it stands so much taller than its surroundings.

On September 29, 2008, the State of North Carolina agreed to purchase Grandfather Mountain for $12 million. The 2,601-acre undeveloped portion of the park, which is where the well-blazed trail system is located, became North Carolina's 34th state park. According to Lewis Ledford, director of the North Carolina State Park system, little change to the trail system is expected. The remaining 604 acres of Grandfather Mountain, including the Nature Museum and Mile High Swinging Bridge, is now operated by a non-profit entity managed by the Morton Family.

Grandfather Trail

19

Grandfather Trail is the classic way up to Calloway Peak, the highest point on Grandfather Mountain. On the way, MacRae Peak offers outstanding 360-degree views. This trail attracts a lot of visitors, particularly at the lower levels, but if you start early, you'll be able to avoid most of the crowds. Ladders and cables add to the thrill of climbing and flawless signage helps to get you up there and back. The trick to getting to the top safely is to follow each and every blue blaze, even if another way looks easier. On the way back take Underwood Trail, a lower trail, for a different view. With the views and challenges this hike offers, you might only cover a mile an hour. Enjoy!

Type of hike: Out and back

Distance: 4.8 miles

Total ascent: 2,000 ft.

Starting elevation: 5,250 ft.

Highlights: Outstanding views, alpine vegetation, ladders and cables

USGS map: Grandfather Mountain

Trail map: Available when you pay your entrance fee

Land managed by: Grandfather Mountain State Park

Getting to the trailhead: The entrance to Grandfather Mountain is located on US 221, 2.0 miles north of Linville and 1.0 mile south of Blue Ridge Parkway milepost 305.

Trailhead GPS Coordinates: N 36° 05.75 W 81° 49.91

The Hike

Grandfather Trail [blue blazes] starts opposite the visitor center, adjacent to the Mile High Swinging Bridge. Almost immediately, you reach a signboard with the rules: stay on the trail and leave the mountain before 6 pm. If you don't yet have a map, you can get one here from the map box.

The trail is rocky from the start. Grandfather Extension Trail comes in from the right at 0.3 mile; it leads to the Lower Trails parking lot and Black Rock Trail. Continue straight and go down a rocky slab and back up with the help of cables. Follow the rocky trail, a gentle uphill walk through open meadows. You'll see the high points you're heading for and reach Grandfather Gap in open country. At 0.5 mile, at the intersection of Underwood Trail and Grandfather Trail, make a right to stay on Grandfather Trail. You'll take Underwood

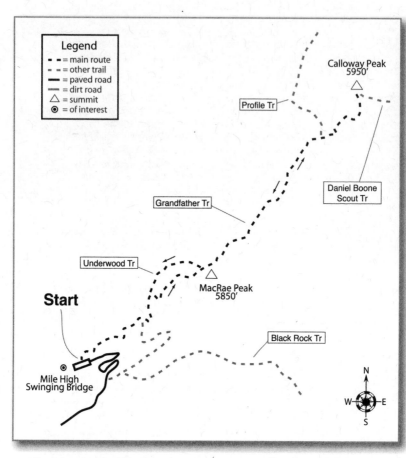

Legend
- = main route
- = other trail
— = paved road
— = dirt road
△ = summit
◉ = of interest

Calloway Peak
5950'

Profile Tr

Daniel Boone
Scout Tr

Grandfather Tr

Underwood Tr

MacRae Peak
5850'

Start

Black Rock Tr

Mile High
Swinging Bridge

N
W — E
S

Trail on your way back.

The trail climbs up steeply on rocks, but ladders bolted into the rock with heavy cables are placed where you'll need them. With the help of a cable, climb to a rock ledge where you'll be surrounded by boulders, creating a cave-like space. Another ladder will help you climb out of the cave.

Go up a series of ladders in quick succession. At the top, pause to see where you came from—the Mile High Swinging Bridge and the visitor center. In late spring, painted trilliums hide in the woods on the few flat spots between rock scrambles.

At 0.9 mile, reach MacRae Peak (5,850 ft. elev.), a free-standing rock, accessible by a tall ladder. The 360-degree views on top are the highlight of this high trail. Looking east, you'll see the Parkway, the transmission tower on Grandmother Mountain, and, in the distance, the Piedmont.

The western views, dominated by Sugar Mountain and its ski resort, will follow you all the way to the top. Public protest against the resort's buildings led to a North Carolina law which now limits the height of buildings on high ridges.

Climb down the ladder and come back on the trail. You'll reach a short, flat stretch which will feel almost like a rest. Farther on more cables and ladders will assist your ascent, and then you'll reach the second intersection with Underwood Trail at MacRae Gap.

In a cavern created by boulders, three ladders, one right after the next, lead you over and under a cluster of rocks—a natural, rocky jungle gym. Climb up the chute, a rock jumble that may be more challenging going down than up, to the Attic Window, the top of a rock mound from which you can see hikers on MacRae Peak.

Climb the last ladder. The trail goes out to a rocky ledge where you may need to use your hands to steady yourself. Just as quickly the trail goes back into the woods. Spring wildflowers—bluets, chickweed, and Wake Robin trillium—bloom here in late May. Summer brings thistle, ironweed, and the rare Heller's blazing star.

At the top of the open rock climb, a column of bare rock on the left is topped with a fringe of moss and other vegetation. The magnificent western view follows you for a while as you continue your climb through blueberries and sand myrtle. The trail passes through a high mountain meadow at 1.5 miles, which in May is ringed with fragrant azalea.

At the next rocky outcropping to the left, you'll see the Sugar Mountain resort from several points. Then head into the woods over gentle terrain covered with ferns under a balsam canopy. Scramble down, carefully following blue blazes into a balsam forest. Heading east in the woods, the trail descends on a pleasant, soft surface. You've left the balsams behind.

Cables and ladders assist your ascent.

At 1.9 miles, you're at Calloway Gap, a muddy, damp spot. Pass a campsite on your right and you'll soon reach the intersection of Grandfather Trail with Profile Trail, which heads west and down to NC 105 (see Profile Trail hike, p. 115). Stay right toward a rock wall that you'll work around, then walk through a grove of red spruce.

At the next intersection, take a left to Watauga View—don't miss this 100-ft. detour. Watauga View, a rocky outcropping, looks down on NC 105 and the community of Foscoe and up to waves of mountain ridges beyond. When the top of Calloway Peak is crowded, Watauga View might be deserted. Then go back to the main trail and turn left to continue to the top of Calloway Peak at 5,950 ft. elev.

On your way back to the start, take the Underwood Trail. Not only will you get another view, but you'll likely have it to yourself, avoiding latecomers starting up Grandfather Trail.

Down from MacRae Peak.

Profile Trail

20

Profile Trail starts west of Grandfather Mountain and provides an easier way (though not necessarily easy—everything is relative) up to Calloway Peak than the traditional Grandfather Trail. The trail will take you through various plant colonies from fern and rhododendron in a hardwood cove to balsam on rocky, exposed tops. This trail also attracts fewer hikers; a permit to hike this trail is free. Read all the information signs and enjoy the amazing trail work.

Type of hike: Out and back

Distance: 6.4 miles

Total ascent: 2,100 ft.

Starting elevation: 4,000 ft.

Highlights: Views, diverse plant colonies, Calloway Peak

USGS map: Grandfather Mountain

Trail map: Available when you get your hiking permit

Land managed by: Grandfather Mountain State Park

Getting to the trailhead: From Linville, drive north on NC 105 for 4.7 miles. Turn right at the Profile Trail sign and drive down to the parking area. Hiking permits are available at several outlets on NC 105 and at the trailhead.

Trailhead GPS Coordinates: N 36° 07.31 W 81° 49.78

The Hike

The trail starts at a trail shelter. The first section meanders through a rich cove forest, filled with fern and wildflowers. You'll cross the head of the Watauga River on solid stonework where in summer jewelweed, asters, and bee balm line the creek. On this pleasant uphill woods stroll, at 0.4 mile you'll find the first of many wooden benches. The trail switchbacks gently up through a rhododendron tunnel, crisscrossing the creek.

At about 1.0 mile, you'll walk through boulders on both sides which form a cavern-like space. You've left behind most of the strollers and casual walkers. The trail is marked with mileage signs every half-mile to mark your progress. The trail continues on flat stones through nettles that have been cut back. Huge rock steps were built in the mid-1980s to replace an old trail dating from the previous century, but the trail was heavily damaged during the 2004 hurricanes. The floods moved stones and even rerouted the stream bed.

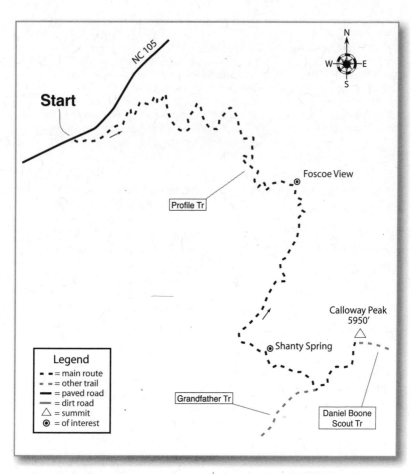

The Grandfather Mountain Trail crew, with the help of the original Trailblazers (a group of trail builders who spent 1985 through 1989 building the profile trail to offer hikers a more gradual ascent up the north slope of Grandfather), relocated boulders to repair steps and stream crossings so hikers can climb comfortably again.

As the trail switchbacks up the mountain, it changes from an easy woods stroll to a more challenging hike.

At 1.7 miles (4,550 ft. elev.), you'll reach a bench at Foscoe View from which you can see the community of Foscoe on NC 105 below.

Boulders get bigger and rock steps get steeper. At the 2.0 marker on the left, there's a flat campsite without water. The trail work is beautiful and amazing, especially considering that only hand tools were used—the original trail builders referred to their methods as "medieval technology."

You'll reach a huge rock wall at 2.2 miles, a forerunner of things to come. Turn the corner at another switchback where the rock wall forms a cave. Boulders on top of boulders create more caverns.

At 2.3 miles, you'll reach the "profile" view of Grandfather Mountain. Shepperd M. Dugger called the rock formation "the great stone face of the Grandfather" in his book, *The Balsam Grove of Grandfather Mountain*, published in 1907. Dugger was part owner of the Grandfather Hotel, which opened in 1885.

At Shanty Spring (2.6 miles, 5,300 ft. elev.), the piped spring in front of a huge rock wall has a sign reading "Last sure water." Shanty Spring takes its name from an old logger's cabin, or shanty, that stood just below the present spring. Like most of western North Carolina, this area was logged about 80 years ago. It is now forever protected by The Nature Conservancy.

At the sign that reads "To Grandfather Trail" make a right on Calloway Trail with a few red blazes. The trail curves around to the right of the wall. At a sign reading "Grandfather Trail," pointing right, and "NC 105," head down and left back to the trailhead. The trail gets rockier and steeper

At 2.8 miles (5,650 ft. elev.), you'll break out of the woods. Turn left on Grandfather Trail [blue blazes]. The trail quickly heads back into the woods and through a balsam grove. At the next intersection, take a left to Watauga View, a few minutes' detour. Watauga View, a rocky outcropping, looks down to NC 105 and the community of Foscoe and out to the western ranges.

When the top of Calloway Peak is crowded, Watauga View might be empty and a good place for lunch. Go back to the main trail and turn left to continue to the top of Calloway Peak at 5,950 ft. elev. Calloway Peak feels like the top of the world. Return the way you came to end the hike.

Variation: If you're lucky enough to have companions who will meet you at the visitor center, take Grandfather Trail back (see Grandfather Trail hike, p. 111). Note that they'll have to pay full price to drive through the main entrance.

Profile Trail offers a more gradual ascent of Grandfather Mountain, free of charge.

Lost Cove Loop offers two swim stops, two waterfall areas, and two creeks, Lost Cove and Gragg Prong, along with a delightful fern valley. For about half the hike, you'll be following the Mountains-to-Sea Trail. If you want to concentrate on summertime swimming and sunning, you can shorten the hike to about five miles, leaving Hunt Fish Falls to the end. There are numerous wet-boot creek crossings. This hike is outstanding in the autumn when the green fern valley changes to gold and sourwoods turn bright red.

Rules/Facilities: None

Closest town: Linville

Website:
www.cs.unca.edu/nfsnc

Type of hike: Loop

Distance: 9.0 miles

Total ascent: 2,300 ft.

Starting elevation: 2,500 ft.

Highlights: Swimming, solitude, fern valley

USGS map:
Grandfather Mountain

Trail map: Linville Gorge/ Mount Mitchell, Pisgah National Forest, National Geographic Trails Illustrated Map #779

Land managed by: Pisgah National Forest, Grandfather Ranger District

Trailhead GPS Coordinates:
N 36° 00.45 W 81° 48.06

Getting to the trailhead:
From Linville, drive south on US 221/NC 181 for 3.7 miles. At Pineola, stay on NC 181 for 2.7 miles and turn left on Pittman Gap Rd. (SR 1471). Go 0.9 mile to Pittman Gap Church and turn left. After another 0.5 mile, turn right at Long Ridge Baptist Church on unpaved FS 464. Go 6.5 miles to Hunt Fish Falls trailhead on the left.

The Hike
Hunt Fish Falls Trail [#263 – yellow blazes], along with the Mountains-to-Sea Trail [#440 – white circle blazes], starts on the west side of the parking area. Go down a steep woods trail into a dark white pine and maple tunnel and cross a small creek at 0.5 mile. The trail switchbacks beautifully, heading north.

At the bottom (0.7 mile, 1,850 ft. elev.), you'll arrive at Hunt Fish Falls. This is the destination for many, since the spot is excellent for swimming, sunbathing, and picnicking. Turn right on Lost Cove Trail [#262 – yellow blazes] which here runs in conjunction with the MST. Cross Lost Cove Creek on rocks and pass a tall, thin waterfall on the right. The trail meanders through a rhododendron thicket and parallels Lost Cove Creek. You may see an occasional yellow blaze or two, but the MST white circles are consistent and frequent. At 1.2 miles, you'll pass a flat campsite area on your left; in midsummer, cardinal flowers fill the area. Immediately after, the trail turns left and crosses the creek—you're going to get your feet wet. Then the MST makes a quick right onto a good, wide trail.

Pass the intersection with Timber Ridge Trail [#261] coming in on your left, where toward the end of the hike you'll come down to close the circle. Farther on, make a left turn following the MST at the confluence of two creeks, Lost Cove Creek and Gragg Prong. You're now following Gragg Prong upstream on your

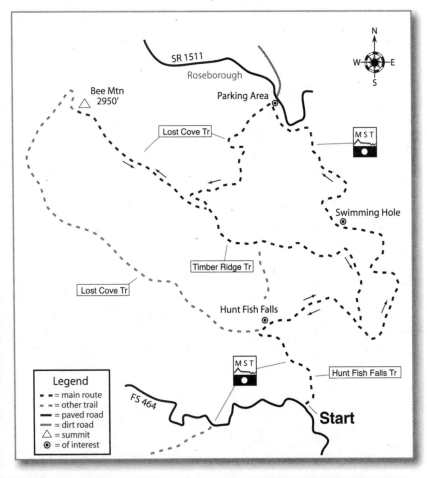

right and passing a house-sized boulder in the river. The creek gets rockier and more active, with many cascades and small waterfalls through the vegetation. Depending on the amount of rain recently, little rivulets from runoff may cross the trail.

At 2.5 miles (2,000 ft. elev.), you'll see a rocky area in the stream that creates several swimming holes—a complex of many small waterfalls, each with its own pool. Toward the bottom of the rocks, a kiddy pool is encircled by rocks. People dangle their feet in the water, swim, and slide down rocks, shrieking as they hit the cold water, while others sit on the upper rocks watching the scene. On a summer weekend, it's a busy place.

The trail continues around the uppermost rock (not over it) and back into the woods. It crosses the creek twice and becomes a jeep road. You'll pass a rocky lookout facing down toward the river; otherwise, the river is obscured by a thicket of rhododendron. At a trail split, follow the right fork which goes uphill, where the MST is clearly marked. Several rocky fingers of bare ground will take you off the trail down to the creek. At 3.2 miles, cross the stream yet again and climb on the other side, where you'll see a few blue blazes along with MST circles. The few yellow blazes at the beginning of Lost Cove Trail have long disappeared, but MST blazes have stayed.

Crossing Lost Cove Creek.

Pick your way carefully over a wet, rocky section on the banks of Gragg Prong. There's an attractive campsite across the stream on your right. Soon you'll reach a wooden sign with an MST blaze that reads "FR 464 3.8 mi." just before a parking area at 3.4 miles, located south of the Roseborough community. Many hikers park here to enjoy the swimming hole about a mile back.

At this point several unofficial trails and a road can cause confusion. Make a sharp left, continue uphill, and stay left, leaving the MST. Follow Lost Cove Trail, without markers. Stay left and cross a little creek, where you'll see Lost Cove Trail on the right, climbing in a forest of rhododendron and mountain laurel, with galax on the ground. At 3.9 miles (2,500 ft. elev.), you'll reach the trail crest. The trail has a different feel when you're away from the stream.

Enter a charming field of ferns. This open fern valley, filled with New York and lady ferns, is a marked contrast from the rest of the hike. Huge boulders on the left are topped with small trees and heath. In the fall, the fern valley turns to a sea of gold.

At 4.4 miles (2,650 ft. elev.), you'll reach a T-junction. Make a right to stay on Lost Cove Trail to Bee Mountain. (After the climb, you'll come back here to take Timber Ridge Trail on your left.) Lost Cove Trail heads west and gently climbs Timber Ridge where fall colors are particularly good. Sourwood trees turn bright red and contrast with yellow oaks and maples. When you reach Bee Mountain at 5.6 miles (2,950 ft. elev.), you'll see several yellow markers on your right, indicating where the trail skirts private land. Lost Cove Trail continues by making a sharp left and descending on a steeply eroded path to Lost Cove Creek.

Retrace your steps to return to the T-junction at 6.6 miles and go straight on Timber Ridge Trail [#261]. It's mostly a gentle downhill stretch; ignore a steep downhill trail coming in from the right. You're deep in the forest, walking through pitch pine and sourwood. At 7.5 miles, the trail turns sharply right. As you continue down, you'll start hearing the creek as the trail becomes gentler and wider. You'll go under an arch created by a huge blowdown. At 7.9 miles (1,750 ft. elev.), make a right onto the MST. The tree at the junction has two orange blazes, the only ones you'll see on this hike. Cross the creek once more to get back to Hunt Fish Falls at 8.3 miles.

You might take time to explore this outstanding waterfall area and even take a second swim. When you can pull yourself away from this spot, return to Hunt Fish Falls Trail and follow its yellow blazes back to your car to end the hike.

⌐Heritage⌐

Wild and Scenic Wilson Creek

The Wilson Creek area lies northeast of Linville Gorge. Though it's not in a wilderness area, it looks and feels like one. There are no facilities and few blazes, other than on the MST. Wilson Creek begins on Calloway Peak on Grandfather Mountain and flows south for over 23 miles into the Piedmont. The Wilson Creek area was inhabited and logged, but after major floods in 1916 and 1940, the people and businesses left. In 2000, Wilson Creek was named a National Wild and Scenic River, ensuring its protection.

Linville Gorge and Falls

Essential Facts

Rules/Facilities:
In Linville Gorge Wilderness, groups cannot be larger than 10 and campfires are discouraged. Linville Falls has a visitor center with restrooms.

Closest town:
Linville

Website:
www.cs.unca.edu/nfsnc

Movies made in the area:
The Last of the Mohicans (1992) with Daniel Day-Lewis

The area was named for William Linville and his son, who were killed by Cherokee Indians while hunting in the area in 1766. The first published account of the incident was in the Pennsylvania Gazette in October 1766 and may have been written by Benjamin Franklin. The Cherokee name for the river was *Eeseeoh*, which means "a river of many cliffs"—a good description of Linville Gorge.

Several Linvilles

Several areas have the name "Linville," which can be confusing. Linville Falls Recreation Area, managed by the Blue Ridge Parkway, has several moderate trails with outstanding views of the falls and river. Linville Gorge Wilderness Area is formed by Linville Mountain on the west and Jonas Ridge on the east. Some call this rugged gorge the Grand Canyon of the East. The Wilderness Area is part of the Grandfather District of Pisgah National Forest. In addition, the

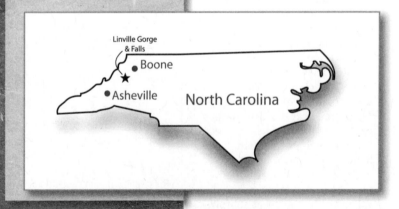

The view of Linville Gorge from Wiseman's View.

small community of Linville Falls is at the intersection of NC 183 and US 221, not to be confused with the town of Linville, 11 miles north on US 221, close to the entrance to Grandfather Mountain.

Linville Gorge Wilderness Area

The Linville River starts at Grandfather Mountain and flows through high valleys into Linville Gorge. Here, the river snakes for 12 miles, slashing through the canyon and ending in Lake James in the Piedmont (see Lake James State Park hikes, p. 48). The gorge is 2,000 ft. deep in places and is so steep and inaccessible that the forest within it has never been logged. The Wilderness Area itself, encompassing more than 11,000 acres of protected land, is a solitary world filled with the roar of the river.

Linville Gorge was first designated a Wilderness Area in 1951 by the Chief of the U.S. Forest Service and became one of three wilderness areas created in the East by an act of Congress in 1964; the other two are Shining Rock in the Pisgah District and the Great Gulf in New Hampshire. Kistler Memorial Highway, an unpaved road despite its name, provides access to the western side of the gorge. FS 210 runs along the eastern side.

Linville Gorge Trail parallels the river on its western side. Though you can get down to the river from its eastern or western sides via several cross trails into the gorge, the western side seems a little more accessible. Spence Ridge Bridge, a relatively new bridge, spans the river at about the middle of the gorge. The most accessible swimming is south of Conley Cove Trail.

The Gorge has several stone monoliths. Two of these, Table Rock and Hawksbill, can be seen from a distance, way beyond the Linville Area. Table Rock was once a sacred ceremonial site to the native Cherokee and is now a popular climbing destination. The trail to Table Rock is short and obvious. The high cliffs are home to endangered peregrine falcons, which have been brought back to the area.

The top of Hawksbill, so named because the rock looks hooked, can also be reached by a short hike, though the trail is not so readily apparent. In 1849, Charles Lanman explained in *Letters from the Alleghany Mountains* that Hawksbill was so named "on account of its resemblance to the beak of a mammoth bird, the length of the bill being about 1,500 ft. It is visible from nearly every part of the valley, and to my fancy is a more picturesque object than the Table Mountain, which is too regular at the sides and top to satisfy the eye."

You can see Table Rock from the Parkway milepost 329.8. Table Rock and Hawksbill are often mentioned in the travel literature of the area, but there's not much about the depths of the gorge itself because it's so rugged.

Linville Falls

Lanman wrote of the falls, "The scenery about them is as wild as it was a hundred years ago— not even a pathway has yet been made to guide the tourist into the stupendous gorge." Lanman would be surprised at the number of visitors coming to the falls today; now a network of trails and paved paths afford views of the falls and the gorge in many places.

Wiseman's View

For a good view into Linville Gorge without any climbing, take in Wiseman's View about four miles from NC 183 on Kistler Memorial Highway (see Getting to the trailhead, p. 125). It was named for LaFayette "Uncle Fete" Wiseman. This was his favorite campsite when taking out salt licks for cattle that grazed on the mountain during the summer. From this viewpoint, surrounded by a stone wall for safety, you can see both Table Rock and Hawksbill in one of the best panoramas in the Blue Ridge Mountains.

Mountain Golden Heather

Many early explorers, including André Michaux and Arnold Guyot, traveled in the Linville Area. Thomas Nuttall (1786 – 1859), who explored much of North America, came to Linville Gorge in 1816. Only days before discovering mountain golden heather *(Hudsonia montana)*, a new species, and thus fulfilling a botanist's dream, he said, "I could not think of a better life than climbing the mountains ...." .

Mountain golden heather is a small, exceedingly rare, needle-leaved shrub with yellow flowers that blooms in early to mid-June. Despite intensive searches by many botanists, no populations of this threatened plant have been found outside Linville Gorge.

Linville Gorge Loop

Wilderness, solitude, rock formations, wading in the river—this loop has it all. The hike takes you into Linville Gorge, down on Babel Tower Trail and up on Conley Cove Trail. You'll find at least two good places to get to the river easily. However, you might average as little as one mile an hour because of the rugged terrain. Just about everything you've heard about Linville Gorge is true. It's rough country, with many snags and blowdowns, and the trails are unblazed although there are a few signposts. Because it's farther away from population centers, it's not as well maintained as Shining Rock Wilderness. The west side of Linville Gorge, where this hike is located, is more remote than the east side of the gorge. But you'll see few people at the bottom of the gorge in any case because, except for the short walk to Wiseman's View, none of the trails off Kistler Memorial Highway is easy. Note: Sandy Flats Trail (which appears on old maps between Babel Tower Trail and Conley Cove Trail) is no more. It was wiped out by hurricanes and the Forest Service has no plans to resurrect it.

Type of hike: Loop

Distance: 9.0 miles

Total ascent: 2,100 ft.

Starting elevation: 3,850 ft.

Highlights: Views, rock formations, Linville River

USGS map: Linville Falls

Trail map: Linville Gorge / Mount Mitchell, Pisgah National Forest, National Geographic Trails Illustrated Map #779

Land managed by: Pisgah National Forest, Grandfather District

Trailhead GPS Coordinates:
N 35° 55.11 W 81° 55.17

Getting to the trailhead:
From the community of Linville Falls on US 221, turn on NC 183S. In 0.8 mile, turn right on NC 1238, Kistler Memorial Hwy. Drive south for 2.9 miles to the Babel Tower trailhead, a wide grassy area on your right. Since the trailhead is not sign posted, you'll need to use driving mileages to find it. If you have two vehicles, you have the option of placing your second car at the Conley Cove trailhead, 2.7 miles beyond the Babel Tower trailhead.

The Hike
From the start of Babel Tower Trail [#240 – no blazes], the only direction is down. The rocky trail, clear and well-maintained, descends through mountain laurel and rhododendron. You'll pass a wide campsite with a large fire ring on your right, then follow a creek on your left.

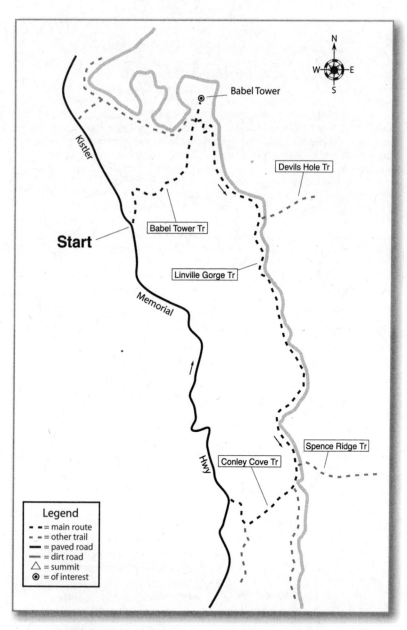

The view opens quickly. Your first view at 0.3 mile looks out at rock columns on the other side of the gorge.

Though it's all downhill, you may find it slow going because of the poor footing over rocks. When trees blow down here, they stay down. The left side offers obstructed mountain views as you walk through galax, trillium, and Indian cucumber root.

Farther down, the trail closes up in a pine, sassafras, oak, and Fraser magnolia forest. Don't be discouraged by the rocky trail at the beginning; the surface improves as the trail descends. You'll reach a huge boulder on your right at 1.1 miles. From the open rocky area, you'll see Hawksbill with its characteristic hook, as well as rocky columns set into the gorge. The striking rock formations here were created by erosion over millions of years.

At 1.2 miles (3,000 ft. elev.), you'll reach Linville Gorge Trail [#231 – no blazes], a narrow, signposted trail. A left on Linville Gorge Trail would take you north and away from your destination. You may hear flowing water but you're quite a long way from the banks of Linville River. You'll come back to this spot, but for now continue straight 0.1 mile on Babel Tower Trail, which quickly swings right and then left.

Look to your left for a flat, rocky outcropping, a good place to see Babel Tower, a tall column of flat rocks. Continue down and straight on Babel Tower Trail to its base. The best view is farther back on the flat rocks that offer good views of Linville Gorge and River.

Return to the intersection with Linville Gorge Trail and make a left going south, heading down toward the river. The trail is rocky and rugged and goes under a rock outcropping which sticks out into the trail.

At a switchback, you'll see Table Rock on the right and several rocky, partly tree-covered columns. Here the trail doesn't go down to the river but turns right and stays above it, bobbing up and down, sometimes gently, sometimes not. You might hear the call of a pileated woodpecker.

When the river is low, sculpted limestone creations poke up out of the water. The trail comes down to several flat campsites; none here are at the water's edge. You'll climb over and under rocks and

Spence Ridge Bridge is an impressive and aesthetically pleasing piece of construction.

fallen trees, but there are good flattish sections as well. At 2.5 miles, the trail skirts a bare rock and looks down on the gorge before going down again.

Continue high above the river, with good views of Hawksbill. At 3.0 miles, you'll reach a point where you can see Hawksbill straight across to your left and Table Rock to the south. Pass a flat campsite close to an intermittent creek. Then, as the trail continues down, you get an unobstructed view of the gorge and maybe even a good breeze.

At 3.5 miles, you'll pass an elaborate campsite and a Linville Gorge Trail sign, leading you right, away from the river. There may be lots of social trails (herd paths) but the official trail is easily apparent—it feels solid underfoot and contours the side of the gorge.

At 3.8 miles, go up and under a huge rock overhang and open cave—it's nice and cool there. Each rock formation could be an inspiration for an expensive stone sculpture in an art gallery.

At 4.3 miles (2,150 ft. elev.), you'll reach a good path leading to the river and the new Spence Ridge Bridge, designed as two individual bridges and separated by a large, flat boulder. Decorative stone columns hold up a split-log bridge with a handrail—an impressive piece of construction. The bridge leads to Spence Ridge Trail on the east side of Linville Gorge. This is the first easy access to the banks of the Linville River.

Pass an open cave created by a horizontal rock that fell on two vertical rocks. The trail, rough and rocky with more blowdowns, hugs the high,

The high cliffs of Table Rock are home to the reintroduced endangered peregrine falcon.

bare walls. You really feel you're in the depths of a gorge.

At 5.0 miles (1,950 ft. elev.), Linville Gorge Trail skirts the river; this is a good place to cool your feet or take a dip before the climb up and out. If you see hikers anywhere in the gorge, you'll probably see them here. Note the stone steps up to a flat area. The William Conley Family, who owned a large plantation nearby, built a small log house here for hunting parties.

Make a right on the signposted Conley Cove Trail [#229 – no blazes]. At first the trail ascends gradually in a maple and oak cove. As it climbs out of the gorge, it's steep and well-switchbacked. Ironweed and white bee balm fill in any open spot. At 5.3 miles, the trail cuts across a small rock slide where you can look up to see your destination—it's a long way up there.

After climbing a half-mile or so, you'll see views on the east side of the gorge. The trail swings right and hugs a huge rock wall. From here, Table Rock sits squarely in front of you and looks flat, living up to its name. You'll also have views of Hawksbill as the trail continues switchbacking. At 5.8 miles (2,900 ft. elev.), you'll reach a T-junction. Make a right to head toward your car. From here, the climb continues as a nice walk in the woods.

You'll reach the road at 6.3 miles (3,000 ft. elev.).

Make a right. If you have a car waiting for you here, your hike is over. If not, walk the gravel road for 2.7 miles to close the loop and end the hike.

Variation: Leave a car at the Conley Cove Trailhead—6.3 miles with 1,400 ft. ascent.

Seen from a particular angle, the peak of Hawksbill resembles the bill of a great bird of prey. For a less-than-two-mile walk, this hike has to be the "best value for your walking buck." The short, steep climb will reward you with views up and down Linville Gorge and, on clear days, all the way to Mt. Mitchell.

Type of hike: Out and back

Distance: 1.4 miles

Total ascent: 700 ft.

Starting elevation: 3,300 ft.

Highlights: Views of Linville Gorge and beyond

USGS map: Linville Falls

Trail map: Linville Gorge / Mount Mitchell, Pisgah National Forest, National Geographic Trails Illustrated Map #779

Land managed by: Pisgah National Forest, Grandfather District

Getting to the trailhead: From the community of Pineola at the intersection of US 221 and NC 181, take NC 181S for 5.3 miles and turn right on Gingercake Rd. (SR 1264). Drive 2.4 miles and at a junction signed, "to Table Rock," turn right on Table Rock

Trailhead GPS Coordinates: N 35° 54.88 W 81° 52.70

Rd. (SR 1261). In 0.8 mile, the road is no longer paved and changes its name to FS 210. In another 1.1 miles, you'll reach Hawksbill parking area on your left. The trail starts to the right.

The Hike

Hawksbill Trail [#248 – no blazes] is a rough trail which ascends in a trench through a rhododendron and mountain laurel tunnel, then quickly opens up to the sky. At about 0.25 mile, ignore the side trail on the left. Pines and hemlock flourish here as the trail narrows and becomes gentler.

At 0.5 mile (3,700 ft. elev.), you'll see a post ahead. About 10 yd. before the post, look for a narrow but still obvious trail on your left. If you reach the post you've gone too far, so go back and look for a side trail (which will now be on your right) going uphill. Many hikers, including this hiker, have blown past this point and missed Hawksbill. At the top of the hill, turn left at the dead end to a flat spot with lots of rocks where the world opens up.

Hawks and vultures circle above on thermal currents. The craggy peak, topped with numerous table mountain pines stunted by harsh weather conditions, offers outstanding views of Linville Gorge. To the left are Table Rock, Shortoff Mountain, and Lake James below to the south. Far below you, the Linville River winds through canyon walls. Rocks jut out at

The top of Hawksbill offers outstanding views of Linville Gorge.

sharp angles, sheltering little pools of water. Sand myrtle, a low-lying shrub with small, light pink flowers, and turkey beard, with its grass-like leaves and white flower stalk, are reminiscent of vegetation much farther north. Retrace your steps to end the hike.

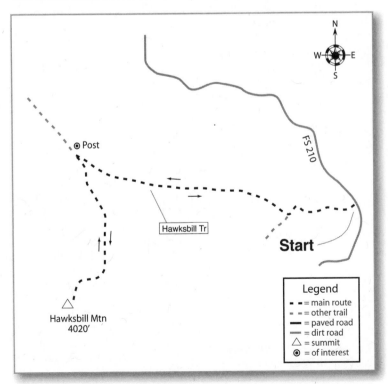

Although finding the trailhead might sound more difficult than the trail itself, this hike is definitely worth the drive. It has two sections; neither is very long but both are steep with outstanding views. The hike to Table Rock Mountain is popular and offers some magnificent 360-degree vantage points. The Chimneys are not a specific set of stone columns but a conglomerate of rock pillars and jumble. For most of the second part of the hike, you'll be able to see Table Rock.

Type of hike: Out and back

Distance: 4.1 miles

Total ascent: 700 ft.

Starting elevation: 3,400 ft.

Highlights:
Views, rock formations

USGS map: Linville Falls

Trail map: Linville Gorge / Mount Mitchell, Pisgah National Forest, National Geographic Trails Illustrated Map #779

Land managed by:
Pisgah National Forest, Grandfather District

Getting to the trailhead:
From the community of Pineola

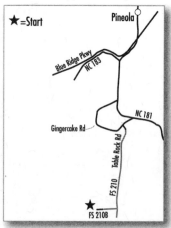

Trailhead GPS Coordinates:
N 35° 53.18 W 81° 53.09

at the intersection of US 221 and NC 181, take NC 181 south for 5.3 miles and turn right on Gingercake Rd. (SR 1264). After 2.4 miles, at a junction signed, "to Table Rock," turn right on Table Rock Rd. (SR 1261). In 0.8 mile, the road is no longer paved and changes its name to FS 210. You'll pass several trailheads. Drive 5.6 miles and turn right on FS 210B, following the sign to Table Rock Picnic Area. Drive for 3.2 miles to the end of the road. You'll pass the entrance to North Carolina Outward Bound School where the road becomes paved again and finally ends at the picnic area, which has pit toilets but no water.

The Hike (Section 1)
The trail starts near the information signboard, with a sign to Table Rock Summit, on the Mountains-to-Sea Trail [#440 – white circle blazes] going trail east. Information plaques along the way describe the uniqueness of this area. In particular, mountain golden heather, a small shrub with yellow flowers, is found only among a few high rocks in this area of North Carolina and has been placed on the federal list of threatened species.

Almost immediately after you start on the steep, rocky trail, you'll have views of the striking rock formations on the western side of the gorge. Except for the trail, there's no sign of civilization. Though you may see enticing side trails, keep to the main trail.

At 0.4 mile, reach a split where the MST goes down and left. Continue right, climbing on Table Rock Mountain Trail.

There are several lookout points where you can see The Chimneys, due south. Stay on the main trail, which here ascends generally to the northeast. The wide trail gets steeper and rockier through table mountain pine, rhododendron, and mountain laurel. At the trail junction at 0.7 mile, go left. Though the trail may look flat here, it will curve around and soon climb again.

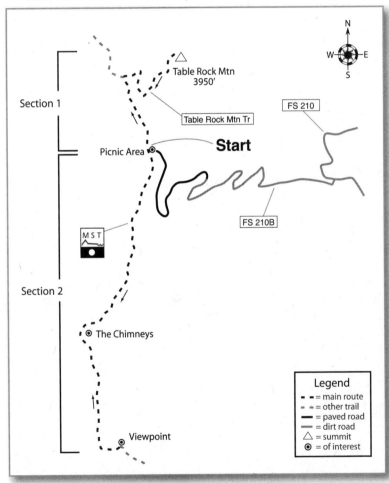

You'll reach the top at 0.8 mile (3,950 ft. elev.). The summit has the stone foundation of an old fire tower with bolts still implanted in the rocks. As you scramble around the rocky ledges, it's very important to stay off the plants. The 360-degree views include Linville Gorge and River. Retrace your steps down the trail to return to the picnic area.

The Hike (Section 2)

Shortoff Trail [#235 – no blazes] to The Chimneys, part of the MST going trail west, starts on the opposite side of the parking area, past the privies. Climb solid rock steps through a picnic area with a lush lawn on the left side. The trail is rocky but well manicured with the same information signs as Table Rock Mountain Trail.

At 0.5 miles (3,500 ft. elev.), you'll reach a flat rock outcropping on the right, surrounded by table mountain pine with spectacular views into Linville Gorge. The rocky areas to the left are collectively referred to as "The Chimneys." The trail goes down and back up on rock steps, then you'll head downhill between two columns of pancake rocks. These columns are made up of flat layers of hard quartzite stacked on top of each other. When the softer rock around them eroded, the columns which make up The Chimneys remained.

At 0.7 mile, the trail descends again with a solid

The trail squeezes between rocks at The Chimneys.

rock wall on your left. You can see more chimney columns on your right. Stay on the trail; peregrine falcons, a North Carolina endangered bird, nest here.

Leaving The Chimneys, you'll descend gently into a hardwood forest cove; the trail is obvious but overgrown. You'll pass two flat campsites at 1.2 miles, one with a good view facing west, away from the gorge. As the trail continues down, look left for an excellent view of Table Rock. MST blazes are intermittent.

The views get better as you approach a flat rock outcropping. A nearby large boulder provides shade. You'll see Linville River, the striated rock across the gorge, and the rocky conglomerate of The Chimneys. The MST continues steeply down on an eroded trail to Chimney Gap and eventually to Shortoff Mountain (see Shortoff Mountain hike, p. 140). However, at 1.3 miles (3,200 ft. elev.), this is the logical place to turn around. Retrace your steps to the picnic area to end the hike.

Variations: To Table Rock and back—1.5 miles with 500 ft. ascent; to the view past The Chimneys and back—2.6 miles with 200 ft. ascent.

Linville Falls drops 90 ft. before its waters start their 12-mile course through Linville Gorge. This hike gives you five different spectacular perspectives of the waterfalls in two short sections and every view is worth the walk. The first section, on the Linville Falls Trail, takes you to three overlooks where you'll appreciate the power of the water that carved the gorge. On the second section, you'll see where the lower falls plunges into a basin and then into Linville River itself. Both sections can be done in a half-day. On a summer weekend, you'll see large groups of people at Linville Falls admiring the views. Please set a good example and stay off the stone walls.

Type of hike: Out and back

Distance: 4.2 miles

Total Ascent: 1,000 ft.

Starting elevation: 3,160 ft.

Highlights:
Waterfalls, Linville Gorge

USGS map: Linville Falls

Trail map: Available at the Linville Falls Visitor Center

Land managed by:
Linville Falls Recreation Area, Blue Ridge Parkway

Getting to the trailhead: On the Blue Ridge Parkway at milepost 316.4, north of US 221 and south of NC 183, take the Linville Falls Spur

★ =Start

Trailhead GPS Coordinates:
N 35° 57.30 W 81° 55.68

Rd. for 1.5 miles to the Linville Falls Visitor Center.

The Hike (Section 1)
Linville Falls Trail starts through the visitor center's breezeway and crosses the quiet Linville River on a concrete and steel bridge. You'll be on a wide road, hearing the river before it goes into the gorge. Holly, hemlock, rhododendron, doghobble, and mountain laurel keep the trail green all year. As the trail undulates, you'll get good views of the river. Ignore the first right turn, which leads to a Forest Service parking area on Kistler Memorial Highway (NC 1238). This side trail is useful if the Blue Ridge Parkway is closed (see Linville Gorge Loop hike, p. 125). Continue left toward the falls.

Go down to the intersection and turn right, uphill, toward Erwins View. The broad trail climbs and offers benches for resting. The blue dots on hemlocks mark trees that are being treated for hemlock woolly

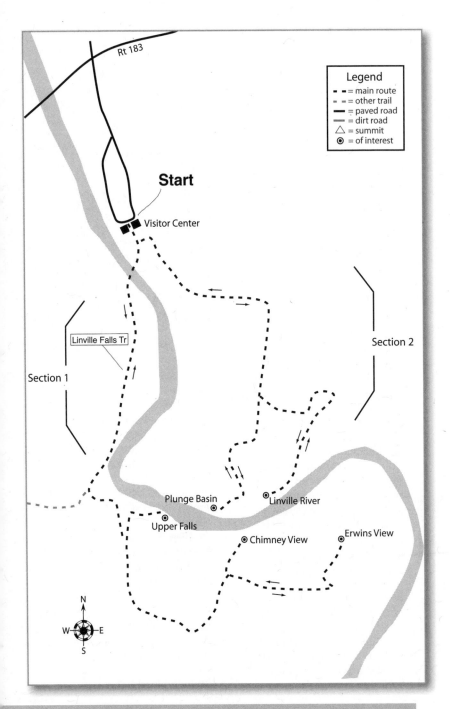

Start

Rt 183

Legend
- - = main route
- - = other trail
— = paved road
— = dirt road
△ = summit
◉ = of interest

Visitor Center

Linville Falls Tr

Section 1

Section 2

Plunge Basin

Linville River

Upper Falls

Chimney View

Erwins View

N
W — E
S

adelgid. At a wooden shelter with two benches, stay right and continue up. At the next intersection (0.9 mile, 3,350 ft. elev.), go up steps on your left to Erwins View.

From high above the falls, you'll see it from the classic (and most photographed) perspective. The power and force of the water rushing through a rock chasm illustrates how the gorge must have been formed. Erwins View is the one farthest away from the trailhead; as you return, you'll stop at closer views.

Come back down the wooden stairs and make a left toward the gorge overlook, surrounded by a stone wall and looking south. When you reach the shelter make a right down the stairs to Chimney View. The first overlook here gives you good views of the falls with the gorge walls straight ahead. At the higher Chimney View Overlook at 1.3 miles (3,250 ft. elev.), you'll see the Upper Falls, which you'll soon reach. This is the best spot to see the upper and lower falls together and also a smaller falls on the lower right side. Hemlock, the dominant tree in the gorge, displays subtly different shades of green.

Return on stone steps to the shelter junction and turn right toward the parking area. A little way down, turn right again toward the Upper Falls Overlook and go down the stairs to the overlook at 1.7 miles. Looking across

On the first section of the hike, you'll have a classic view of Linville Falls.

the river to the gorge walls, you'll see the upper twin falls on your left spilling into a large pool. Downstream, the water whirlpools through a rocky chasm to form the lower falls. Return to the junction and retrace your steps to the visitor center.

The Hike (Section 2)

The second section of the hike takes you to the Plunge Basin Overlook and the Linville River itself. Take the trail to the left of the visitor center and go up the steps. At the junction make a right, away from Dugger's Creek, and head uphill. You'll pass through a green rhododendron and doghobble tunnel where songbirds abound. The trail flattens out a little and at the intersection (2.6 miles) goes straight to the Plunge Basin Overlook.

After passing two small concrete structures low to the ground that once supported a bench, go down stone and concrete steps to an overlook that seems to be suspended halfway down into the gorge. From here you can see the lower falls plunge into a huge pool surrounded by rocks. Because the rock walls form such a perfect rectangle, the scene looks artificial, like a quarry or a pool on an Italian estate.

Returning from the Plunge Basin Overlook, turn right toward the Linville Gorge Trail. The trail starts uphill, but you know it's got to go down soon. This is a quieter area than Linville Falls Trail because the hiking is much rougher. Still, this section of trail down to the river gives you a good feel for the gorge without having to go into the wilderness area, which is more challenging (see Linville Gorge Loop hike, p.125).

Go down rocky steps where you can hear the force of the water as you turn the corner. Look for a switchback to the right; you should never have to bushwhack. Pass a rock wall on your right with a splotch that looks like yellow paint—it's actually lichen.

You'll reach the Linville River at 3.4 miles (3,100 ft. elev.). The high rock walls of the gorge tower above you on both sides. Rhododendron and mountain laurel grow out of the wall's ledges and boulders have formed islands in the river. Go back up the way you came and at the intersection, turn right to go back to the visitor center to end your hike.

Variation: Linville Falls Trail only—2.2 miles with less than 500 ft. ascent.

You can see the river from between the boulders.

Shortoff Mountain is the hike to take if you want a good preview of Linville Gorge. This rock mass at the lower end of the gorge looms dramatically over the foothills and Lake James. And what a wonderful panorama! As you climb, you'll have constant views of Lake James. From the top you'll be able to see Linville Gorge and the Black Mountain Range, including Mt. Mitchell. You can also combine this hike with the Overlooks hike (p. 48) in Lake James State Park, where you'll see the blunt end of Shortoff Mountain from below. This hike starts on an access trail which connects to the Mountains-to-Sea Trail, going trail east.

Type of hike: Out and back

Distance: 3.3 miles

Total ascent: 1,650 ft.

Starting elevation: 1,800 ft.

Highlights: Views

USGS map: Ashford

Trail map: Linville Gorge / Mount Mitchell, Pisgah National Forest, National Geographic Trails Illustrated Map #779.

Land managed by: Pisgah National Forest, Grandfather District

Getting to the trailhead: From I-40, take exit 90 for Nebo/Lake James and head north. At 0.5 mile, turn right onto Harmony Grove Rd.

Trailhead GPS Coordinates: N 35° 49.45 W 81° 53.37

and follow it for 2.0 miles to a stoplight. Proceed straight across the intersection, past Nebo Elementary School to a stop sign. Turn right on NC 126 and follow signs to the Lake James State Park entrance, 2.3 miles on the left. Continue another 8.8 miles on NC 126 and turn left on Wolf Pit Rd. Take the road for 2.5 miles to where it ends in a parking circle.

The Hike
The trail begins on the north side of the circle at the Wilderness Area sign. Start climbing a rough trail where almost immediately you'll see the remnants of a forest fire, which closed the area in the early summer of 2007. The fire left open views of the hills to the north, but pine and mountain laurel are already starting to regenerate the forest. The trail turns right and you'll get your first look at an arm of Lake James below you (see Lake James State Park hikes, p. 48). These views keep improving as you go higher. At 0.7 mile (2,350 ft. elev.), to the

left (south) is Grant Mountain, a private mountain with transmission towers and to the right is the South Mountain range. The town of Morganton lies below but the prominent feature is always the lake.

At 1.1 miles (2,600 ft. elev.), you'll reach the intersection with the MST [#440 – white circle blazes], which here runs concurrent with Shortoff Trail [#235]. Even though this is a wilderness area, the MST circles are frequent. Continue straight on uphill, following MST trail east, ignoring an old eroded, blocked-off trail to the right. You'll see huge boulders on both sides of the trail. As you climb around the western flank of Shortoff Mountain, the views of Lake James get better and better.

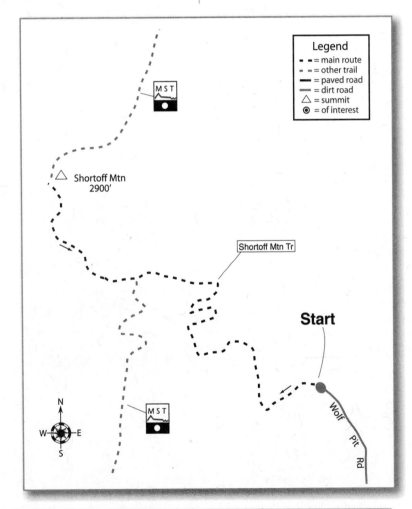

The Lake James views are replaced by views of the Black Mountains in the distance across the gorge. The trail approaches the edge of the cliff. There's nothing artificial here—you're truly in the wilderness.

Now at the edge of the gorge, the trail leads to several flat rocky outcroppings. You'll reach a small piped spring where the trail narrows in a tunnel of lush rhododendron. This is where the 2007 fire must have stopped. Around the corner, you'll pass a campsite and reach another layered rocky outcrop fringed with pitch pine and table mountain pine.

The last overlook at 2,900 ft. is *the* view on Shortoff Mountain, which is at one end of a large plateau. You can see Table Rock, Hawksbill, and Sitting Bear, the most striking features of the eastern side of the gorge. From this angle, the bill of Hawksbill is not visible.

Looking across the gorge on your left, the most prominent rock face is Wiseman's View on Kistler Memorial Highway. If you visit Wiseman's View, you'll see the classic scene of Linville Gorge and look straight on at Table Rock.

This is the turnaround point for this hike. However, if you want to continue to explore, stay on the MST, which here is almost flat. Most of the burned area will be behind you. A peregrine falcon nesting

Shortoff Mountain is at one end of a large plateau.

Topped out on Shortoff.

area to the left of the trail is closed much of the year to protect this endangered bird.

As you retrace your steps to end the hike, you'll be walking facing views of Lake James, each view better than the next.

5

Hot Springs

*A more delightful location for
a hotel or an internment camp
could hardly be found even in
the mountains of this region.*

— Jacqueline Burgin Painter, *The
German Invasion of Western North
Carolina: A Pictorial History*, 1997

Hot Springs/ Appalachian Trail

Essential Facts

Rules:
None
Websites:
www.hotspringsnc.org;
www.appalachiantrail.org
Related books:
The German Invasion of Western North Carolina: A Pictorial History and *The Stackhouses of Appalachia: Even to our Own Time* by Jacqueline Burgin Painter; *The French Broad* by Wilma Dykeman

The Cherokees knew all about the natural hot mineral springs long before white settlers stumbled on them. Warm Springs, as it was first called, was well known as a resort destination from the 1830s. The Warm Springs Hotel, also known as Patton's White House, the first large hotel there, attracted almost a thousand visitors at a time, many of them from Charleston. The warm water was thought to heal numerous ailments, from sore eyes and vertigo to barrenness and impotence. The hotel burned down and was rebuilt several times under different names, each time with more modern amenities.

As you drive through the imposing curved entrance leading to the site where the grand hotel stood on the banks of the French Broad River, you can imagine women carrying parasols and men with walking canes strolling along the river. The mountain town and the elegant hotel appealed to those looking for upscale social life

in the summer. The resorts provided a venue for the display of wealth, the exchange of views on fashion and politics, and a chance for courtship.

An even warmer spring was discovered in the 1880s and the town was renamed Hot Springs. At the height of Hot Springs's popularity, the recommended treatment cure consisted of three weeks of massages and baths.

Hot Springs is located on the Buncombe Turnpike, a road built in 1828 from Greenville, SC, to Greeneville, TN. The turnpike was the superhighway of its time, allowing goods and people to flow into and out of the mountains. More than 100,000 hogs and other livestock were driven along the turnpike each year, heading for either the coast or the Ohio Valley. Heading north, the turnpike's route is approximated by US 25 until you reach Hot Springs. Before crossing the French Broad, the old route turned and paralleled the river to Paint Rock at the state line. The river (known as a "Broad") was called "French" because it flowed into French-held territory before the French relinquished all their holdings east of the Mississippi River in the Treaty of Paris in 1763.

In the early 20th century, rich vacationers lost interest in "taking the waters" at mineral springs. During World War I, the hotel housed German sailors—prisoners of war who were unlucky enough to have been working on a luxury liner in New York at the beginning of the war. Or maybe they were quite lucky: they spent the duration of the war in Hot Springs, building a picturesque German village from bits and pieces of scrap lumber. Most of the wooden buildings were blown up in the exuberance of Armistice Day. The grand hotel burned in 1920, never to be rebuilt, and although two smaller lodging establishments succeeded it, they too were destroyed by fire. After that, Hot Springs never regained its prominence with fashionable society of the Low Country.

Today, with fewer than 700 year-round residents, the town is quiet in winter. Gift shops, most restaurants, and even the tourist office close, but the springs still exist in the form of a hot tub-style spa.

The Appalachian Trail

The Appalachian Trail goes right down the town's main street. Outside of western North Carolina, few people have heard of Hot Springs—except A.T. thru-hikers. For them, Hot Springs is a major destination, one of only a handful of places where the A.T. passes through a town.

Most long-distance hikers spend a few days in town to rest, restock their supplies, do laundry, and catch up with trail friends. Every April, Hot Springs organizes Trailfest, a weekend festival of music, food, parades, and talks by celebrity hikers—and yes, there are celebrity hikers. Trailfest is scheduled for when the bulk of hikers who start on Georgia's Springer Mountain reach Hot Springs after walking 270 miles. Many who haven't arrived in town by that time or have already passed it hitchhike into Hot Springs to participate in Trailfest, then after their wild weekend, thumb back to where they were on the A.T. and continue walking. Some hikers see it as a reunion, others as a resting place for weary feet and hungry stomachs.

Extending from Georgia to Maine, the 2,175-mile A.T. may be the most famous footpath in the world. If you've been trying to figure out if you have the right stuff to walk the distance, Leanna Joyner, who thru-hiked the A.T. in 2003 and now works for the Appalachian Trail Conservancy, offers the following advice. "Success has to do with enjoying your surroundings and having a positive attitude despite uncomfortable circumstances—rain, cold, tired feet. Yes, the 'right gear' always helps, but having an openness to learn, to be challenged, and to be adaptable is very important."

Most people who thru-hike the A.T. do it at a point of transition in their lives: graduation, retirement, losing a job or a partner. When you complete the trail, you will be forever known as a 2,000-

Crossing Max Patch Bald

miler—you can put that on your transcript and your tombstone.

How long it takes you to thru-hike depends on how much you walk per day and how many zero (nonhiking) days you take. If you average 13 miles a day, six days a week, it will take you about six and a half months, conventionally done between March and October. Most backpackers walk more than that since they have such long hiking days— they don't spend time driving to the trailhead. On the seventh day, you don't rest; you do laundry, take a shower, buy and repackage your food, and send postcards home. Postcards? If you call home too often you run the risk of being pulled back into family life, leaving the trail to go to your cousin's wedding, worrying about your sister's divorce, and all the rest. For this adventure, other A.T. hikers become your family.

Most hikers take a trail name, a moniker to show that they have taken on a new identity on the A.T. Hikers are known by names like *Sunshine*, *Wanderer*, or *Tulip*. Trail names show you belong in the A.T. club.

Walking the A.T. is not a solitary experience and meeting other hikers is part of the fun. If you start out by yourself—and most successful thru-hikers do it solo—you'll meet people at shelters and be able to choose your companions at different points. Shelters, planned about a day's walk apart, are three-sided structures with a tin roof and the fourth side open to the elements. Most shelters only accommodate eight hikers. You may be the ninth, so you still need to carry a tent.

But you don't have to give up your job or drop out of school to complete the A.T. and become a 2,000-miler. You have a whole lifetime to hike it in sections. It takes more organization to plan an A.T. section hike, year after year. You have to be in top physical shape, since you can't use the first week of hiking to get in shape. If you're limited by vacation time your schedule is less flexible, so you have to finish each section by a certain date. Most section hikers hire shuttlers, locals who will drive them to the beginning of the hike. Less than a quarter of the 2,000-milers who finish walk the A.T. in sections.

Benton MacKaye was the visionary who, in 1921, first proposed the A.T. as a path stringing together a set of planned wilderness communities where people could go to renew themselves, away from the excesses of the modern world. Ironically, it was the automobile which made a linear trail feasible. Before that, outdoor activities were typically concentrated at mountain resorts with loop trails.

But it was Myron Avery, a maritime lawyer, who became the first 2,000-miler in 1936. Avery worked feverishly for decades to turn a utopian dream into the white-blazed trail we hike today. He organized volunteers, worked with the government, and developed local hiking clubs, and he walked and measured every step of the trail.

Earl Shaffer, a World War II veteran from Pennsylvania, was the first thru-hiker; in 1948, he performed a feat that had been considered impossible. His recommended equipment included a sheath knife and small axe to cut wood for his cooking fire. He carried a poncho which he used as a raincoat, parka, ground cloth, and shelter. He hiked the trail two more times, the third time finishing two weeks before he turned 80.

This classic Appalachian Trail hike on the North Carolina/ Tennessee border wiggles between the Cherokee National Forest and Pisgah National Forest and leads to 360-degree views on grass-covered Big Bald. You'll be hiking trail north toward Maine in this section, with the trail heading compass east. Wildflowers blanket the forest floor under a canopy of maple and oak. You'll see fences and many old roads and trails taking off from the A.T., even an abandoned mine—all evidence that the land was once worked and farmed. Because the trail is well-maintained, the hike feels easier than its distance and ascent might indicate.

Type of hike: Out and back

Distance: 13.0 miles

Total ascent: 3,100 ft.

Starting elevation: 3,750 ft.

Highlights: Spectacular views, grassy bald, meadows, wildflowers

USGS map: Sams Gap

Trail map: Appalachian Trail Guide to Tennessee-North Carolina

Land managed by: Pisgah National Forest, Appalachian District

Getting to the trailhead: From I-26 exit 3, turn east on Bear Branch Rd. (SR 1346) and cross over the highway. Turn left on US 23A north for 3.2 miles. Park in the large parking area at Sams Gap before the road goes under I-26.

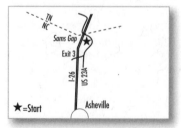

Trailhead GPS Coordinates: N 35° 57.15 W 82° 33.66

The Hike

From the parking area, cross US 23A and go through a wooden stile. The A.T. [white rectangle blazes] is well-signposted here. You'll walk through a field of asters, goldenrod, chicory, and Queen Anne's lace as you parallel I-26. The trail switchbacks right and up.

Go through a metal gate, leading from the highway into forest in a quarter-mile. The trail continues wide and flat under a hardwood cove forest of maple and oaks. You might still be able to hear cars on the highway.

At 0.4 mile, you'll pass a flat area on the right, a campsite that's illegal because it's too close to the trail. At 0.8 mile you'll pass two springs where the trail goes gently up and down. You can't count on getting water from any spring on this section, even though the area looks fertile and green.

At 1.3 miles, two faint trails take off from a flat area on the left, crossing an intermittent creek. Then the trail climbs steeply through poison ivy, jewelweed, and Christmas ferns to an enormous permanent blowdown on one side. There's a huge drop-off to the right as the trail goes up good wooden steps. At 1.4 miles (4,100 ft. elev.) you'll reach the top of an abandoned talc mine on the left. Look for an old excavation site about a hundred feet deep. The hole has new growth of trees and vegetation.

A little above the mine, an old overgrown road heads left. With some imagination, you'll see a clearing through the trees. At 1.8 miles (4,450 ft. elev.), the trail reaches a flat area with illegal campfire rings and a fence to your right. The trail then makes a soft left into an open field and goes down through a pasture with excellent views of ridge after ridge of mountains.

The pasture has been mowed and you'll see evidence of horses. The trail goes back into the woods and descends steeply on rock steps. A huge rock wall rises on your right and, to your left, a gravel road ascends to meet the trail at Street Gap (2.4 miles, 4,150 ft. elev.). To your left the road takes off toward Flag Pond, TN, and right toward Puncheon Fork Rd. in North Carolina.

Go through a metal barrier meant to keep vehicles off the trail and continue through a wildflower-filled meadow. At the top of the rise as you pass under power lines, you'll see cars zipping by on I-26 to your left, below a range of Tennessee mountains in the distance. Here you're on a

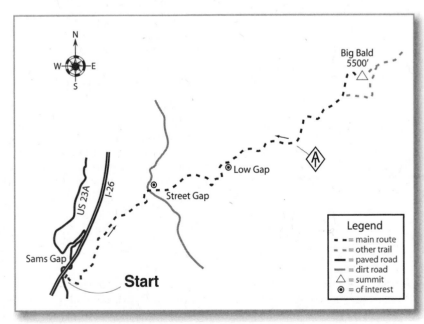

A large meadow offers open views on the way to Big Bald.

wide, flat road under a maple, oak, and buckeye canopy without much of an understory. As you climb, you'll see small pieces of quartz on the ground.

At 3.6 miles, a side trail goes sharply left and down to a campsite. Continue gently downhill on the A.T. to Low Gap at 3.8 miles (4,300 ft. elev.). This gap may be indistinct, but when you reach it you'll start going up seriously. A blue-blazed trail to the right leads to a spring.

At 4.3 miles, pass an intermittent spring on the right where rocks could be wet and slippery. You'll reach a road leading to power lines at 4.6 miles (4,900 ft. elev.). Beyond the crest of a sidehill at 5.1 miles where the trail starts to descend, a beech tree with exposed roots grows out of a rock on your left. The maple

canopy is so thick that there's little undergrowth other than wildflowers, nettles, and ferns.

At 5.7 miles (5,050 ft. elev.) you'll pass a board, now full of graffiti, which directs you left on the A.T. or right onto a blue-blazed trail, used in bad weather. The blue-blazed trail avoids Big Bald's open top. As a dayhiker, in bad weather you may decide to return to the start of a hike or not begin at all. However, long distance backpackers don't have that option; they need to keep moving forward. So bad-weather bypasses have been created on the A.T., allowing hikers to go around sections deemed dangerous in rain, fog, or lightning storms.

The trail climbs steeply for the last 500 ft., passing a couple of springs. As the trail gets rockier, you'll pass a huge craggy boulder on your right with trees and fringes of vegetation. The climb moderates at 6.1 miles (5,400 ft. elev.). After taking you past an abandoned orchard, the trail opens up into a field filled with grasses, cow parsnip, filmy angelica, and blueberry bushes almost as big as trees.

As you climb more gently, turn around for your *wow* moment. You're surrounded by mountain ranges as you follow wooden posts to the top. These posts are particularly helpful in guiding hikers through open fields in foggy and wet weather. Below and to your right lies Wolf Laurel Resort, a large residential gated community and ski center. However, the ranges are mostly empty of development and that emptiness dwarfs the effect of the few houses you'll see.

At 6.5 miles you'll reach Big Bald (5,500 ft. elev.), a grassy bald with one of the finest 360-degree views in the Southern Appalachians. It's always windy here. On a good day you'll see Mt. Mitchell, the highest peak east of the Mississippi, the Black Mountain Range to the southeast, and the Smokies to the west. A round metal benchmark has been hammered into a stone on the ground near the post at the highest point.

The top has a large gravel parking area connecting to a private road to Wolf Laurel Resort. Return the way you came to end the hike.

Varied terrain includes large rock outcroppings on the trail.

This challenging hike combines outstanding views with solitude through most of the day. From Hot Springs, you'll take Roundtop Ridge Trail, which climbs to the summit of Rich Mountain and its lookout tower with excellent views. Then you'll descend on the A.T., heading trail south through Tanyard Gap and passing the meadows of Mill Ridge and a small pond on your way to Pump Gap. You'll climb again to the Lovers Leap Ridge and enjoy great views of Hot Springs. After that, it's down, down, down to the French Broad and back to your car. If you're staying in Hot Springs, you could walk out from your lodging and hike without a vehicle. In mid-April, you'll see thru-hikers heading out to the A.T. from Hot Springs.

Type of hike: Loop

Distance: 13.0 miles

Total ascent: 2,950 ft.

Starting elevation: 1,300 ft.

Highlights: Views from tower, French Broad, solitude until close to Hot Springs

USGS map: Hot Springs

Trail map: Harmon Den & Hot Springs Area Trail Map, USDA Forest Service

Land managed by: Pisgah National Forest, Appalachian District

Getting to the trailhead: From the center of Hot Springs, drive on US 25/70 north across the bridge and make an immediate left on SR 1304. Turn left onto Silvermine Rd. at the first intersection, go under the bridge, and park on the right in a grassy area.

Trailhead GPS Coordinates: N 35° 53.57 W 82° 49.30

The Hike

From the trailhead, take the paved road SR 1304, which goes under the US 25/70 bridge. Turn right on Reservoir Rd. at 0.4 mile. The trail climbs gently past several houses and crosses a drainage pipe in front of the last house. Take the dirt road on the left to enter Pisgah National Forest. Soon you'll see a "Road Closed" sign. At 0.9 mile, pass a green water tower on your left. You'll be on Roundtop Ridge Trail [#295 – yellow blazes], heading east with good views on the right, following a stream shrouded in rhododendron.

The trail may not be well-maintained but because it was the old A.T. up to Rich Mountain, it's still quite clear as it switchbacks up the mountain. Every so often you can see Hot Springs and hear roosters crowing below. As you go deeper into the forest, the sound changes to jungle calls of pileated woodpeckers. The trail climbs through a dry white pine forest with an understory of blueberry bushes, and Rich Mountain Tower can be seen above. In the spring, the trail is lined with cut-leaved toothwort and wild lily-of-the-valley.

The ridge you see to your right is the one you'll descend on your way back to Hot Springs. At about 3.4 miles, the meadows on Mill Ridge, which you'll pass on the way down, are visible across the valley. At 4.2 miles (3,200 ft. elev.), make a left on the A.T. [white blazes], heading trail north. You'll come back to this point after visiting the tower. The soil is damper here; you'll see rue anemone, halberd-leaved violets, and irises in springtime.

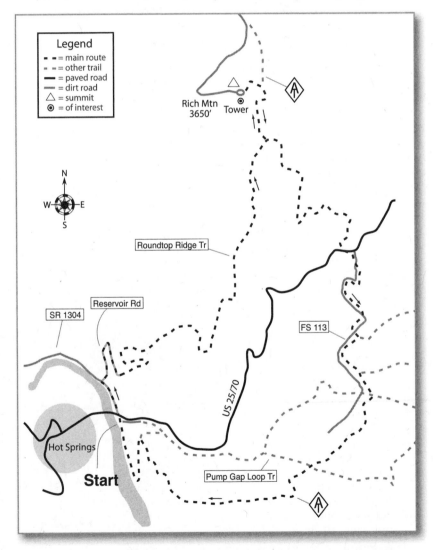

When the A.T. goes right at 4.7 miles (3,500 ft. elev.), stay left and continue uphill toward the Rich Mountain Lookout Tower, passing open fields on both sides. Cross NC 467B, the road to the tower. The tower has a dunce-cap roof and an open-air room on top. Enjoy the panorama from the Smokies to the Black Mountains.

Retrace your steps from the tower. Don't take the first left on the A.T. but continue on, heading trail south. At 5.6 miles, at the junction with Roundtop Ridge Trail, stay on the A.T., which switchbacks pleasantly downhill through a moist landscape rich with mountain laurel, rhododendron, and galax. Look for a piped spring in a crevice on your left. As you descend into a narrow glen, you'll begin to meet other dayhikers and dog walkers and arrive at the small Tanyard Gap parking area.

At 7.6 miles (2,300 ft. elev.) you'll cross a bridge above US 25/70. Walk on a road for a short while and go up the steps on the left to stay on the A.T. A sign says "Hot Springs 3.8." The trail climbs steadily as motorcycle noises fade away; FS 113, a dirt road, is on the right below. Soon you'll reach a grassy, open area on the right. At 8.2 miles, the road comes up to meet the trail. Walk on the dirt road to reach a sign on the left that reads "Mill Ridge Trail Parking." Stay right through a meadow and pass a wooden information board on the left. The fields of Mill Ridge were once planted in hay and tobacco. The land was bought by the Forest Service in 1970 and now attracts turkey, grouse, and other wildlife.

Turn right off the road to stay on the A.T. Back in the woods, a pond on the left side, created by an old dam, attracts anglers of all ages. When you reach an old road coming from the right, stay left on the A.T. Cinquefoil, bluets, and dwarf crested iris grow profusely on this southeast-facing slope.

At 10.1 miles, the A.T. intersects Pump Gap Trail and hugs the ridge, Hot Springs disappears, and Rich Mountain Lookout Tower is visible again. When the trail cuts over to the left, you'll hear the rush of the French Broad.

Rich Mountain Lookout Tower has a distinctive dunce-cap roof.

Hot Springs is located on the Buncombe Turnpike, built in 1828. It was the superhighway of its time.

Pass an unofficial campsite on your left. At 11.8 miles, make a left on a short trail to the first view from Lovers Leap; Lovers Leap Ridge has several views. In another 0.2 mile the A.T. intersects Lovers Leap Trail, leading to Silvermine Trailhead. Stay left on the A.T., where there's another lookout down into Hot Springs. The trail switchbacks down to the French Broad, close to rocks on the left. You'll parallel the French Broad and pass a gauging station and perhaps people cooling their feet in the river. The water runs too fast here for swimming. After the Nantahala Outdoor Center take-out point, you'll find your car on the left to end the hike.

Laurel River Trail follows Big Laurel Creek on an old railroad bed to the historic ghost town of Runion and the French Broad. Depending on the water level, you may find several good wading spots along the way. Over 250 vascular plants have been identified here. This out-and-back hike is good any time of year. The gentle trail, also a bike trail, is almost flat, which is unusual in the Blue Ridge Mountains.

Type of hike: Out and back

Distance: 7.5 miles

Total ascent: 300 ft.

Starting elevation: 1,450 ft.

Highlights: Creek views, wading, wildflowers, logging artifacts

USGS map: Hot Springs

Trail map: Harmon Den & Hot Springs Area Trail Map, USDA Forest Service

Land managed by: Pisgah National Forest, Appalachian District

Getting to the trailhead: From the center of Hot Springs, take US 25/70 south for 5.4 miles. After the road turns right, look for a wide parking area on the right. The trail starts on the southern end of the parking lot.

Trailhead GPS Coordinates: N 35° 54.75 W 82° 45.41

The Hike
Laurel River Trail [#310 – yellow blazes] follows the creek generally south and stays mostly level. Disregard the first right turn as you go down to the creek. Wildflowers are plentiful here; so is poison ivy. You'll pass a private house on your left.

At the creek, you'll enter a gorge with a huge rock wall on your left and variegated boulders jumbled in the streambed. Coneflower, jewelweed, and Joe-Pye weed line the creek. Fishing is popular here.

Hikers and waders have created rock sculptures in the river bank by stacking flat rocks on top of each other. At 1.8 miles you'll pass a muddy spot where you can get into the creek easily, but continue less than 0.1 mile to a better spot. Here, a promontory with a rocky beach provides easy access to the creek. Pass a campsite on the left, a flat area nestled against the rock at about two miles. The rocks seem to have disappeared, though you're still in the gorge. Cook Branch, a tributary, comes in from the right.

At 2.5 miles, hikers have placed several rope swings over the creek. The water seems a little deeper here with fewer rocks, then gains momentum and speeds downhill around boulders, creating several cascades. The force of the water has bleached and smoothed boulders and created potholes. When the water level is low, you'll see the effects of water wearing against rocks.

The trail moves farther up and away from the creek. At 3.0 miles, you'll reach the remains of Runion, an old mill town. Three walls and

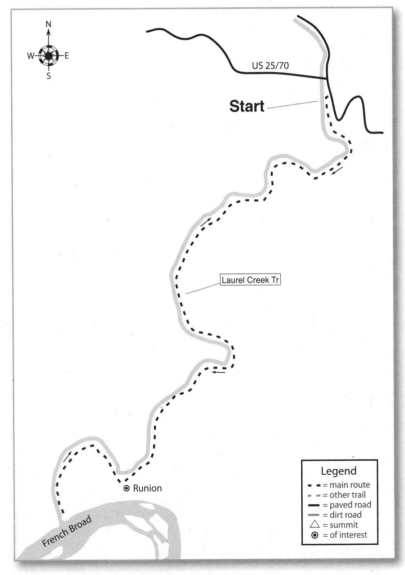

An angler tests the waters of Laurel Creek.

the railroad tracks of Norfolk-Southern Railroad, still in active use; do not cross the tracks. Here Laurel Creek empties into the French Broad. Return the way you came to end the hike.

scattered concrete structures are all that's left of a once thriving community. Old stone foundations and pillars are now fringed with vegetation and mosses; metal rods are embedded in rocks. If you take a left on one of several narrow trails, you'll see more stonework and evidence of a railroad. A pump house stands off to the left.

As you continue, you'll leave behind most of the ruined mill. Some concrete blocks still lie along the creek and a few old brown bricks are scattered on the trail. You'll pass a flat campsite by the creek at 3.5 miles where a small cascade flows through a break in the rock and around a boulder. You might see a solitary great blue heron flying in the gorge. Reach the end of the trail and

Heritage

The Stackhouse

The Stackhouse is so intimately connected with the area that you might want to have a look at the outside of this beautiful private house. In the 1870s, Amos and Anna Stackhouse, originally from Pennsylvania, established the settlement that bears their name. The Stackhouse, built in 1904 by Amos, Jr., had 10 rooms and a circular tower.

In 1897, Amos Stackhouse leased land to North Carolina Land & Timber Company. The company built a sawmill, church, school building, and houses for

The 1904 Stackhouse, built by Amos Stackhouse, Jr., is still occupied by his descendents.

community life in Runion shrank as the school, stores, churches, and post office closed.

In 1991, the site of the original mill towns became part of Pisgah National Forest and Runion turned into a ghost town. However, the Stackhouse home is still occupied by the family that bears its name.

their workers. More land was bought as the village expanded. When the company went bankrupt, the Laurel River Logging Company came into Runion to continue the cutting, logging, buying, and selling of timber. At its height, over 500 people lived in Runion and neighboring Stackhouse. In addition, many workers walked in from other communities. Runion was a company town where workers were paid in paper scrip; the average worker made $1.50 for a 10-hour day.

The mill became the largest employer in Madison County. The railroad brought both logs and workers from Runion to the mill. In those days, trees seem to be in endless supply and it was thought that forests would last forever. But in 1925, the company went bankrupt and many families had no choice but to move away and look elsewhere for work. Little by little,

To get to the Stackhouse:

From the Laurel River trailhead, make a right on US 25/70 and drive 1.9 miles. Turn right on Stackhouse Rd. and drive 2.5 miles to the end of the road, crossing the railroad tracks. The road ends at the French Broad and a public day-use area. The Stackhouse is across the tracks.

The sawmill at Runion.

This hike has a wonderful variety of terrain, from the famous open summit of Max Patch to flat meadows, distant ridges, and a new Appalachian Trail shelter with modern trail conveniences. You'll climb to Max Patch for panoramic views of the Smokies, the Black Mountains, and the Balsams. But soon you'll leave most casual hikers behind to explore the side trails: Max Patch Trail, missing from some maps, and Buckeye Ridge Trail. You'll want to get an early start for this hike because on a good weekend, the parking lot fills up quickly.

Type of hike: Loop

Distance: 5.9 miles

Total ascent: 800 ft.

Starting elevation: 4,300 ft.

Highlights: 360-degree views on the bald, spring flowers, shelter

USGS map: Lemon Gap

Trail map: Harmon Den & Hot Springs Area Trail Map, USDA Forest Service

Land managed by: Pisgah National Forest, Appalachian District

Getting to the trailhead: Take I-40 to exit 7 (Harmon Den). Turn right at the exit and follow Cold Springs Rd. for 6.7 miles. Stay left and on the main gravel road. Turn left on SR 1182 and drive for less than 2.0 miles to the Max Patch parking area.

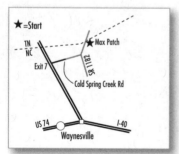

Trailhead GPS Coordinates: N 35° 47.78 W 82° 57.76

The Hike

At the trailhead, go over the stile and take the trail to the left, following the wand that says "Max Patch." This wide jeep trail heads up and north where flame azalea blooms in mid-June. In 0.5 mile, turn right on the A.T. (trail south) and climb to the summit of Max Patch. There's the occasional cow parsnip, but the top of Max Patch at 4,600 ft. is kept bald by the Forest Service with mowing and controlled burns. Casual hikers climb this hill for its outstanding views. From the top of Max Patch on a clear day, looking west you can see Mt. Cammerer and Mt. Sterling in the Great Smoky Mountains National Park and to the east the Balsam Range. In fact, it feels as if from this spot you can see the whole world.

Continue on the A.T. in the same direction. Take one last look at the top of Max Patch as the A.T. turns left. The trail is lined with blackberry cane as it goes down on good wooden steps. Poison ivy doesn't typically thrive above 3,000 ft., but here it is on the side of the trail at 4,600 ft. Poison ivy flourishes on disturbed land and does well at the edges of the mowed areas.

Leave the A.T. and turn left on Max Patch Trail. An information sign says "2.0 miles," pointing left to the Max Patch trailhead where you're going. This wide road through the trees soon comes out into the open below Max Patch. Look up to the left to see Max Patch from a different perspective.

At 1.7 miles (4,300 ft. elev.), stay left when you intersect Buckeye Ridge Trail, which goes up and to the right. When Max Patch Trail joins the A.T., continue straight, heading trail north toward Roaring Fork Shelter. The trail enters a rhododendron tunnel with rusty barbed wire on the left. Go through a stile and cross an old forest road; you'll come back to this point toward the end of the hike. Make a sharp left to stay on the A.T., which follows Roaring Fork Creek on the right on a rocky trail. A blue sign points to "Water." Go right to the creek for a look if you want; otherwise turn left to stay on the A.T. toward Roaring Fork Shelter. Turn right at the

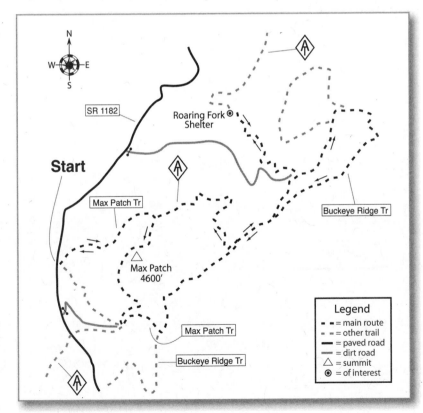

shelter sign. At 2.9 miles (4,000 ft. elev.), you'll arrive at the Roaring Fork Shelter, designed and built by the Carolina Mountain Club. It replaced an old shelter at Lemon Gap which had been trashed by nonhikers. This shelter, access trail, and privy were all built to meet requirements of the Americans with Disabilities Act. After a break at the shelter, retrace your steps on the A.T. On the way back, instead of following the sign to water, go up and to the right.

At 3.3 miles (4,200 ft. elev.), make a left on the unnamed old forest road after a gate. There's no sign, but the wide forest road is unmistakable. Soon make a right and go up on Buckeye Ridge Trail [#304 – yellow blazes], a horse trail, which climbs gently into the forest. You'll see the wand for Buckeye Ridge Trail only after you've made the turn. After cresting a rise, the trail flattens out through a meadow filling in with blackberries, cohosh, and cow parsnip, with Max Patch looming in front of you. There are wands at regular intervals to guide you through the field.

When you see white blazes to your right at 4.5 miles, rejoin the A.T., heading into the woods. The two trails run together for a short while. Make a right to stay on the A.T., which climbs up in an enclosed maple and oak forest with huge umbrella plants and Solomon's plume. You'll pass a campsite on your right just before you come out into the open. At 5.4 miles, leave the A.T. and turn right to go back down to your car and end the hike.

A group hike across Max Patch Bald, famous for its open views.

On this hike you'll go deep into the Pigeon River Gorge on the Rube Rock Trail, which may be as close as you can get to untouched nature without actually bushwhacking. Though you will hear the sounds of cars on I-40 as you near the bottom of the Gorge, you won't actually reach the interstate. Then you'll climb to a shelter on Groundhog Creek Trail, using the old route of the Appalachian Trail. You'll hike a small section of the A.T., stopping at Hawks Roost, where there is an overlook and a large information board explaining the natural regeneration of the forest.

Type of hike: Loop

Distance: 8.9 miles

Total ascent: 2,000 ft.

Starting elevation: 3,500 ft.

Highlights: Gorge, solitude, Hawks Roost

USGS map: Waterville

Trail map: Harmon Den & Hot Springs Area Trail Map, USDA Forest Service

Land managed by: Pisgah National Forest, Appalachian District

Getting to the trailhead: Take I-40 to exit 7 (Harmon Den). Turn right at the exit and follow Cold Spring Creek Rd. (FS 148) for 3.3 miles. Make the first left turn on FS 148A, a gravel road and drive for 1.3 miles to the intersection of two forest roads at Brown Gap. Park at a wide spot near the intersection.

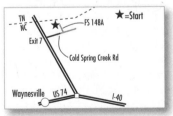

Trailhead GPS Coordinates: N 35° 46.39 W 82° 59.75

The Hike
At Brown Gap, walk down FS 148A, the road you just drove up, and in less than a quarter-mile turn right on FS 357, a gated forest road. It's a gentle up and down with a great variety of wildflowers, including aster, gentian, goldenrod, jewelweed, ironweed, and Joe-Pye weed. Pass a boulder on the right. At 1.4 miles (3,650 ft. elev.), Rube Rock Trail [#314 – yellow blazes] comes in from the right. Continue on the road for another 0.1 mile and take the continuation of Rube Rock Trail on the left.

It's a bit overgrown, but there should be a brown carsonite sign just as you go into the woods. The trail is narrow, thick with nettles and sometimes poison ivy. After zigzagging downhill in a deep, solitary forest with lots of vines, on your right you'll parallel the road you just left. Cross the road at 1.8 miles where there are clear blazes to guide you back on the trail.

The trail is beautiful and easy to follow, heading gently downhill through deep forest

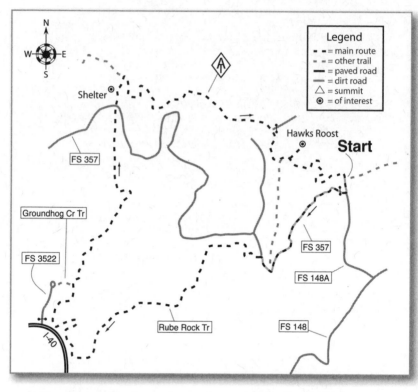

Legend

- = main route
- = other trail
- = paved road
- = dirt road
△ = summit
⊙ = of interest

Shelter

FS 357

Groundhog Cr Tr

FS 3522

Rube Rock Tr

Hawks Roost

Start

FS 357

FS 148A

FS 148

I-40

with a canopy of oak, maple, and tuliptrees. The trail turns sharply right as you parallel a small creek on your left, past a big patch of rhododendron, galax, and fern around the creek. It's much more moist here than at the beginning of the hike. Cross a tributary of Rube Rock Branch and crisscross the creek several more times, passing huge, ramrod-straight tuliptrees. Rhododendron is thick around the creek, which gets wider as you continue down. The forest is silent and green, with untouched moss-covered logs, Christmas and New York fern, and club moss.

At 2.7 miles (2,950 ft. elev.), you'll pass a good, flat campsite with streams on both sides. Farther down, boulders in the stream create cascades and waterfalls through the rhododendron. You'll crisscross small creeks as you descend more seriously and begin to hear traffic on I-40 in the Pigeon River Gorge. The trail is now smoother, wider, and covered with soft pine needles. You may even see the interstate through the trees, but you won't be dropping all the way to the highway. Instead, you'll skirt around Hickory Ridge as the trail undulates gently. In the fall, you may find the fruit of the strawberry bush, which breaks open to expose its red seeds when ripe. Because of the way the seeds burst out, the plant is referred to as "hearts-a-bustin'."

After passing a flat area above the interstate, the trail makes a sharp right and completely changes its feel. You'll now walk on the grade of an old railroad which went from Waterville, NC, to Newport, TN. Note the indentations in the ground, the only remaining evidence of the long-gone railroad ties. Cross Rube Rock Branch at 3.6 miles (2,100 ft. elev.) on rocks, which may be a challenge if the water is high. As you walk farther away from the sounds of traffic, the hill is on your right and the vegetation has changed to mostly hemlock. It's a beautiful, solitary trail. Go around a second minor cove.

At 4.1 miles (2,250 ft. elev.), Groundhog Creek Trail [#315 – blue blazes] comes in from your left then heads down into the gorge. Continue straight and slightly right on Groundhog Creek Trail, heading north. The trail is well-maintained and lined with occasional boulders; there may be some confusing places at creek crossings. You'll reach a tributary of Groundhog Creek as the trail returns to the railroad grade and leads around a hill on your left.

Cross the creek again on a jumble of rocks with a pool toward the top. The trail makes a sharp right, then goes left and climbs more seriously. Trillium and iris carpet the ground in spring. Note the grooves on the trail bed again, showing the path of the old railroad. At 5.2 miles, the trail goes down

An information board at Hawks Roost explains Champion International Corporation's role in logging and managing land around the Pigeon River.

wooden steps, crosses the creek, and goes back up.

Cross FS 357 and continue straight. At 5.5 miles (2, 900 ft. elev.), you'll reach Groundhog Creek Shelter with several good camping spots around the shelter and a rickety picnic table in front. A string hung with empty cans is provided so campers can suspend their food bags away from mice and other small rodents.

Beyond the shelter the climb becomes steeper, passing old-growth hemlock. When you reach the A.T. [white blazes] in another 0.2 mile, make a right, heading trail north (you'll head compass east on the North Carolina/Tennessee border). A sign points to Brown Gap, your destination; Snowbird Mountain is on your left. The A.T. climbs up and down the ridge with few views and meets an abandoned overgrown lumber road at 7.4 miles (3,650 ft. elev.); you'll see a gate on your left. The A.T. makes a right that's obvious in the spring, but overgrown later in the year. The A.T. leaves the road within 100 ft. and goes up on wooden steps. You'll reach an intersection with Rube Rock Trail which comes in from the right at 7.9 miles (3,900 ft. elev.). The A.T. swings left and down.

At 8.0 miles, take a short diversion (less than 0.1 mile) on a blue-blazed trail going left and down to Hawks Roost. An information board explains that Champion International Corporation managed the land below. In 1908, the company established a pulp and paper mill along the banks of the Pigeon River in Canton, and became one of the biggest loggers in the area. The plant was closed in 1997, after which Champion employees purchased it and formed Blue Ridge Paper Company. It is now owned by Evergreen Packaging.

Just beyond the sign is a small rock outcrop with good northeastern views toward Max Patch, but you can't see the signature bald of Max Patch because of the hills in between. Unless the Forest Service cuts down some trees, this view is not going to last much longer.

Return to the A.T. and make a left to continue trail north. The trail goes down where you reach a sign for Brown Gap, and soon your car, to end the hike.

Heritage

The Pigeon River: A Return to Aquatic Health

The Pigeon River takes its name from the passenger pigeon, an extinct bird that was once plentiful in the region. This species, perhaps once the world's most abundant birds, died out as a direct result of human activity.

In the mid-1800s, passenger pigeons traveled in huge flocks. John James Audubon lived during their heyday. In *Birds of America,* he wrote, "The multitudes of

Wild Pigeons in our woods are astonishing….The air was literally filled with Pigeons; the light of noon-day was obscured as by an eclipse, the dung fell in spots, not unlike melting flakes of snow; and the continued buzz of wings had a tendency to lull my senses to repose."

But the bird was considered an agricultural pest and it also made for good eating. Hunters could easily shoot down nesting flocks. Even Audubon killed the birds he used to create his famous painting of two pigeons feeding each other. Much of the passenger pigeon's habitat was destroyed by extensive logging. By the end of the 19th century, there were too few remaining for the species to maintain itself. The last known passenger pigeon died in 1914.

The East Fork of the Pigeon River starts high on Graveyard Ridge and follows US 276 on the east side of Shining Rock Wilderness. The West Fork of the Pigeon River starts on Pisgah Ridge and parallels NC 215 on the west side of the Wilderness. The two forks flow north and join in Canton to become the Pigeon River, which then roughly parallels I-40 through the

Pigeon River Gorge. At Waterville, the river is impounded by a dam before entering Tennessee, where it runs into the French Broad River.

Champion Paper will forever be linked to the Pigeon River. The company's giant paper mill in Canton became the area's largest employer—and polluter. Champion used the river as a dumping ground for its industrial waste; the river was once considered one of the most polluted in the country. But because of environmental action and advances in wastewater treatment, the water quality has improved tremendously in the last 10 years. The Pigeon River now sustains native aquatic species that had not been seen there for decades. Snails, mollusks, minnows, darters, and various shiners have been reintroduced; these are indicator species used to measure a river's aquatic health. In early 2007, the last advisory against eating fish caught downstream of the paper mill was lifted. The company has undergone a couple of name changes and is now called Evergreen, having become a member of a large multi-national corporation. To most locals, however, it is still known as Champion.

6

Pisgah
Appalachian District

When I was a child in the 1950s, US 70 from
Black Mountain to Old Fort was always an
adventure. You never knew which hairpin
curve would produce a flatbed apple truck or
a Greyhound bus; neither could be passed by
a car in the narrowest part. You might see a
bear crossing the road or munching apples in
the orchards on the side of the mountain.

— Tommie Moffit Boston, 2007

Hump Mountain

32

Starting on Roaring Creek Rd., the trail climbs to Yellow Mountain Gap, where the Overmountain Men passed through on their way to victory at the Battle of Kings Mountain. Here you'll join the Appalachian Trail, which travels over open meadows and ridges to Little Hump Mountain and Hump Mountain. On the return to Yellow Mountain Gap, you'll take in a short section of the historic Overmountain Victory Trail. The outstanding views, grassy balds, and fields of wildflowers make this hike one of the best on the A.T.

Rules/Facilities: None

Closest town: Burnsville

Website:
www.cs.unca.edu/nfsnc

Type of hike: Out and back with a small loop

Distance: 8.4 miles

Total ascent: 2,050 ft.

Starting elevation: 4,250 ft.

Highlights: Views on open ridges, high mountain meadows, historic trail

USGS map: Carvers Gap, White Rocks Mountain

Trail map: Cherokee and Pisgah National Forests, National Geographic Trails Illustrated Map #783

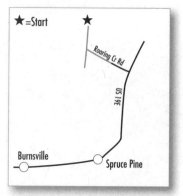

Trailhead GPS Coordinates:
N 36° 07.02 W 82° 02.94

Land managed by:
Pisgah National Forest, Appalachian District

Getting to the trailhead:
From Burnsville, take 19E north for 30.4 miles and turn left on Roaring Creek Rd. Drive 5.1 miles to the end of the road. (At the intersection, continue right to stay on Roaring Creek Rd.). Park at the gate.

The Hike
The hike starts at the end of Roaring Creek Rd. at gated FS 5545 in a sea of bee balm, jewelweed, and spiderwort. Turn right at the first turn onto a blue-blazed trail, a wide jeep road lined with white snakeroot. A large wooden post has been placed in the middle of the trail to prevent vehicles from driving on it. As you reach an open field filled with coneflowers and larkspur, the Overmountain Victory Trail, which you will take on the way back, comes in from the right.

You'll reach the Appalachian Trail [white blazes] at 0.8 mile (4,650 ft. elev.) at Yellow Mountain Gap. Two plaques explain the significance of the

Overmountain Victory National History Trail. The Overmountain Men crossed Yellow Mountain Gap on Sept. 27, 1780, on their way to the Revolutionary War Battle of Kings Mountain.

The Overmountain Shelter sits west and down in a clearing. This shelter, also known as Yellow Mountain Barn, can be reached on a side trail 0.3 mile from the A.T. Once a hay barn, it is one of the A.T.'s largest shelters, accommodating at least 35 people. Tennessee Eastman Hiking and Canoeing Club has refurbished the shelter several times.

Turn right on the A.T. going trail north (compass east). Soon you'll come out into open fields, filled with coneflowers in the summer. Looking back, you'll see the balds on Roan Mountain. Big Yellow Mountain is due south of the A.T. on your right. The trail climbs through blackberry, ironweed, and honeysuckle, which attract butterflies and bees. It then heads back into the woods, passing good sitting rocks, boulders, and barbed wire fence and posts left over from old farming days.

Stay on the A.T. and ignore an overgrown road coming in from the right. At 2.0 miles, the trail comes out into the open to expose Little Hump Mountain, a

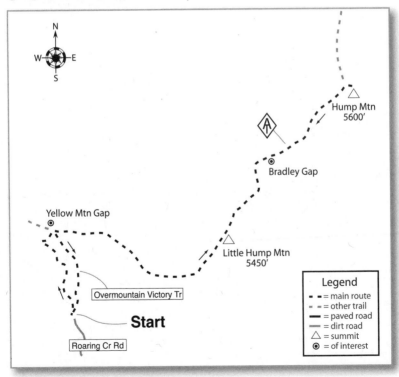

At 5,450 ft. elevation, Little Hump Mountain has 360-degree views.

beautiful bald with a trail going through its middle. Looking right (east), you'll see the profile of Grandfather Mountain, which will follow you all the way. Your walk toward Little Hump Mountain will take you through fields of tall grasses and an old orchard with a few boulders.

At 2.4 miles (5,450 ft. elev.), you'll reach Little Hump Mountain with its 360-degree views. Grandfather Mountain rises to the right (see Grandfather Trail and Profile Trail hikes, pp. 111 and 115). The Doe River Valley communities of eastern Tennessee lie to the left. Hump Mountain, your next destination, looks a lot higher. You can see Linville Gorge and its signature peaks, Table Rock and Hawksbill. (See Hawksbill and Table Rock/Chimneys hikes, pp. 130 and 132.)

Coming down from Little Hump Mountain, the A.T. descends steeply at first on a dry, dusty path through silver birch woods, but soon changes to a gentle downhill. Watch out for hawthorn trees with sharp thorns on their trunks. You'll pass a sign to the right, pointing to water at 2.9 miles. The creek may be dry, so it's best not to depend on it. When you come out in a field of blackberries and wildflowers, you'll see the false summit of Hump Mountain straight ahead. The true summit is farther beyond.

At Bradley Gap (3.3 miles, 5,000 ft. elev.), you'll stare

directly at Hump Mountain. Once you're on the bald itself, the fields don't seem that bald—they're filled with tall grasses and wildflowers. A few rocks have tumbled on the side of the trail, looking a bit like Roman ruins. At 3.8 miles you'll go through a log fence. Domestic animal grazing prevents blackberries and trees from growing on the bald. Past the log fence, the trail veers west.

At 4.1 miles (5,600 ft. elev.) you'll reach the top of Hump Mountain, a bald with no shade. On a clear day, views don't get much better than this. You're surrounded by mountains with little sign of civilization. Looking southeast, the profile of Grandfather Mountain looks very close. Farther south is Grandmother Mountain with its tower. The Roans are to the west. Look northeast to Mt. Rogers, the highest mountain in Virginia. If you go down just beyond the top of Hump Mountain, you'll find the Stan Murray memorial plaque. Murray (1923 – 1990) was founder and director of the Southern Appalachian Highlands Conservancy, which has protected thousands of acres in the Roan Highlands.

Return the way you came on the A.T. Beyond Little Hump Mountain, the trail is almost all downhill or level. At Yellow Mountain Gap at 7.4 miles, turn left on the blue trail and at the split stay left on the Overmountain Victory Trail.

The bald of Hump Mountain is covered with tall grasses and wildflowers.

Yellow Sneezeweed
Helenium autumnale

Staying right would take you the way you came up. The trail is overgrown; it has not been heavily used since 1780. It soon turns into a wide road under an oak forest and goes through a grassy field, veering left. At a wand signposted "Overmountain Victory," the trail turns sharply right and heads downhill, paralleling a creek on your left. You'll reach the trailhead at a gate just below the gate for FS 5545, and end the hike where you started.

Heritage

The Story of the Overmountain Men

The Overmountain Men settled in Sycamore Shoals, TN, now Elizabethton, in the 1770s. In doing so they defied King George's Proclamation of 1763, which stated that English settlers must not move west of the Blue Ridge Mountains. To establish their own rule, the settlers created the Watauga Association, which may be considered the first (male) majority-rule American democracy.

In the summer of 1780, the British Royal Army aimed to conquer the South. Assuming the South would be more loyal to the British Crown than the North was, they thought it would be quick work. The plan was that after the South was subdued, southern Loyalists would be recruited to help the British Army in its battle with the North.

Instead, western settlers from eastern Tennessee and southwest Virginia, dubbed Overmountain Men, marched through these mountains east to Kings Mountain, SC. As true volunteers, they provided their own horses, food, and guns. They defeated the Tories on October 7, 1780. This American victory freed the American South from British domination and was a turning point in the Revolutionary War.

The Overmountain Victory National Historic Trail starts in Abingdon, VA, and goes through Elizabethton, TN, over Yellow Mountain Gap, down to Cowpens National Battlefield in South Carolina (site of another major encounter with the Tories), ending at Kings Mountain National Military Park. There's also a branch of the trail from Elkin, NC. Most of the route is now on roads, but on this hike you can walk some of it.

The Overmountain Victory Trail is managed by the National Park Service. For more information, visit www.nps.gov/ovvi.

The Blacks

Essential Facts

Rules/Facilities:
In Mt. Mitchell State Park, pets must be on a leash. The park has a snack bar, museum, restaurant, and gift shop.

Closest town:
Burnsville

Website:
www.cs.unca.edu/nfsnc

Related book:
Mount Mitchell and the Black Mountains: An Environmental History of the Highest Peaks in Eastern America by Timothy Silver

The story of the Black Mountains is the story of explorers who came to the mountains, some from the surrounding areas and others from overseas. It's the story of superlatives, of first and highest. This history is also reflected in the names of the mountains and plants.

Deer hunting first brought the Cherokees to the Black Mountains. Later, Europeans became enthralled with this area of diverse flora and dark, brooding mountains. Most saw the Blacks from a distance. André Michaux, a botanist from France, first came in the 1780s to "botanize"—to find new plant species which he took back to King Louis XVI. He named what we now call the Blacks *La Montagne Noire,* because the fir trees were so thick that they made the mountains look black. He kept meticulous records of his travels as he picked plant specimens. The Carolina lily (*Lilium michauxii*) and Michaux's saxifrage (*Saxifraga michauxii*) are two plants named for him.

The Black Mountain Range includes both Big and Little Butts. This photo is a view of the Blacks from Little Butt.

But it's the mild-mannered college professor and minister Dr. Elisha Mitchell, originally from Connecticut, who is most associated with Mt. Mitchell, the highest mountain in the Blacks and east of the Mississippi. He taught science and math at the University of North Carolina at Chapel Hill and he preached on Sundays. Having read Michaux's notes, Mitchell was fascinated by the western North Carolina mountains. He had climbed present-day Mt. Jefferson, the Roans, and Grandfather Mountain, and it was from the summit of Grandfather that he first came to his belief that the Blacks might be higher than Mt. Washington in New Hampshire.

If you look at the Blacks from above, you'll see a "J" with Celo Knob at the north end of the "J." The range runs south to Potato Knob and then curves north to include Big and Little Butts, now accessible from the Blue Ridge Parkway. Trying to discern the various cones, pinnacles, and peaks in the 15-mile mountain range is not easy.

Mitchell made several trips to the area, climbing different mountains, guided by local people. He first measured the altitude of Morganton in the foothills and then ventured to the peaks, measuring altitudes by looking at differences in barometric pressure between known and unknown altitudes. He always stayed with locals in the mountains because he was not comfortable camping overnight.

By the 1850s, access to the peaks became easier as horse trails were extended. This brought in a new wave of explorers, including Thomas Clingman, a North Carolina native and former student

A plaque in memory of mountain guide "Big Tom" Wilson marks the top of the peak, near Mt. Mitchell, named for him.

Search parties were dispatched all over the Blacks to look for Mitchell's body. "Big Tom" Wilson, a legendary bear hunter and great storyteller, retraced Mitchell's most likely route and followed human footprints. At the base of the waterfall, he found Mitchell's body, which was brought back to be buried in Asheville. Public sentiment moved quickly to name the highest mountain in the east after Elisha Mitchell, and his body was later reburied at the top of the mountain that now bears his name. A mountain named "Big Tom" for Wilson stands nearby.

Arnold Guyot, a Swiss geologist who taught at Princeton University, had also been exploring the Southern Appalachian mountains. According to Timothy Silver in *Mount Mitchell and the Black Mountains*, "Guyot's methods were time consuming, physically demanding, and far more meticulous than those employed by either Mitchell or Clingman." Guyot was willing to stay in the mountains for days. His measurements stood the test of time well into the 20th century. Guyot did not have a Black Mountain named for him but was honored with Mt. Guyot in the Smokies, the second highest mountain in the park after Clingmans Dome.

of Mitchell. Clingman, who became a representative in Congress and then a senator, was a bold promoter of western North Carolina, which enjoyed a steady stream of visitors from the lowlands. In 1855, Clingman claimed that Mitchell had measured another peak and that he, Clingman, was first on top of the highest mountain in the east. The argument was not which mountain was the tallest but who had climbed it first. In addition, because the Blacks are a mountain range, one peak can blend into another, confusing the matter further.

Mitchell himself had doubts about which mountains he had climbed. In 1857, when he was 64, he came back to climb the Blacks again. Staying in a cabin on the mountain now called Mt. Mitchell, he had set out by himself when it started to rain and thunder. He reached a waterfall (now called Mitchell Falls and located on private land), slipped, and fell to his death.

Fast forward to the early 20th century. The Blacks had long been known to loggers, who cut trees indiscriminately. They built roads and then railroads which allowed them to denude the forests even more efficiently. Governor Locke Craig of North Carolina, appalled at the destruction he saw, pushed to protect the area around the Mt. Mitchell peak. In 1915 it became the first state park in North Carolina, which now comprises almost 2,000 acres.

Mt. Craig, also within the state park and the second highest peak east of the Mississippi, honors Governor Craig. Mt. Mitchell State Park is surrounded by Pisgah National Forest, which can still be logged today. The point at which you leave the state park with its well-marked trails and amenities and enter the national forest will be clear to you as you hike. The majority of visitors drive to the top of Mt. Mitchell, where there is a snack bar, museum, and gift shop, and walk the couple of hundred feet to the new Mt. Mitchell tower, never exploring the trail further.

Natural History

The climate of the Black Mountains is more like that of Canada than North Carolina. During the Ice Age, plants now found only in northern latitudes grew all the way down to the Southern Appalachians.

As the area became warmer, these cold-adapted species restricted themselves to the highest peaks and many plants on Mt. Mitchell resemble those native to more northern alpine environments. However, the Fraser fir, the distinctive tree that grows above 6,000 ft. in these mountains, is a species confined to the Southern Appalachians. Unfortunately, the balsam woolly adelgid, a tiny aphid-like insect originally from Asia, has reduced many Fraser fir trees to stark skeletons. Red spruce, characteristic of New England and the Canadian Maritime Provinces, is also found in the Blacks above 5,500 ft. Both species have been further stressed by acid rain and high ozone levels.

Maple Camp Bald

33

Starting at Mt. Mitchell, the highest mountain in the east, this counterclockwise hike takes you down through a spruce-fir forest more typical of New England than North Carolina. You'll then meander on a gentle trail with a variety of wildflowers (and in season, an abundance of blueberries and blackberries) to the great open views of Maple Camp Bald. You'll climb up to Deep Gap Trail, the backbone of the Black Mountains, past Big Tom and Mt. Craig, the second highest mountain in the East, back to Mt. Mitchell. After the hike, shed your pack and head for the Mt. Mitchell tower, where with luck the fog will have burned off to reveal outstanding views.

Type of hike: Loop

Distance: 7.4 miles

Total ascent: 1,450 ft.

Starting elevation: 6,550 ft.

Highlights: Views, wildflowers, blueberries, the two highest mountains in the East

USGS map: Mt. Mitchell

Trail map: Linville Gorge / Mount Mitchell, Pisgah National Forest, National Geographic Trails Illustrated Map #779. A Mt. Mitchell State Park map is available at the visitor center.

Land managed by: Pisgah National Forest, Appalachian District, and Mt. Mitchell State Park

Trailhead GPS Coordinates:
N 35° 45.99 W 82° 15.90

Getting to the trailhead:
From Blue Ridge Parkway milepost 355.3, turn up NC 128 (Mt. Mitchell Rd.). Drive to the top and park.

The Hike
When you park at the top of Mt. Mitchell Rd., you know that it can only be downhill from there. Take Balsam Nature Trail to the left of the parking lot as you face the museum and gift store buildings. This short trail goes through a dark spruce-fir forest with information signs explaining the woods around you.

At 0.4 mile, turn left on Mt. Mitchell Trail [#190 – blue diamond blazes], which here runs concurrent with the Mountains-to-Sea Trail [white circle blazes]. You'll walk through balsams on slippery rocks and wooden steps covered with moss. The dead Fraser firs are victims of the balsam woolly adelgid, an exotic aphid-like insect that reached this area in the 1950s. Boulders and caverns will add interest to your downhill walk.

At 1.3 miles, you'll come out into the open just long enough to enjoy blackberries on the left as the trail makes its way back into the forest. You'll reach a large, flat campsite at 1.7 mile (5,800 ft. elev.), filled with asters and coneflowers.

The enclosed stone structure may look like a spring, but there's no water coming out of it; there's no water close by.

Turn left and down on the MST through a gate, then turn left on the Buncombe Horse Range Trail [#191

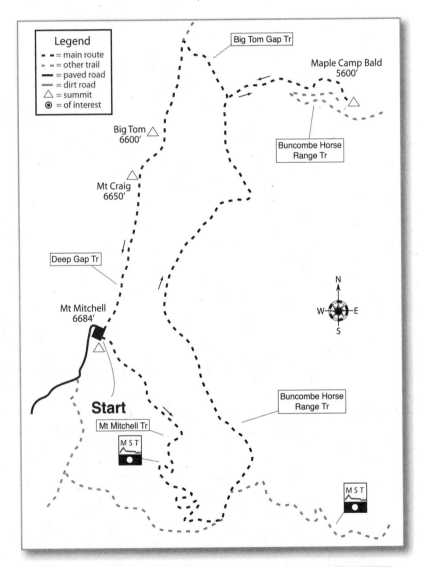

– white blazes]. There are no blazes on this jeep road, but the trail is wide and obvious and a little wet in places because of horses.

You might be lucky and find grass-of-Parnassus, a rare flower with delicate green veins on its white petals. The kidney-shaped leaves look like wild ginger. In summer, Joe-Pye weed, turtleheads, and an abundance of blueberries and blackberries flourish. Little cascades come out of fissures in rocks and at 2.8 miles a large, bare rock slide on the left creates a waterfall when it rains. Altogether, it's a very pleasant walk.

At 3.6 miles, you'll reach an open area as the trail turns left, a good place to stop for a snack or a rest. Then the terrain turns less rocky as rhododendrons take over. You'll pass a wooden sign for Big Tom, but continue straight on Buncombe Horse Range Trail to Maple Camp Bald; you'll come back to this point. The trail narrows and may be overgrown, but it's still flat. Bush-honeysuckle, a native plant, has taken over. Dodder, a parasitic invasive vine without chlorophyll, has attached itself to blackberry canes and other host plants. Ignore a trail shooting off to the left and stay on Buncombe Horse Range Trail where a wand points the way toward the right.

You'll reach Maple Camp Bald, now not very bald, at 4.7 miles (5,600 ft. elev.). The area has filled in with

Climbing up to Big Tom.

rhododendrons and blueberry bushes. Large rocks suitable for sitting make this a good spot for lunch where you can admire southwestern views of the Black Mountain ridge.

Return to the junction with Big Tom Gap Trail [#191A – blue blazes] at 5.4 miles and turn right to start the climb. Big Tom Gap Trail heads northwest; it's narrow and rocky and a little obscure in places, with intermittent blue blazes painted on rocks. As you go up, you'll feel a breeze, reaching a stand of Fraser fir and then the junction with Deep Gap Trail [#179 – orange triangle blazes] at 5.7 miles (6,250 ft. elev.). Turn left toward

Big Tom, and you'll be back in Mt. Mitchell State Park. A right would take you to Deep Gap and continue on Black Mountain Crest Trail [#179] over several peaks over 6,000 ft. and eventually to the community of Bowlens Creek. Some have dubbed the hike from Bowlens Creek to Mt. Mitchell "the death march" because of its 6,000-ft. cumulative ascent.

The trail goes down a little and then starts climbing up. Heavy ropes attached to boulders with bolts may help you negotiate the uphill, though they're probably more needed for the downhill direction.

At 6.2 miles (6,600 ft. elev.), you'll arrive at Big Tom. The views are spectacular. On the way to Mt. Craig, you'll have another great view of ridge after mountain ridge at a flat rock outcropping. You're now walking in an ecologically important alpine area, reminiscent of a Canadian forest. Please stay on the trail. Cut logs have been placed on both sides of the trail to discourage walkers from straying and trampling the sensitive vegetation.

At 6.5 miles (6,650 ft. elev.), you'll reach the top of Mt. Craig, with its open 180-degree views. To the left, the Mt. Mitchell parking lot, tower, and buildings are visible. If you reach this spot in mid-afternoon, you'll have plenty of company because many people make this their destination.

The trail takes you back into the woods on an easy walk to Mt. Mitchell. Volunteers from Carolina Power & Light have installed rock steps to accommodate the high hiking traffic. The trail goes through the picnic area. Cross the road and go up stone steps to the parking lot. Head to Mt. Mitchell tower for more views to end the hike.

Mt. Mitchell tower stands at the top of the highest mountain in the East.

Big Butt Trail starts above 5,000 ft. and climbs to outstanding views of the Black Mountains. The trail follows Brush Fence Ridge, separating Buncombe and Yancey Counties, through balsams that appear healthy and free of the balsam woolly adelgid. You'll be walking perpendicular to and away from the Blue Ridge Parkway in a very quiet area of Pisgah Forest. In late spring, fields of trillium and mayapple carpet the forest floor. Autumn, when colors spread over the Black Mountain Range, is also a great time for this hike.

Type of hike: Out and back

Distance: 6.0 miles

Total ascent: 1,600 ft.

Starting elevation: 5,350 ft.

Highlights: Views, solitude, spring flowers

USGS map: Mt. Mitchell

Trail map: LinvilleGorge / Mount Mitchell, National Geographic Trails Illustrated Map #779

Land managed by: Blue Ridge Parkway and Pisgah National Forest, Appalachian District

Getting to the trailhead: Big Butt Trail starts at Balsam Gap Overlook on the Blue Ridge Parkway at milepost 359.8.

Trailhead GPS Coordinates: N 35° 44.91 W 82° 20.03

The Hike

Two trails start at Balsam Gap Overlook. The Mountains-to-Sea Trail [#440 –white circle blazes] goes up from the middle of the parking area. This hike on the Big Butt Trail [#161 – white rectangle blazes] starts from the left side, in back of a wooden sign which says "Little Butt 3 miles," a slight overestimation. The trail descends north through a fir spruce forest, perpendicular to the Parkway. But soon you're off Parkway land and into Pisgah National Forest. The trail skirts private land on your right, owned by the Cane River Hunt Club and protected by a conservation easement. After 0.2 mile, the trail goes up, following a few white splotches for blazes. There's no mistaking the boundary with its many private property signs and red paint.

At 0.5 mile you'll reach the top of a knob with obstructed views to your right (east). The trail descends steeply, then when it meanders gently back up, you'll get your first views of the Blacks. In less than 0.5 mile, a short side trail to the right takes you to an obstructed view, a hint of views to come. The trail leaves the balsams and enters hardwoods for a short while. The wide, flatter path doesn't last long, though, and soon you're back walking through balsams.

The trail zigzags down between two humps. Both Little Butt and Big Butt are now clearly visible and you may wonder when you'll start climbing. At 2.1 miles (5,400 ft. elev.) you'll reach a gap where

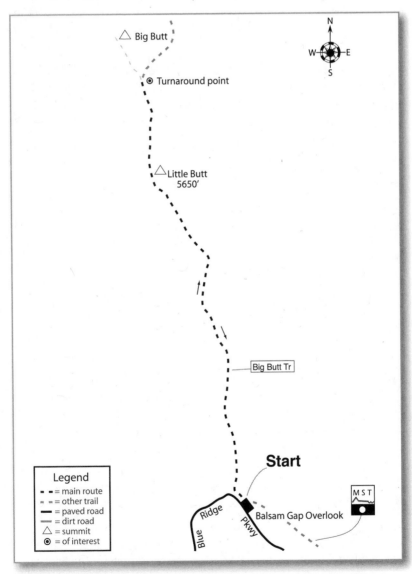

From Little Butt, outstanding views to the east reveal the whole Black Mountain Range.

you'll find a flat, dry area for camping. Then the trail rises steeply to go around several boulders supporting beech trees whose roots seem to grow right out of the rock. This rocky section is slippery when wet. You'll reach a wooded area of rhododendron and mountain laurel. Rock tripe, a leafy lichen that looks and feels like rubber, covers the exposed rock.

At 2.4 miles (5,650 ft. elev.), a short path to the right leads to Little Butt—a wide rock outcropping, perfect for a snack break. Looking across the Cane River, the outstanding eastern views reveal the whole Black Mountain Range. Starting on your right, the mountain with the transmission tower is Clingmans Peak. Mt. Mitchell, the highest peak, is in the middle. Continuing left, Mt.

Craig and Big Tom are the next two mountains, very close to each other (see Maple Camp Bald hike, p. 182). The view displays Black Mountain Crest Trail [#179] beautifully, with its many peaks over 6,000 ft. Hikers affectionately refer to Black Mountain Crest Trail as "the death march" for its many ups and downs. A small stretch of Mt. Mitchell Rd., which goes from the Parkway to the top of Mt. Mitchell, is visible between Clingmans Peak and Mt. Mitchell.

After leaving Little Butt, the trail continues on the ridge with winter views of the Blacks and passes a couple of boulders. The trail splits at 2.9 miles. Take the left fork and descend through a rhododendron tunnel; there are no trees here. The knob ahead is Big Butt. Through a cut in the rhododendrons on your left, you'll get your first western views of Craggy Dome and Craggy Pinnacle on the Parkway. The small community of Barnardsville is spread in the valley below. The trail continues up gently, following white blazes.

At 3.0 miles, a faint trail starts off to the left in the direction of Big Butt, once known as Yeates Knob. Big Butt has no trail or views. This is a good place to turn around and head back to where you began. The Big Butt Trail skirts the western side of Big Butt and continues right for another three miles to Cane River Gap on NC 197.

Variation: To Little Butt and back—4.8 miles with 1,300-ft. ascent.

This section of the Appalachian District of Pisgah National Forest is solitary and secluded. Even the drive is an adventure, which gives you a good feel for the remoteness of the Big Ivy area with its old-growth hemlocks. Though the hike is titled Douglas Falls, it continues up to Cascade Waterfall and eventually to the Mountains-to-Sea Trail. The trail offers a great display of wildflowers and wonderful fall colors. You could start at Craggy Gardens and do the hike in reverse, but you'd have a long uphill at the end of the day and you'd miss the drive through the small communities of Big Ivy and Dillingham. For a fuller day hike, you may want to continue to Craggy Gardens and back.

Type of hike: Out and back

Distance: 5.8 miles

Total ascent: 1,250 ft.

Starting elevation: 4,400 ft.

Highlights: Waterfall, hemlock forest, several cascades, solitude

USGS map: Montreat, Craggy Pinnacle

Trail map:
Linville Gorge / Mount Mitchell National Geographic Illustrated Map #779

Land managed by:
Pisgah National Forest, Appalachian District

Related movie: *Winter People* (1989) with Kelly McGillis

Trailhead GPS Coordinates:
N 35° 43.72 W 82° 22.46

Getting to the trailhead:
Take US 19/23 north of Asheville to exit 15 toward Barnardsville on NC 197. Proceed 6.2 miles, pass the post office on your left, and turn right onto Dillingham Rd. (SR 2173). Proceed another 5.2 miles, where it turns to gravel and changes its name to FS 74. In 9.5 miles, you'll pass Walker Falls on your left. Continue until you reach the trailhead at the end of the road at 13.3 miles.

The Hike
Several trails begin from the far end of the parking area. Douglas Falls Trail [#162 – white on map, yellow on the trail] is the trail farthest to the right, the lowest one. It starts out flat and rocky where huge old-growth hemlocks, which somehow survived the loggers, create a dark, spooky atmosphere. Fly poison, white snakeroot, bowman's root, and several types of fern line the trail. Roots from large blowdowns lie perpendicular to the trail, forming interesting patterns. When you get close

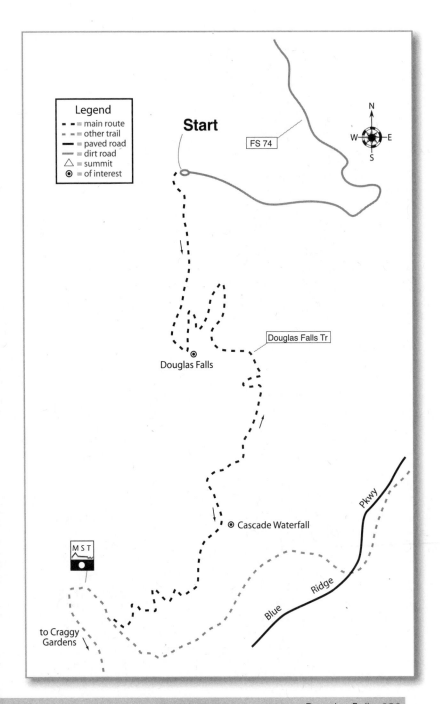

At 70-ft. Douglas Falls, you can walk behind the falling water without getting wet.

to Douglas Falls, note a blaze on a trail heading left; that's where you'll come back to.

At 0.6 mile you'll reach Douglas Falls, a huge rock wall. Water from a tributary of Waterfall Creek makes a 70-ft. freefall from the top of the rock, and you can walk behind the waterfall without getting wet. The falls were probably named for William O. Douglas, Supreme Court Justice and environmental advocate. They've also been referred to as Carter Creek Falls because Waterfall Creek is a tributary of Carter Creek.

To continue on Douglas Falls Trail, retrace your steps on the trail (look for yellow blazes) and make a right turn. The trail switchbacks up and passes a huge rock wall with trees growing on top on the left and a flat area that would be good for a campsite. You'll climb steeply through stinging nettles and Solomon's plume. Cross the creek on large stones and reach a flat area at 1.4 miles (4,750 ft. elev.). In autumn, look for doll's eyes, a cluster of white berries with a characteristic black dot in the center. This plant, also known as white baneberry, has white flowers on a tall stalk in the spring.

At 2.0 miles, cross Waterfall Creek at Cascade Waterfall on large flat rocks. Cascade Waterfall is a long slide above and below the crossing, which can be very slippery. You'll see remnants of old cables and handrails lying on the rocks; these were meant to help hikers cross the creek. Then the trail climbs more steeply with only occasional faint yellow blazes. The hemlocks have disappeared and stands of rhododendrons have taken over. You'll cross another tributary of Waterfall Creek. The trail opens up through a beech forest with Solomon's plume, turtleheads, and bee balm covering the hillside. A few hundred feet from the top, a rock to the left looks like a turtle's back with several trees growing out of it. You'll reach the Mountains-to-Sea Trail [#440] at 2.9 miles (5,300 ft. elev.). Return the same way to end your hike.

Variation: To continue to Craggy Gardens, turn right on the MST going trail west. Here the rugged trail goes generally up. At 1.0 mile, reach a T-intersection and turn right to stay on the MST. A left would take you to the visitor center. Go up to the shelter and Craggy Gardens, a heath bald. In mid-June rhododendron, mountain laurel, and azalea explode with color. Continue down to a parking area with picnic tables and restrooms. This variation adds 3.8 miles and 1,050 ft. of ascent, round trip, to the hike.

At Cascade Waterfall, you'll see remnants of old cables originally meant to help hikers cross the slippery creek.

Catawba Falls

36

The Catawba River is a major river in the Carolinas which provides water for the city of Charlotte and beyond. But here at its headwaters, the Catawba is creek-size, flowing wild and free. The walk to the Lower Falls is moderate. However, reaching the Upper Falls is very difficult and should not be undertaken lightly. Ropes assist with the rockiest part; you'll need to pull yourself with your hands on other sections. This is a good hike any time of year. However, if you plan to go to the Upper Falls, you'll want to avoid yellow jacket season, usually in the early fall. Please stay on the trail—that's a good rule in general, but especially where waterfalls are involved.

Rules/Facilities:
Daytime access only

Closest town: Old Fort

Website: www.foothillsconservancy.org, www.cs.unca.edu/nfsnc

Type of hike: Out and back

Distance: 3.8 miles

Total ascent: 700 ft.

Starting elevation: 1,650 ft.

Highlights: Waterfalls, old dam, power plants

USGS map: Moffitt Hill

Trail map: None

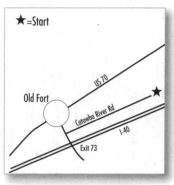

Trailhead GPS Coordinates:
N 35° 36.89 W 82° 13.79

Land managed by: Pisgah National Forest, Grandfather District; Foothills Conservancy (www.foothillsconservancy.org)

Getting to the trailhead: From Old Fort, take I-40 exit 73 and immediately make a hard right on Catawba River Rd., which parallels the interstate for a short while. Drive 3.2 miles to the end of the road, where there's a wide parking area on the left.

The Hike
At the trailhead, go through the gate and stay on the trail. There's a barn to your right. Cross the Catawba River at 0.3 mile and you'll come to a flat area. Pass a concrete building on the right that looks half-built and the remnants of a power plant across the river.

The wide, flat trail, which used to be a stage coach road, climbs gently, paralleling the Catawba River on your left. Most of the land is scrub, filling in with rhododendron and hemlock.

At 1.1 miles (1,850 ft. elev.),

you'll pass a huge rock wall on your right and soon reach a dam that fed the first power plant, which you passed at the beginning of the hike; this is not the Lower Falls. On your right, a concrete wall is all that remains of the second power plant. The trail follows the river closely. You'll walk between the Catawba on your left and Chestnut Branch on your right; a dam on Chestnut Branch fed the second power plant.

Cross the Catawba River on slick, flat rocks. The trail turns right and goes up steeply. Do not cross the river again. At 1.5 miles (2,000 ft. elev.), you'll turn left to reach a flat area at Lower Catawba Falls,

a cascade which drops into a pool. Most people stop here, enjoy a break and snack, and hike back the way they came.

The way to the Upper Falls is steep, rocky, eroded, and slippery. Two ropes secured to tree trunks will assist you in climbing up. Only one person should use these ropes at a time. One experienced hiker said of climbing to Upper Catawba Falls, "It didn't get this technical up to the base camp on Mt. Everest." You might find it harder going down than up.

The trail hugs the sides of the Lower Falls. You'll go under a permanent blowdown to reach the top of the Lower Falls, where you can rest.

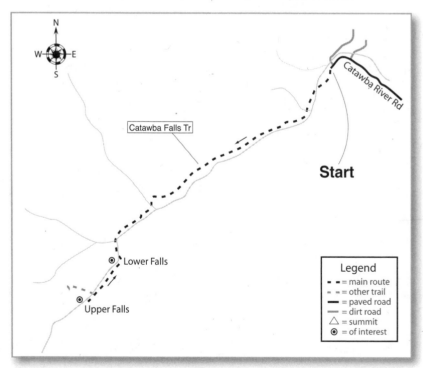

The trail continues through rhododendron and moves away from the creek. Though you can barely see the creek through the green heath thicket, you can certainly hear the falls. For a while, the obstructions disappear and you'll walk on a smooth trail, anticipating the Upper Falls, until the trail suddenly descends.

Turn left toward the river at 1.8 miles (2,350 ft. elev.), ignoring another trail going up steeply to the right. You'll be at Upper Falls, but if you want to get closer, look for a path on your left through the bushes which goes up toward a rock wall and down to the falls. A cairn close to the falls indicates the end of the trail. The waterfall hugs the rock and cascades into a pool ringed by rhododendron. Trees grow out of huge boulders. Several flat rocks give you a ringside seat at the falls. Return the way you came to end the hike.

Upper Catawba Falls

Heritage

The Catawba River

The 225-mile-long Catawba River winds through the heart of the Carolinas, providing water and power for more than 1.3 million residents. Along the way, it has been dammed to form several lakes, including Lake James, Lake Norman, and Fishing Creek Reservoir near Great Falls, SC. Eventually it flows into the Lake Wateree reservoir and downstream of the reservoir it becomes the Wateree River. The Catawba River was named for the Catawba Indian nations, whose traditional homes were along its banks in what is now North and South Carolina. The path of the river provided a trail for the Cherokees, then in the 1800s it became a stagecoach route to Asheville which followed the Catawba and then Chestnut Branch, a tributary, to Swannanoa Gap.

Rufus Morgan, a portrait and stereograph photographer, photographed the Catawba Falls in the 1870s, encouraging people to hike along the river to see them. Today, after years of being off-limits, the falls are on their way to becoming open to the public.

In the early 1900s, Colonel Daniel W. Adams, a pioneer in the development of hydroelectric power, bought thousands of acres of land in the Old Fort area, including the falls. In the 1920s he built the dams you'll pass on the hike, which generated electricity for the town of Old Fort. In 1928 he sold the power plant to a small power company. Eventually Duke Power Company took it over and closed the Catawba facility.

Catawba Falls was always privately owned; hikers could get to the falls only with permission of the landowners. The falls themselves were acquired by Pisgah National Forest in the late 1980s from the Adams family. However, a short access trail stayed in private hands and the falls became landlocked.

When the access land was put on the market, the Foothills Conservancy acted quickly to buy it with loan funds to secure public admittance to the trail. The Conservancy has turned over this path to Pisgah National Forest.

An old dam on the Catawba River

Kitsuma Peak

37

A steady, moderate climb up on Youngs Ridge Trail will take you to Kitsuma Peak where, on a good day, you'll have views of the eastern ridges including Mt. Mitchell. Then it's all the way down first to Swannanoa Gap on the Kitsuma Peak Trail, then to Ridgecrest Conference Center. You'll take Old US 70, now an abandoned road, which was the way up the mountain before I-40 was built. The railroad line, visible from the trail, is still active and goes through numerous tunnels.

Rules/Facilities: None

Closest town: Old Fort

Website:
www.cs.unca.edu/nfsnc

Related book:
The Road by John Ehle

Type of hike: Loop

Distance: 10.1 miles

Total ascent: 1,550 ft.

Starting elevation: 1,600 ft.

Highlights: historic railroad, abandoned road, valley views

USGS map: Old Fort

Trail map:
Linville Gorge / Mount Mitchell, National Geographic Trails Illustrated Map #779

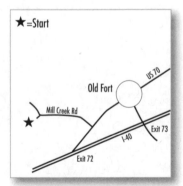

Trailhead GPS Coordinates:
N 35° 38.09 W 82° 13.21

Land managed by:
Pisgah National Forest, Grandfather District

Getting to the trailhead:
From Old Fort, take US 70 west. Make a right on Mill Creek Rd. at the Andrews Geyser sign. At 2.6 miles, turn left into the picnic area. The parking area is 0.1 mile farther.

The Hike
From the parking area, walk past the information board and water fountain and stay left toward the closest privy. You'll see a trail wand which reads "Youngs Ridge." Start up Youngs Ridge Trail [#206 – yellow blazes], following the stream which alternates between strenuous and moderate sections; the trail stays right. You can hear cars on I-40 as you climb.

In mid-spring, as you reach about 3,000 ft., you may be lucky and hit a triple flowering: rhododendron, mountain laurel, and flame azalea all blooming at the same time. As the trail makes a sharp left and descends at 3.0 miles, look to your right for the huge white cross of the

Ridgecrest Conference Center, a Christian retreat. Enjoy this temporary downhill and look up and left to Kitsuma Peak, a wooded bump which is your destination. Toward the top, ignore a couple of side trails.

You'll reach the top of Kitsuma Peak at 3.8 miles (3,200 ft.), a flat area where people have camped, though there's no water close by. It's all downhill from here on Kitsuma Peak Trail [#205 – no blazes]. Start down through a rhododendron tunnel and ignore the trail going up to your right. To your left, looking east and down, you'll see I-40; you can certainly hear it. Go right to a rocky outcropping to look down toward Ridgecrest.

Come back to the main trail and continue down.

The trail switchbacks down to I-40. Several steep herd paths cut through the switchbacked trail and add to the erosion problem. Here, the trail is dry, with Solomon's plume, galax, and Robin's-plantain.

At 4.5 miles (2,800 ft.), you'll reach the bottom where you're paralleling I-40, going west on a grassy path with a wire fence and a metal barrier on your left between you and the interstate. Trucks struggle up the hill to the Eastern Continental Divide at 2,786 ft. At 4.8 miles, at the parking area, a confusing sign says "Youngs Ridge/Kitsuma Peak 4 mi," but it's been less

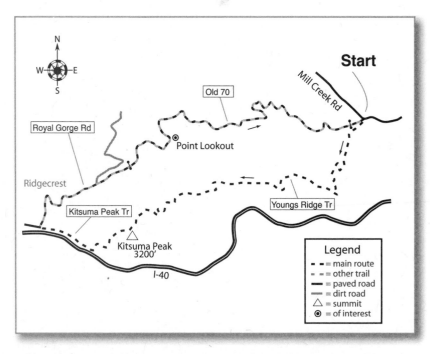

than a mile from Kitsuma Peak. Walk past several small, neat houses facing I-40.

At the stop sign, make a right on Royal Gorge Rd. in Swannanoa Gap. The Ridgecrest Cross is straight ahead at a side entrance to Ridgecrest and the Swannanoa Tunnel at Swannanoa Gap is down on your right.

Walk on the side of the road, which here still has some light traffic. Pass a road on your left which heads up to the Inn on Mill Creek Bed and Breakfast. At 5.9 miles, walk around the barrier. Mountain bikes coming from the last parking area might be pumping up this old road, but you'll no longer have to worry about automobile traffic. In another mile you'll reach Point Lookout, a wide spot on your right with benches and a flagpole. Look east for an expansive view. On the opposite side, there's a stairway up to what may have been a little store. The Southern Railroad line goes in and out of tunnels and the Swannanoa Creek is on the right, way down below.

Pass a house and cross a barrier at 9.6 miles to get back on an active road. Turn right at the Pisgah National Park picnic area at Old Fort and walk back to your car to end your hike.

Taking in the scenery at close range.

Heritage

A County Rich in History

The Mountain Gateway Museum in Old Fort presents a unique history of the conflict between the Cherokee and the colonists before the Revolutionary War. When war was declared between the colonials and the British, the Cherokee sided with the British, forcing the colonials to fight enemies on two fronts. In 1776, General Griffith Rutherford led a band of over 2,000 militiamen in a campaign against the Cherokee, starting from Old Fort and crossing the Blue Ridge into what is now Swain County. As you travel through western North Carolina, you may see historical markers referring to the Rutherford Trace. Rutherford and his men attacked and destroyed thirty Indian towns, along with crops and stored food. The Cherokee never fully recovered from the devastation. Rutherford may have been the originator of the first "scorched earth" warfare in the Americas, later used by General Sherman in the Civil War. This museum building was constructed on the site of the fortifications built by General Rutherford.

Bringing the railroad from Marion up the mountain to Swannanoa Gap was both an engineering and organizational feat. According to the North Carolina Gazetteer, the Swannanoa Tunnel was cut in 1879 at a cost of $600,000 and 120 lives. The tunnel marked the completion of this section of the railroad.

John Ehle's *The Road* is a historical novel about the people who built the railroad in western North Carolina, an epic of men (literally) against mountains. The men doing the manual labor were mostly African-American convicts from eastern North Carolina, adding racial issues into the mix. The construction of this tunnel involved one of the area's first uses of nitroglycerine for blasting rock.

Opposite the entrance to the picnic area, a North Carolina historical sign refers to Andrews Geyser, 2.1 miles away on Mill Creek Rd. The geyser's water comes from the lake at the Inn on Mill Creek Bed and Breakfast. The Innkeeper turns the geyser on by operating a lever which opens a pipe. The water drops down the mountain with so much pressure that it spouts up 80 ft. out of a small pipe at the geyser. The geyser was built in the early 1880s to honor Alexander Boyd Andrews, a railroad vice-president.

Point Lookout, which looks down on Royal Gorge, adds another perspective to the area. It was a famous tourist stop from the mid-1920s until 1954, when a four-lane highway, the predecessor of I-40, was built. According to Wendell Begley, who writes historical pieces for the *Black Mountain News*, Point Lookout is credited with popularizing the scenic overlook concept later used in the construction of the Blue Ridge Parkway.

The Swannanoa Tunnel was cut in 1879 by African-American convicts from eastern North Carolina at a cost of $600,000 and 120 lives.

Hickory Nut Gorge

The strange occurrences began in the western part of our great American State of North Carolina. There, deep amid the Blue Ridge Mountains rises the crest called the Great Eyrie.

— Jules Verne, *Master of the World*, 1904

Hickory Nut Gorge

Essential Facts

Rules/fees/Facilities:
Varies; see individual hikes.
Closest town:
Chimney Rock
Websites:
www.ncparks.gov, www.
chimneyrockpark.com
Related movies:
A Breed Apart (1984)
with Kathleen Turner;
Dirty Dancing (1987)
with Patrick Swayze and
Jennifer Grey; *The Last
of the Mohicans* (1992)
with Daniel Day-Lewis

The spectacular Hickory Nut Gorge was carved by the Rocky Broad River, which drops 1,800 ft. in elevation over eight rugged miles from Hickory Nut Gap to the banks of Lake Lure.

US 74A, historically known as Drovers Road and now a state scenic byway, was used long ago by farmers to drive their flocks to market through Hickory Nut Gap. Chimney Rock had always been a famous landmark at the eastern gateway to western North Carolina. The road is squeezed in between steep, rocky canyon walls with the boulder-strewn Rocky Broad River cutting through the gorge. Country gift shops and cabins with small fishing ponds hug the walls of the gorge, but there's not a chain motel in sight.

Starting your trip from Asheville, US 74A east goes through Fairview and soon passes Sherrill's Inn. Now a private residence, this historic inn and tavern catered to weary travelers, settlers, and Civil War soldiers between 1834 and 1909.

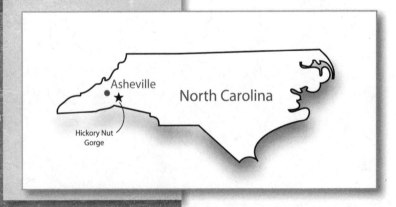

Asheville

North Carolina

Hickory Nut
Gorge

A classic view of Chimney Rock from Skyline Trail.

Farmers also stopped there as they drove their livestock through the gap on their way to eastern markets.

You'll climb to Hickory Nut Gap (2,880 ft.) at the Eastern Continental Divide, the dividing line between water flowing to the Atlantic Ocean and to the Gulf of Mexico. As the road descends, pass the tiny village of Gerton, the turnoff for Florence Preserve on your left.

Farther along, the entrance to Bat Cave on the right is beyond the Bat Cave Apple House, a snack stand with picnic tables. Next is the village of Chimney Rock, with a good assortment of coffee shops and gift shops and the entrance to Chimney Rock Park. You can see Chimney Rock and Hickory Nut Falls from several points on the main street. The narrow gorge ends at Lake Lure, a picture-postcard town created in the 1920s by the damming of the Rocky Broad River. The road continues on to Rutherfordton and the Piedmont.

The literature of the area also mentions the Bottomless Pools. These three pools became famous early in the 20th century for their beauty and geological oddity; their depths have never been successfully measured. They will eventually be incorporated into Chimney Rock State Park.

The Development and Preservation of Chimney Rock

Chimney Rock opened as a tourist attraction in 1885 when

Jerome Freeman, who owned it, built a trail to the base of the chimney and a stairway to the top. But the story of Chimney Rock is most intimately connected to its modern champion, Dr. Lucius Morse. Originally from St. Louis, Morse was fascinated by the rock when he wandered on horseback through Hickory Nut Gorge in the late 19th century. Dr. Morse bought Chimney Rock in 1902 and constructed the bridges, roads, and trails in use today. Morse increased access by taking on the engineering challenge of adding an elevator to the top of the Rock. When it opened in 1949, the new 26-story elevator was the highest in North Carolina. Morse was also responsible for damming Lake Lure in 1926.

The lakes in western North Carolina are all artificial; they were created to store water or generate electricity, except for Lake Lure which was envisioned from the beginning as a resort. Morse had grand plans for hotels, an amusement park, golf courses, hundreds of mountain lake-front homes, even a casino. The prospectus for Lake Lure property said that "world travelers have been lured by the infinite variety of scenery at Chimney Rock country years before the advent of the automobile." It was "a great natural vacation land" and, most important, he was offering "land bought at farm acreage values and saleable at resort real estate prices." Morse completed the dam but with the stock market crash of 1929 and the Great Depression, most of his other plans never materialized.

Early visitors to Chimney Rock enjoy the "Opera Box."

Chimney Rock might have been an anachronism—a private park charging admission near public land with thousands of miles of trails—but it was always popular because of the elevator to the top of the chimney and the wonderful views.

In 2006, the Morse family put Chimney Rock up for sale, with an original price tag of $55 million. In most cases like this, people—including conservationists—don't get irate until they see the first house being framed on a mountaintop. Then they blame the developer, but by then it's too late. In this case, the public lost no time in telling Governor Mike Easley that they wanted the State to buy the property. Less than eight months later, the State of North Carolina and the landowners came to an agreement that was celebrated as a conservation victory. Today the State, working in concert with several conservation groups, protects the steep cliffs and caves that are the habitat for the Indiana bat and the crevice salamander, known to live only in this gorge.

Chimney Rock State Park also comprises less famous (but no less ecologically important) purchases including Worlds Edge and Rumbling Bald. Chimney Rock Company will continue to operate the park for a few years while the state parks system develops a use plan. To maintain the amenities installed when it was privately owned, the original Chimney Rock Park will probably always charge an entrance fee.

There are many myths and stories about bizarre events in the gorge. Strange apparitions have appeared on the face of the mountain: in 1806, a woman and her children saw a large crowd of people of every size, and five years later, in the same spot, people saw a battle between two troops of ghostly cavalry. Cherokee legend holds that when magical "little people" guarded the only pass through the mountains and refused to let the Indians through, a medicine man tore down the cliffs, crushing the little people; the boulders that fell now lie in the riverbed. For most of us, though, the reality is magical enough—bats, salamanders, wildflowers, breathtaking views, and new hiking and climbing opportunities.

Hikers at Chimney Rock's Inspiration Point circa 1920.

Florence Preserve

Florence Nature Preserve is a small, 600-acre treasure surrounded by private property. This jewel is hidden away on the slopes of Little Pisgah Mountain, off the Drovers Road Scenic Byway. The Preserve only has a few miles of trail, all well signposted. A rushing stream with small cascades traverses the property, which has a meadow and several rock outcrops. This land is owned by the Carolina Mountain Land Conservancy but is open to the hiking public. The Preserve is so new that the trails don't have names yet, just colored diamond-shaped blazes.

Rules/Facilities: None

Closest town: Chimney Rock

Website:
www.carolinamountain.org

Type of hike: Loop

Distance: 6.5 miles

Total ascent: 1,650 ft.

Starting elevation: 2,500 ft.

Highlights:
Waterfalls, views, solitude

USGS map: Bat Cave

Trail map: Available at www.carolinamountain.org

Land managed by: Carolina Mountain Land Conservancy

Getting to the trailhead:
From Asheville, take I-240 east to exit 9 (Bat Cave and US 74A east). Follow US 74A east to Gerton. From the

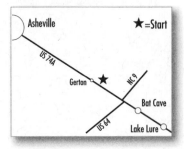

Trailhead GPS Coordinates:
N 35° 28.40 W 82° 19.94

Eastern Continental Divide, drive 2.4 miles to a parking area on the left in front of a stone chimney. The trail starts to the left of the parking area as you face the chimney. Parking is 6.4 miles west of Chimney Rock State Park.

The Hike
Yellow Trail starts to the left of the parking area and climbs steeply, passing an old cabin on the right. Follow signs for Little Mt. Pisgah Trail for 0.6 mile. When you reach the intersection with Blue Trail, make a right to start the loop. Note the pink paint on the hemlocks, which marks trees that have been treated for hemlock woolly adelgid.

Here you'll walk on the high sides of a ditch created by previous horse traffic. Hopefully, horse riders will avoid Blue Trail now that it's been rehabilitated. At 0.9 miles (3,100 ft. elev.), you'll reach a stone foundation. According to a Carolina Mountain Land Conservancy volunteer, Blue Trail may have been part of an offshoot of the Drover's Road, and the stonework is the remains of a way station, an inn for travelers.

Yellow Trail takes off to the left. Stay on Blue Trail. Pass a little cave on the right, overhanging a bubbling creek. Many sections of this trail have been relocated away from older, poorly maintained trails; you'll see piles of twigs and debris closing off those old sections of trail.

Step over the narrow creek and turn left to cross a log bridge. The trail leaves the creek and goes through a rhododendron tunnel with little undergrowth. White Trail goes off to the left. Continue on Blue Trail, which enters a different ecosystem. Here the land is much drier and more open, with white pine, maple, and oak trees.

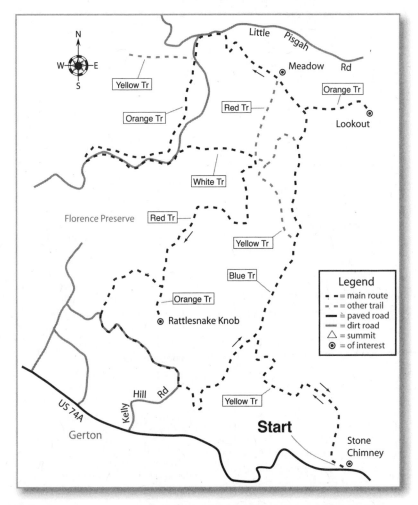

An old stone foundation at Florence Preserve.

At 1.4 miles (3,350 ft. elev.), turn right on Orange Trail for a short detour of less than 0.5 mile, out and back, to an overlook. It follows the remains of an old jeep road, going first downhill and then up, heading east toward a set of flat boulders. Looking southeast, Hickory Nut Gorge is below, though you're more likely to hear the whistling wind than traffic noises. To your left is privately owned Little Pisgah Mountain. Return to Blue Trail, make a right through a rhododendron tunnel, and cross a wide wooden bridge.

At 2.0 miles you'll reach a meadow where the Red Trail comes in from the left. Explore the meadow and note the chestnut trees, each one encircled by a wire fence. The American Chestnut Foundation has planted trees from seed to regenerate the species after it almost disappeared following the chestnut blight of the early 20th century. The blight doesn't attack the roots; it's in the air, which may explain why there are many small, scrawny chestnut trees in the woods which never reach maturity. This dry site is ideal for chestnut regeneration, but it can also be full of poison ivy.

Continue right on Blue Trail, now an old road. A flat homesite on your left is filled with yucca. There is also a *Cunninghamia lanceolata*, sometimes called a "china fir," a large conifer with long, flat needles. This exotic tree comes from the mountains of Taiwan and is common in city parks in Taipei, but not in the mountains of western North Carolina.

Go around a chain-link fence and turn left on unpaved Little Pisgah Rd. Stay to the left on the road; there's not much traffic. Pass the Yellow Trail on the right. A few feet later, make a right on the Orange Trail. Soon the trail becomes an old logging road lined with hemlock. As the trail descends, Bearwallow Mountain, the highest mountain in the area, is visible to the southwest on your left; the mountain has a gated housing development. Make a left on Little Pisgah Rd. at 3.1 miles. A right turn would take you onto private property. After about 0.4 mile, turn right on White Trail. You'll be enclosed in rhododendron and hemlock as the trail starts gently downhill.

Make a right on Red Trail at Kathleen Corner, named for a woman who was lost and then met up with her group here. At 4.5 miles, turn left and head up on Orange Trail to two rocky outcroppings and lookouts. The climb is steep but very short to a right turn leading to the first lookout. Look southwest down into the gorge and across to a cleared field, houses, and the ridge line. Go back on Orange Trail and continue right to the second lookout, Rattlesnake Knob. It's a wide, rocky slab shaded by trees, with good winter views of Bearwallow Mountain on your left.

Return to Red Trail and make a left under mountain laurel. You'll soon pass a steep trail on the right which goes to the Florence family home and property. Please respect their privacy and stay on Red Trail, which turns left at a blaze and continues downhill.

At a T-intersection (5.1 miles), make a left on an old road with no blazes. You'll pass two houses on the left at the edge of the Preserve, then the road becomes passable by car. Go downhill to reach an old fenced-in parking area. Turn left on Blue Trail. Cross a log bridge and go up steps with the help of a rope banister. Generally stay left; other unmarked trails will intersect the designated trails. Again cross the creek coming down from the slopes of Little Pisgah Mountain, then continue gently uphill through mountain laurel.

Just before the third bridge, there's a little cascade on your right ending in a pool. The old trail, which went straight uphill, is still visible. Cross the bridge and go up wooden steps through a rhododendron thicket to reach an intersection with Yellow Trail. Make a right on Yellow Trail and follow it back to US 74A and the trailhead to end your hike.

Heritage

Florence Nature Preserve: Setting a Standard for Land Conservation

The Florence Nature Preserve shows what a land conservancy can do to protect land, even when everything else around is being developed. Tom and Glenn Florence kept 22 acres for their home and donated 600 acres to the Preserve. It's a mixture of dense forest with rhododendron tunnels, two meadows, a stream with a small waterfall, and rock overlooks, one of which faces Bearwallow Mountain. The Florences created the trails, then the Carolina Mountain Club upgraded them and built several bridges. Kieran Roe, Executive Director of Carolina Mountain Land Conservancy, emphasizes that Florence Preserve "is not a public park, because we don't have that kind of management. We encourage hikers to become members of the Conservancy and sensitive to our goals of preserving natural resources."

Many hikers and conservationists have heard about Bat Cave Preserve, but they don't know exactly where it is or how to get to it. To hike there, you need to make reservations with The Nature Conservancy (see details below), which oversees it. The reward for planning ahead is a short walk with a guide who'll show you endangered plant species and perhaps a rare salamander. You'll venture to the entrance of the largest granite fissure cave in North America and be chilled by natural air conditioning, but you should know in advance that you won't go into the cave or see the bats. This excursion is suitable for children who enjoy short, steep climbs and have a sense of adventure and imagination.

Rules: To go to Bat Cave you must take a guided trip with The Nature Conservancy.

Website: www.nature.org/ wherewework/northamerica/ states/northcarolina/

Type of hike: Out and back

Distance: 1.4 miles

Total ascent: 500 ft.

Starting elevation: 1,450 ft.

Highlights: Fissure cave, rare and endangered plant species, natural air conditioning

USGS map: Bat Cave

Trail map: None

Land managed by: The Nature Conservancy

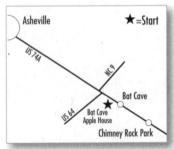

Trailhead GPS Coordinates: N 35° 26.89 W 82° 16.61

Getting to the trailhead: Directions are from the entrance to Chimney Rock Park in the village of Chimney Rock. To reach Chimney Rock Park from Asheville, take I-240 east to exit 9 (Bat Cave and US 74A east) and travel east on US 74A for 20 miles. Look for the park entrance on the right.

The meeting point for the hike is north of the community of Bat Cave at the Bat Cave Apple House, 1.9 miles west of Chimney Rock Park. To make reservations, call (828) 350-1431. The hikes are held every Wednesday and Saturday, June through August. The cost is $10 for adults, $5 for children 12 and under.

The Hike

There's something intriguing about a hiking area that's gated and locked. What is going on and why can you only go there with a guide? Just such an area will be your first glimpse of this hike, and it will soon become clear why the restrictions exist.

After signing a waiver and paying your fee, you'll

walk up stairs to a bridge with a metal fence and a solid wooden door with two locks. The leader opens both locks. After the group walks through and you're on the other side of Rocky Branch, everything is locked up again.

The guide will lead you through the mature hardwood forest that cloaks the rugged slopes of Hickory Nut Gorge, pointing out various plants, including poison ivy—there's a lot of it on the sides of the trail. The furry poison ivy vines, which wrap around tree trunks, should also be avoided. The walk attracts many visitors, some from western states who may not be familiar with the plant and the rash it causes.

The preserve has an abundance of spring wildflowers, including bloodroot, toothwort, trillium, and violet. Summer brings spiderwort, blue cohosh with its blue berries, and black cohosh which is used to treat rheumatism and menopausal symptoms. Farther into the preserve, ground pine, a type of club moss, covers the trail banks. These club mosses look like tiny pine trees and are said to predate dinosaurs; their fossils are found in the carbonaceous material that makes up coal beds. You'll also see some unusual plants such as broadleaf coreopsis (on the endangered list for North Carolina) and the mandarin plant with orange seed pods.

The preserve is not immune to the hemlock woolly adelgid, a non-native, invasive insect which is killing hemlocks in the region. The Nature Conservancy has decided not to treat the Eastern hemlock, only the less common Carolina hemlock. The area also harbors invasive plant species such as multiflora rose and honeysuckle. When college interns are not guiding groups through the preserve, they spend their time pulling out invasive plants, both exotic and native. Native nuisance plants include poison ivy and Indian plantain.

The guide shares lore and myths as well as botanical information. For example, rattlesnake fern supposedly

Taking a peek into Bat Cave.

points in the direction of ginseng. It's said you might have to walk five hundred miles in that direction to find it, but it will be there.

As you climb and enter a cove forest covered with Carolina rhododendrons, the area becomes rockier, with large boulders. If you're lucky, you'll see a Yonahlossee salamander, informally called a crevice salamander, hiding in a hole. North Carolina may have the greatest variety of salamanders in the United States.

On a side trail, you'll suddenly start feeling chilly, as if air conditioning has been switched on. In fact, cool, moist air is blowing out from the nearby cave. When hot air outside the cave is drawn inside, where the temperature is a constant 45 to 50 degrees, it is cooled and then blown out through openings in the boulders.

Back on the main trail, the guide will warn the group about the steep climb to come, which pumps up everyone's adrenalin. The top section is steep and rocky for about 0.3 mile but there's no need to be scared by the warnings. The path, lined with a jungle of vines, narrows as it goes up. The "air conditioning" pours out of rocks as they close in on the trail toward the cave opening

The cave you will be facing is the largest known granite fissure cave in North America. Fissure caves are formed by rock splits, boulder movements, and other motions of the earth,

Summer interns from Warren Wilson College lead guided walks at Bat Cave twice a week.

while most other caves are formed by water dissolving and abrading rock.

The first small cave you'll visit, which has five or six openings, is home to about a thousand Indiana bats. The public is not permitted to enter the cave because these endangered bats can't be disturbed. The bat population is declining for many reasons, including commercialization of caves, destruction by vandals, disturbances caused by increased numbers of spelunkers, bat banding programs, and possibly insecticide poisoning. The main chamber inside the cave is a dark cathedral-like space, more than 300 ft. long and approximately 85 ft. high, where bats hibernate during the winter.

You'll walk a little farther up to a second, larger cave where you're permitted to go part of the way in. Before you do, the guide will inform you that in 1994, a 63-ton boulder wedged in the top of the cave fell down—and another boulder could fall any time!

The hike up to the cave takes over an hour. Retracing your steps back down takes less than 20 minutes.

Heritage

Bat Cave: Cooperative Conservation

Margaret Flinsch and her family have owned the Bat Cave property since the 1920s. She began having problems with trespassers and vandals, yet she wanted the public to have controlled access, so she turned to The Nature Conservancy for help. Although no one remembers exactly when discussions first started, an official relationship was established in 1981. The preserve is now co-owned by Mrs. Flinsch and The Nature Conservancy.

College interns from nearby Warren Wilson College, a small private college with an outdoor leadership program, lead walks twice a week during the summer. The walks attract visitors from all over the country, most of whom are vacationing in the Chimney Rock area.

Chimney Rock has only a few miles of trails, but they are spectacular and varied. This loop leads you from the Nature Center on the wooded Four Seasons Trail to the bottom of Hickory Nut Falls. Then a counterclockwise loop takes you through several rock outcroppings to the top of the waterfall, the film location of the dramatic ending in *The Last of the Mohicans.* Coming down, you'll enjoy views of Lake Lure all the way to the Chimney Rock itself, where most tourists congregate. Leaving the crowds, you'll climb down an elaborate stairway and retrace your steps.

Chimney Rock, one of the newer members of the N.C. State Park system, is operated by Chimney Rock Management, LLC, in a manner consistent with the way the park was run by the Morse family when it was privately owned. Because of all the amenities, an entrance fee is still charged. The exposed trails are closed in winter, so check before you go.

Type of hike: Loop

Distance: 5.2 miles

Total ascent: 1,500 ft.

Starting elevation: 1,500 ft.

Highlights: Views, rock formations, wildflowers

USGS map: Lake Lure, Bat Cave

Trail map: Available at the park. Note that the trail map incorrectly shows the park as north of US 74A when it is really to the south.

Land managed by: Chimney Rock State Park

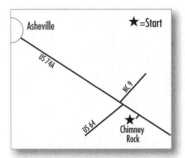

Trailhead GPS Coordinates: N 35° 25.85 W 82° 14.57

Getting to the trailhead: From Asheville, take I-240 east to exit 9 (Bat Cave and US 74A east). Drive on US 74A for 20 miles to the village of Chimney Rock and turn right at the park entrance.

The Hike

Park at the first parking area past the ticket plaza, close to the Nature Center building. Cross the road and go through a wooden archway to start on Four Seasons Trail. On the left, you'll find the Great Woodland Adventure. In April, the smooth path is flanked by a glorious display of mountain laurel. Cross a wooden bridge and head up stone steps where the trail climbs through an oak and maple forest. Turn right to reach a wide, flat intersection and continue straight. You'll pass a maintenance building on your right.

In late March, the ground is covered with sessile-flowered

maroon trillium. The trail crosses a bridge over a ravine and goes up on log steps. Boulders seem to have been plopped down here and there; as the trail descends, go around a huge boulder with three tree stumps for seats. This may be the best trail for wildflowers, including Solomon's plume, bloodroot, black cohosh, star chickweed, and Canada violets. Chimney Rock Park offers several nature courses which use Four Seasons Trail for wildflower identification.

At 0.6 mile (1,900 ft. elev.), at the end of Four Seasons Trail, make a right on Hickory Nut Falls Trail which leads to the bottom of the falls. You'll come back to this point. This old jeep road has Carolina rhododendron, smaller and less common than rosebay rhododendron. There are good views across the gorge looking north and up to Bearwallow Mountain, recognizable by its tower.

As you turn the corner where the trail is graveled, you can hear the falls and feel that it's cooler as you continue to climb on stone steps. You'll go across a wooden plank and reach a rock platform at the bottom of the waterfall at 1.3 miles (2,100 ft. elev.). Hickory Nut Falls is like a thin

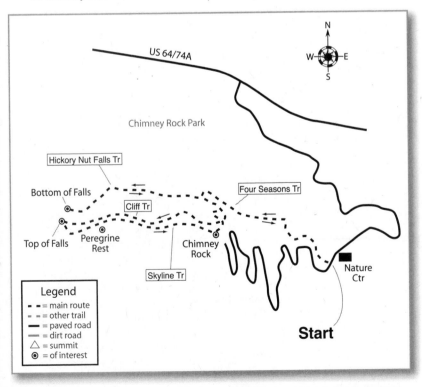

ribbon running over a huge, bare rock. You're too close to the falls here for a good photograph; that will have to wait until you get to Inspiration Point. According to the park information, the falls are 404 ft. high, but Kevin Adams, author of *North Carolina Waterfalls*, claims that the best estimate may be no higher than 350 ft.

Return to the junction with Four Seasons Trail on your left at 2.0 miles and continue straight ahead to take an elaborate stairway to your right. The trail going straight leads to an intermediate parking lot where most people park to see the bottom of the falls. Heading up the stairs, pass a deck with two picnic tables overlooking the gorge and continue up. At the top of the stairs on the left, you'll find restrooms and a high-end gift shop called The Cliff Dwellers. Most tourists park here and take the elevator to the observation deck on Chimney Rock itself.

Continue right on a wrap-around deck, hugging a boulder. At a split, continue to the Needle's Eye, a spiral stone stairway with several lookouts down to the gorge. Go up into the Needle's Eye. At the top of the stairs, a left would take you down through the Subway, a rock tunnel which heads back down.

Continue past the opening to the Subway and stay right toward Cliff Trail, which will take you to the top of the falls. Cliff Trail starts out as a broad walkway heading up to a set of

Hickory Nut Falls is a thin ribbon of water running over a huge, bare rock.

stairs underneath huge rocks; you'll pass a sign reading "35 minutes to Hickory Nut Falls." On your climb up, you'll get great views of Hickory Nut Gorge, the road through the gorge, and the village of Chimney Rock. Across the gorge, you'll see the start of more housing developments.

When you pass through a slit in the rock at Wildcat Trap, you may have to take your pack off. Looking northwest, you will have a clear view of Bearwallow Mountain. After passing through a rain shelter, the trail alternates between rocks and steps. This is the place to take the classic photo of Hickory Nut Falls, both the top and the bottom.

You'll pass Nature's Showerbath, a small stretch with continuous "rain" from the top of the rock. Watch your head on some of these low rocks. Beyond them, you'll notice a door which allows the park to close Cliff Trail in the winter.

At 2,450 ft. elev. you'll reach the top of Hickory Nut Falls with outstanding gorge views; the dramatic ending of *The Last of the Mohicans* was filmed here. You're not at the top of the trail yet, though. Go around a multi-level cascade and a tiny "Bridge of Sighs" to smaller cascades. You'll be on Skyline Trail where you'll begin to encounter people coming toward you. Stop at Peregrine Rest for yet another outstanding view of the gorge and Bearwallow Mountain, as well as your first southern views of Lake Lure. The high point of the hike is at 2,600 ft. elev., and then Skyline Trail descends, with more excellent views of Lake Lure. Continue on to Exclamation Point, a wide outcropping, covered with table mountain pine, that has panoramic views up the gorge and down the lake.

Here the trail starts down more steeply on a series of steps over the rock face. The trail has been designed to make it easy to get to vistas without having to climb hand over hand on rocks.

Make a left for a diversion to Devil's Head, a rock shaped like a human head. Return to the stairway for another left to Opera Box for amazing vistas. Continue on Skyline Trail, the main trail, where you'll see Chimney Rock itself—and lots of people. At 4.0 miles (2,300 ft. elev.), reach the top of Chimney Rock, only a few steps from the observation deck, which has great views of Lake Lure. A plaque set into the ground recounts a short history of Chimney Rock and the Morse family.

To your left, Sky Lounge accommodates a snack bar, small gift shop, and restrooms. Tourists who've taken the elevator from the Tunnel Entrance come through the back of Sky Lounge, but you'll take the steps to the right of Chimney Rock, down and under rocks on The Outcroppings. This trail diverts at several more vistas looking toward Lake Lure, including Pulpit Rock and Vista Rock. Continue right down steep stairs and take the short diversion into Moonshiner's Cave, formed by a freeze-thaw cycle which caused the rock to split and fall apart.

Before reaching the restrooms and parking area at The Cliff Dwellers, make a left down the stairs and retrace your steps—without going back to the falls, of course. At the bottom of the stairs at 4.5 miles, make a left on Hickory Nut Falls Trail to its intersection with Four Seasons Trail. Turn right and follow Four Seasons Trail to your car to end the hike.

Rumbling Bald

41

On this hike, you'll walk on a wide jeep road with great views on both sides. At Eagle Rock and Party Rock, the bookends of the hike, you'll get a top-of-the-world feeling as you look down on Lake Lure. The jeep road goes up and down over hill and dale, getting lower at each point until Party Rock. You'll start at 3,150 ft. elev. and end at 1,300 ft., with some uphill stretches in between. In the early spring, fields of bloodroot cover the sides of the trail. You'll also see sessile-flowered maroon trillium, Robin's-plantain, and yellow and purple violets in abundance. In late March, redbud trees are in bloom.

Type of hike: Shuttle

Distance: 4.6 miles

Total ascent/descent: 700 ft./2,350 ft.

Starting elevation: 3,150 ft.

Highlights: Views and rock formations

USGS map: Lake Lure

Trail map: None

Land managed by: Chimney Rock State Park

NOTE: Access to Rumbling Bald was acquired by Chimney Rock State Park in 2008. Previously the Nature Conservancy led a guided hike, which is described here. As of this writing, a formal plan for trail/hike development is in progress with a currently undetermined date of completion. To check the status of public access at Rumbling Bald, visit: www.hikertohiker.com or www.ncparks.gov/Visit/parks/chro.

Getting to the trailhead: The instructions are from the entrance to Chimney Rock Park, in the village of Chimney Rock. From Asheville, take I-240 east to exit 9 (Bat Cave and US 74A east). Drive on US 74A east for 20 miles and look for the park entrance on the right.

To place a car at the end of the hike: From Chimney Rock Park, take NC 9 south/US 74A east, drive 0.8 mile, and make a left on Boys Camp Rd. Drive 2.9 miles to its end and park on the side of the road opposite the entrance to the Blue Heron Point housing development.

To place a car at the beginning of the hike: Go back to NC 9/US 74A, make a right, and go past Chimney Rock Park. From the entrance to Chimney Rock Park, drive 2.8 miles to the NC 9/US 74A split. Make a right to stay on NC 9 north for 2.2 miles. Take a right on Shumont Rd., go 4.3 miles to its end, and park on the side of the road.

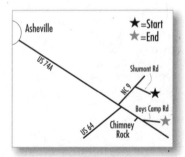

Trailhead GPS Coordinates: N 35° 28.39 W 82° 14.66

The Hike

Go through the gates of The Nature Conservancy property and head east on an old jeep road. At the split take a left, which leads to Eagle Rock. At 0.5 mile (3,500 ft. elev.), look up to see a small wooden bridge among the rocks. If you scramble up Eagle Rock, you'll see cleared land readied for development but also areas of untouched forest land below.

Continue across the bridge with good views down to Lake Lure. Down through the trees on the right, there is a miniature Chimney Rock, a rock formation resembling the top of a chimney. Up and to the right, the three humps of Rumbling Bald form the route you'll be taking. The metal pillars driven into the rock are from an old fence at the edge of the trail. According to a state

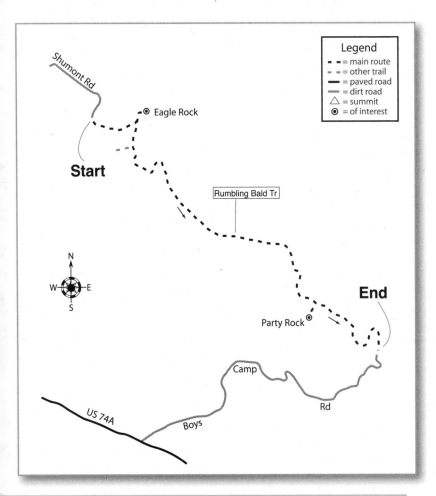

The view from Eagle Rock.

park employee, people used to hang-glide from that point and land on the golf course, which didn't please the golfers below.

Retrace your steps from Eagle Rock back to the jeep road. Make a left and stay left as the trail descends. Few vehicles can drive this road because it's badly eroded. At a fork at 1.3 miles, continue to the left on the main road. Turn around for one last look back at Eagle Rock. At the next intersection, go right and down. There are winter views on both sides as you descend in an easterly direction.

The meadow you see on the right (to the southwest) is a parking lot for Chimney Rock Park. Farther down, there are good views of Lake Lure on the right. Continue left, uphill.

At 2.8 miles, the trail becomes steeper, rockier, and rougher. It would be tricky for an SUV to drive here. At 3.1 miles, take a short side path to the right to an old hunter's cabin set on a rock foundation. Through the broken windows, you can see four bunk beds and a kitchen complete with sink, counters, and cabinets. After getting back to the main trail, follow it for 0.2 mile, and then stay left at what looks like a split in the trail.

At 3.4 miles (2,200 ft. elev.), take a right off the main trail toward Party Rock. The side trail goes through a flat area with a fire ring, and then continues to a rock outcropping above Lake Lure. Party Rock is a monadnock with thin soil cover. From here, you'll have good views of Lake Lure with its islands and a 180-degree view of the main roads and houses on the lake. You won't have any doubt about the name of the rock—the word *Party* is painted on it in huge letters. Retrace your steps to the junction with the jeep road and make a right to continue down.

Now the trail is much rockier and the walking is slow going. As you go down steeply, you'll feel as if you're going to end up in the lake. At times the trail becomes a trench; it might be easier to walk on the side of the trench instead of in it. There are side trails and dead-ends, but the main trail keeps descending. As you get farther down, building material, sewer piping, and other evidence of housing construction lines the trail. Shortly thereafter, you'll reach your car to finish the hike.

Heritage

Rumbling Bald: Fact and Fiction

In the early 20th century, without ever visiting western North Carolina, Jules Verne wrote a science fiction novel set in Linville Gorge and the surrounding area. Verne was inspired by a famous series of rumblings that occurred in Rutherford County

Heritage continued

in 1874. Over the course of six months, county inhabitants felt more than a hundred shocks around Bald Mountain, the old name for Rumbling Bald. At the time, people thought it might be a volcanic eruption, an idea Verne incorporated to heighten the thrill factor in his book.

The rumbling from Bald Mountain caused a panic. Residents heard booming sounds and saw what they believed was smoke coming from the mountain. The *New York Times* headlined a story "A Volcano in North Carolina/ Terrible Sights and Sounds/The Terror-Stricken Residents Praying During Sixteen Days." However, no volcano erupted; geologists later suspected the rumbling was caused by a barrage of minor earthquakes. The rumbling was caused when huge boulders, jarred loose by the quakes, fell inside caves, and the "smoke" was believed to be dust that billowed up through rock crevices.

In *From the Banks of the Oklawaha,* Frank FitzSimons collected anecdotes of the incident. According to one resident, The Reverend Pose Conner was holding a prayer meeting when an earthquake struck during the sermon. The minister called for everyone to fall on their knees and ask for forgiveness because the end of the world was coming.

Worlds Edge

42

Worlds Edge is a high bluff above Lake Lure in Polk County on the eastern edge of the Blue Ridge Escarpment. From the top looking southeast, the view includes the South Mountains, Kings Mountain, and Paris Mountain in South Carolina. There's no public access at the trail's low point; this hike starts at the top, going down and then back up before it reaches Lake Lure, staying on state park land. It's not easy to end a hike going uphill, but the pleasant downhill at the beginning makes the climb back up a little easier. On the way down, you'll make out several features outlining Hickory Nut Gorge, including Chimney Rock and Rumbling Bald. The overlook is at the end of the hike. At this time, the trails don't have names or blazes.

Type of hike: Out and back

Distance: 6.2 miles

Total ascent: 1,300 ft.

Starting elevation: 3,000 ft.

Highlights: Views

USGS map: Bat Cave

Trail map: None

Land managed by: Chimney Rock State Park

NOTE: As of this writing, if you want to hike at Worlds Edge you must take a guided trip with the Carolina Mountain Land Conservancy (www. carolinamountain.org).

Trailhead GPS Coordinates: N 35° 23.54 W 82° 15.69

However, plans are in the works for Worlds Edge to be open to the public as part of Chimney Rock State Park. To check the status of public access at World's Edge, visit www.hikertohiker. com or www.ncparks.gov.

Getting to the trailhead: From I-26 exit 49A, take US 64 east (Chimney Rock Rd.) toward Bat Cave, for 7.3 miles. Turn right on Gilliam Mountain Rd./SR 1602 and drive for 2.5 miles. Turn left on Sugarloaf Mountain Rd. and continue for 2.5 miles as the road wiggles left and right. When Sugarloaf Mountain Rd. turns sharply left, stay straight on Worlds Edge Rd. (also SR 1602). In 1.0 mile the road dead-ends; park there. The jeep trail starts straight ahead.

The Hike

Start on the jeep trail going northeast, and after about 100 ft. take the first left on another jeep trail. Soon you'll reach a flat circular area. Make a right turn on a wide jeep road, which should have yellow state park signs posted on trees.

From there, the trail goes north and down. At 0.9 mile, a little creek crosses the trail. This forest was logged but it has rebounded and filled in with rhododendron, hemlock, and mountain laurel. White and Virginia pines now line the trail as you zigzag down. First the land falls away to the right, then to the left, as the switchbacks descend.

As the right side of the trail opens up again, it exposes the Pool Creek watershed. Pool Creek flows northeast into Lake Lure after feeding the Bottomless Pools (see introduction to Hickory Nut Gorge hikes, p. 205). Minor runoffs, depending on the rain level, head for Pool Creek. At 1.7 miles (2,500 ft. elev.) a side trail on the right is closed off by two metal posts meant

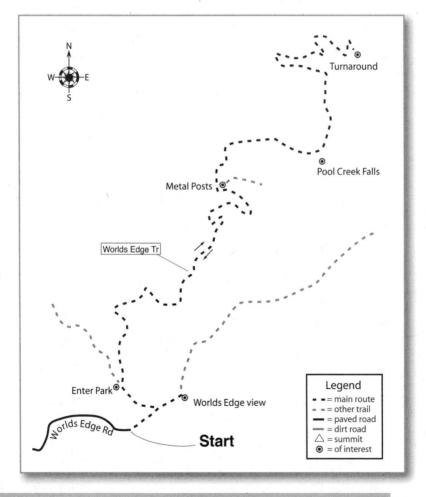

From the top of the Blue Ridge Escarpment with the valley below, it feels as if you're standing on the edge of the world.

to discourage vehicles. As you descend, ignore a steep trail going up on your left. The trail begins to narrow.

At 2.2 miles, on your right you may see the top of Pool Creek Falls, depending on how thick the vegetation is. The cliffs on the back side of Chimney Rock are straight ahead with a rocky finger—a mini-chimney—sticking up. To its right is Rumbling Bald Ridge above a few isolated houses. Continuing right, Judes Gap is in the distance, and then the top of the Worlds Edge escarpment where the hike started. The terrain has changed, with fewer trees. Huge rocks have fractured into many shapes and landed in a narrow cove tucked away from the sun.

At 3.1 miles, veer right, away from the main Worlds Edge Trail on a narrow, flat trail. Two solitary boulders on the right look like a nose of a ship. A fire ring in the middle of the trail designates your turnaround point. Retrace your steps. Farther up, on your right, the prominent ridge is Sugarloaf Mountain at 3,950 ft. elev. with an intermittent waterfall halfway up the mountain.

When you reach the flat circular area at the top, continue left; at the split, stay left, and turn left again onto the main trail. At a wide roundabout previously used by four-wheelers to turn around, stay right, taking it counterclockwise. It won't take you long to reach a flat area with an outstanding view. From the top of the Blue Ridge Escarpment with the valley below you, it feels as if you're on the edge of the world. In the distance, starting from the left, are the South Mountain ridges. Farther right are Kings Mountain and Paris Mountain. Below on the extreme right is Lake Adger, created by damming the Green River. Retrace your steps and stay left on the jeep road back to your car to finish the hike.

Pisgah District

*Biltmore could be made to
prove what America did
not yet understand—that
trees could be cut and the
forest preserved at one
and the same time*

—Gifford Pinchot,
Breaking New Ground, 1947

When George Vanderbilt first traveled to Asheville from New York City for a short vacation in 1885, he was enthralled by the vistas and fresh air of the mountains. It was then that he began to envision what is now the Biltmore Estate. He came back the following year and started buying land so he and his mother could visit each winter. He ended up with 146,000 acres, stretching from the Biltmore House to beyond what is now US 276—much more than needed for a winter getaway.

Vanderbilt, born in 1862, was the grandson of Cornelius Vanderbilt, known as the Commodore, who had made the family fortune in ships and railroads. When the Biltmore House was opened on Christmas Eve 1895, George Vanderbilt's jaded city relatives were overawed by his house, the biggest ever built in the United States and the largest private home in the country. Unlike the other Vanderbilt houses in New York City

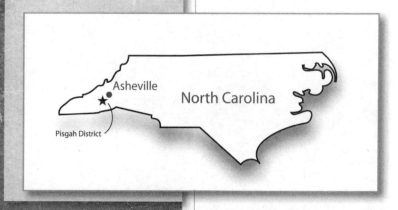

Asheville

North Carolina

Pisgah District

and Newport, RI, Biltmore was modeled on French chateaus like those found in the Loire Valley. George's goal was to run his duchy as a self-sustaining estate.

The Beginning of Forestry

There is evidence that humans have lived along the Davidson River for over 4,000 years. Legend has it that Pisgah was named by James Hall, a chaplain who joined General Rutherford in 1776 on his expedition against the Cherokee Indians. Impressed by the rich forest land, Hall compared it to the Promised Land that Moses saw from the biblical Mt. Pisgah (now in Jordan).

The land Vanderbilt bought was in poor shape, but he thought he could improve it over time. Many of the properties he acquired had been owned by absentee landlords and cleared for crops, livestock, and dwellings. The land had been slashed, burned, and overgrazed. Soil had washed away into streams. Trees were girdled to die in place so light could reach crops planted around them. As their properties deteriorated, many residents sold out and moved on, leaving the land in the hands of real estate speculators.

Enter George Vanderbilt, who invited Frederick Law Olmstead, famous for designing urban parks, including Central Park in New York City, to look over his new property. He hired Olmstead assuming he would turn the land into a park. Instead, Olmstead encouraged Vanderbilt to create a forest and improve the land left devastated by poor farming practices. Olmstead advised that "the topography is most unsuitable for anything that can properly be called park scenery. It's no place for a park. You could only get a very poor result at great cost in attempting it. My advice would be to make a small park into which to look from the house … and make the rest a forest, improving the existing woods and planting the old fields."

Olmstead recommended Gifford Pinchot, a European-trained forester, to manage the long-term health of the forests. Pinchot replanted old farm fields and improved the way the timber was harvested, showing it was possible to upgrade the physical condition of the forest and still make a profit. Although silviculture, scientific forestry, was centuries old in Europe, it was unknown in the United States, where the supply of land and trees seemed inexhaustible. After three years, Pinchot left the Biltmore Estate to become head of the Division of Forestry, later renamed the U.S. Forest Service.

Dr. Carl Schenck succeeded Pinchot as Vanderbilt's chief forester. When he arrived from Germany, he saw that the estate surrounding the Biltmore house was made up of 50 decrepit farms and 10 country places owned by impoverished Southern aristocracy. He was concerned that Vanderbilt was buying up too much land and removing tenants, leaving no one around to fight fires or do forest work. So he suggested a feudal system like that in Europe, with farms rented out in areas that needed protection. Schenck saw transportation as integral to good forestry management and built a road system to move timber out into the marketplace.

In 1898 Schenck started this country's first school of forestry, with mostly sons of local landowners for students. He taught a practical curriculum with lectures in the morning and field work in the afternoon. The school graduated men who went on to introduce scientific methods of forestry all over the country. By 1913, university-based forestry programs were growing, and Schenck's school closed because it couldn't attract enough students. He returned to Germany.

George Vanderbilt's fortune was not without limit. Even though he had inherited seven million dollars plus the income from a five-million dollar trust, which was passed down to his daughter, five years after he moved onto the estate, he ran out of money. To alleviate his financial problems, he negotiated a contract in 1912 with Louis Carr to log Pisgah Forest. The 30-year contract remained in force long after the land became part of Pisgah National Forest. Carr harvested timber and turned it into various wood products. The Carr Lumber Company placed railroad lines up several valleys and built sawmills, a train yard, and employee housing and even installed a telephone line.

Trees from almost every section of the Pisgah District were fair game for the saw. South of Vanderbilt's property, Gloucester Lumber Company, owned by Joseph Silversteen of Brevard, logged the headwaters of the French Broad River. West of the Blue Ridge, Suncrest Lumber Company harvested spruce trees and

Dr. Carl Schenck

built a logging town, now buried under Lake Logan.

George Vanderbilt died in 1914 at the age of 52 after an appendectomy. Within three months, Edith Vanderbilt started selling land to the National Forest Preservation Commission for $5 an acre. She kept selling land; the current Biltmore Estate consists of 8,000 acres. The Weeks Act, passed in 1911, allowed the Federal Government to purchase lands for stream-flow protection and to maintain those lands as national forests. Pisgah National

Forest became the first national forest east of the Mississippi.

The Cradle of Forestry in America

The history of the first forestry school in America is well preserved at the Cradle of Forestry on US 276, just below the Pink Beds trailhead. The 6,500-acre Cradle of Forestry Historic Site within Pisgah National Forest was set aside by Congress to commemorate the beginning of forestry conservation in the United States. The Forest Discovery Center houses many exhibits. A helicopter simulator recreates the experience of flying over a forest fire, an underground exhibit displays how animals live under the forest floor, and an 18-minute film explains the beginning of forestry in America. You can get a good feel for life as a forestry student by walking two paved loops, each about a mile long. The Biltmore Campus Trail meanders past seven historical buildings, including a schoolhouse, commissary, and student quarters. The Forest Festival Trail includes Dr. Schenck's forestry experiments, a portable saw mill, and a logging locomotive you can climb on.

Beyond Vanderbilt's Pisgah

Pisgah National Forest consists of three ranger districts: Pisgah, Appalachian, and Grandfather. Pisgah Ranger District, the subject of this chapter, has over 400 miles of trail.

The Appalachian District, located north of Asheville, is an arc formed by two discontinuous pieces of land, including Mt. Mitchell and sections of the Appalachian Trail (see the Pisgah–Appalachian District chapter for hikes there). The Grandfather Ranger District runs from the McDowell/Buncombe county line just east of Asheville over to US 321 between Lenoir and Blowing Rock. The Vanderbilt property was not the first piece of land east of the Mississippi purchased by the Forest Service; that distinction belongs to Curtis Creek located in the Grandfather District. Linville Gorge and Wilson Creek are considered the highlights of Grandfather Ranger District (see the High Country chapter for hikes there).

Your First Hike in the Pisgah District

Mt. Pisgah (2.6 miles, 750 ft. elev. gain) is a good first hike to do in the Pisgah District because it will orient you to the area. The trailhead is on the Blue Ridge Parkway at milepost 407.6. From the observation platform on top, you'll see Cold Mountain, Looking Glass Rock, and the Frying Pan Mountain tower. Mt. Pisgah is recognizable from many other points in the mountains because of its tower.

This hike encircles Coffee Pot Mountain. You'll go up Trace Ridge Trail, a dry trail with eastern winter views, to Beaver Dam Gap on the Blue Ridge Parkway. After looking at various peaks from the overlook, you'll return on Spencer Branch Trail, following and crossing several streams in a forest with a variety of trees. The end of Spencer Branch Trail leads you to the old Hendersonville Reservoir and Dam. You'll return on a road paralleling the North Fork of the Mills River.

Type of hike: Loop

Distance: 8.3 miles

Total ascent: 1,500 ft.

Starting elevation: 2,400 ft.

Highlights: Streams, Blue Ridge Parkway, old Hendersonville Reservoir

USGS map: Dunsmore Mountain

Trail map: Pisgah Ranger District, Pisgah National Forest, National Geographic Trails Illustrated Map #780

Land managed by: Pisgah National Forest, Pisgah District

Getting to the trailhead: From I-26 exit 40 (Airport Rd.), take NC 280 west for 3.9 miles and turn right on North Mills River Rd. (SR 1345). At 4.9 miles,

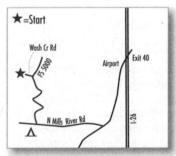

Trailhead GPS Coordinates: N 35° 25.22 W 82° 39.41

you'll enter the North Mills River Recreation Area and soon pass a parking area on your left. Immediately turn right on Wash Creek Rd. (FS 5000). Drive 2.1 miles and turn left. You'll cross a one-lane bridge and in 0.5 mile reach the Trace Ridge trailhead.

The Hike

From the trailhead, make the first right toward the eastern side of the parking area at a "road closed" sign on Fletcher Creek Rd. After a few feet, take a right on Trace Ridge Trail [#354 – orange blazes]. The trail soon makes a sweeping arc to continue left and up. This is an old, rocky jeep trail which also allows bikes and horses. The trail curves northwest around Coffee Pot Mountain, going uphill gently through an oak and maple forest dotted with pitch pines.

The trail, now enclosed by rhododendron, dips down only to go up again; it's bare red soil with a few roots. This is a rough section of Pisgah Forest where logging has left a maze of trails. At 1.1 miles, the trail climbs on a ridge for winter views on both the east and west sides.

The trail has few blazes, but once you're on it, you'll have no problems finding your way. At 2.8 miles (3,350 ft. elev.), Spencer Branch Trail [#140 – yellow blazes] comes in on your left. You'll take that trail back down, but for now continue on Trace Ridge Trail. Soon after, Spencer Gap Trail [#600] takes off to your right as you continue straight. The trail becomes rocky, steep, and enclosed by oak, maple, and tuliptrees, with an understory of sourwood.

At 3.1 miles (3,500 ft. elev.), you'll reach a wand for Trace Ridge Trail. You'll be close to the Parkway but not quite there. In another 0.1 mile

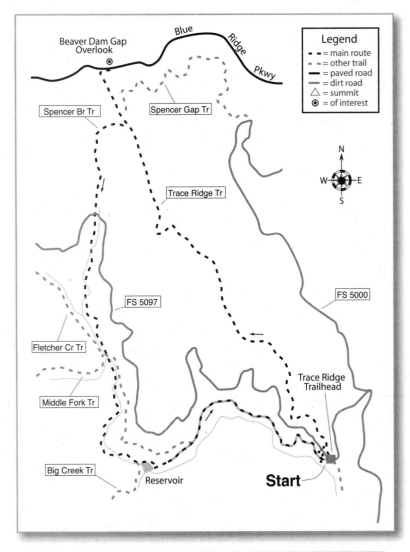

(3,600 ft. elev.) you'll reach the Parkway and make a right to Beaver Dam Gap Overlook. Across the road, the Mountains-to-Sea Trail [#440] runs along the edge of the parking area.

Beaver Dam Overlook offers views of wave after wave of mountain ridges. Trace Ridge is the near hump, closest to you on the left as you face the overlook. Behind it, the next ridge is Laurel Mountain, which separates North Mills River drainage from South Mills River drainage.

Retrace your steps on Trace Ridge Trail and turn right on Spencer Branch Trail at 3.8 miles. This wide, rocky trail starts down steeply on wooden steps but soon moderates. In a half-mile, you'll reach a flat area with tall, straight tuliptrees. A little farther down, you'll be in a little hemlock valley. The line of small hemlocks looks like a Christmas tree farm. At this writing, the young trees look healthy; with luck they won't succumb to the hemlock woolly adelgid. Cross a stream, cross FS 5097, and continue straight to parallel Spencer Branch on your left. On your right you'll pass a fence holding black plastic silt cloth, placed there to control erosion. Walk on an old road until you cross Spencer Branch at 5.0 miles (2,750 ft. elev.).

Spencer Branch flows into Fletcher Creek, which takes off to your right then returns and crisscrosses the trail several times. To your

The sight and sound of rushing water is one of the great pleasures of hiking.

right, fields are filling in with bushes and vegetation. You'll come to a large beaver pond, more like a huge beaver estate. A steep side trail on your left allows you to skirt around the beaver pond and not have to swim across. Then the trail veers away from the beaver pond. Walk southeast on a flat trail through mountain laurel and rhododendrons. At 5.6 miles, Fletcher Creek Trail [#350], a horse trail, crosses Spencer Branch Trail.

Cross Fletcher Creek again and continue left, following yellow blazes. A yellow marker and wand show you where to cross again. The creek, now below you on the left, is wide and active, with cascades and ripples. The trail continues to follow the creek downstream. At 6.2 miles, you'll enter an alleyway of hemlocks. The trail snakes through the cove following the creek.

At 6.7 miles (2,550 ft. elev.), Big Creek Trail [#102] comes in from your right. Depending on the water level, there may be a little beach and on your right a waterfall.

The spillway for the old Hendersonville Reservoir, which feeds into the North Fork of the Mills River, is not often used. When you reach it, turn left and walk on Hendersonville Reservoir Rd. (FS142), now closed to traffic, and pass the end of Fletcher Creek Trail on your left. It's a pleasant road walk which follows Big Creek, passing a waterfall on the left. Big Creek is down below in a bed of rhododendron. At 7.6 miles, North Mills River Trail [#353] comes in from the right. Several narrow benches on the right overlook a wide campsite off North Mills River Trail. The road climbs gently and steadily, skirting the mountain, to take you back to your car as you finish the hike.

The spillway for the Old Hendersonville Reservoir feeds into the North Fork of the Mills River.

Cantrell Creek Lodge

The hike to the Cantrell Creek Lodge site is a beautiful, easy river walk on South Mills River Trail. Most of the South Mills River Watershed is classified as Outstanding Resource Waters because of its excellent water quality and recreational significance. There are many great campsites on the river. You can go as far as you want and set up camp, so it makes a perfect excursion for beginning backpackers or when testing new equipment. Several bridges were demolished by Hurricanes Frances and Ivan in 2004, but they have been replaced. Cantrell Creek Lodge is now preserved at the Cradle of Forestry; only the chimney is still on site. On this gentle hike, you'll see also how the forest has recuperated from logging.

Type of hike: Out and back

Distance: 8.0 miles

Total ascent: 700 ft.

Starting elevation: 2,650 ft.

Highlights: River, beautiful campsites, Cantrell Creek Lodge site and chimney

USGS map: Pisgah Forest

Trail map: Pisgah Ranger District, Pisgah National Forest, National Geographic Trails Illustrated Map #780

Land managed by: Pisgah National Forest, Pisgah District

Getting to the trailhead: From the community of Pisgah Forest, drive 5.2 miles east on NC 280. Turn left on Turkey Pen Rd. at the Transylvania/Henderson County line and drive 1.4 miles to the parking area.

The Hike
From the parking area, go down to the left of the information board on South Mills River Trail [#133 – white blazes]. It's a multi-use trail; bikers and horses take the parallel trail on the right to avoid log steps. At the first split, turn left to stay on the trail and continue down into a rhododendron-lined cove. A creek on your left flows into the South Mills River. At 0.4 mile (2,400 ft. elev.), turn left to cross South Mills River on a wide suspension bridge. Straight ahead is Bradley Creek Trail [#351], which heads north and crosses the river without a bridge.

After the bridge crossing, the trail climbs and makes a sharp left; it's a wide road which goes up gently. You'll follow the river upstream as you walk through hemlock, white pine, rhododendron, and mountain laurel. Soon you'll

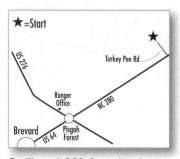

★ =Start

US 276

Turkey Pen Rd

Ranger Office

NC 280

Brevard

US 64

Pisgah Forest

Trailhead GPS Coordinates:
N 35° 20.57 W 82° 39.57

pass Mullinax Trail [#326] on the right. Stay left where the trail gently descends to meet the river. At 0.9 mile, a trail on your left leads to the riverbank, which might be a good destination for a child's first backpacking trip, particularly with a fishing pole. Soon the trail zigzags under a canopy of hemlock and crosses one of many runoffs into the river. In the winter, icicles hang on shaded rocks long after the trail is clear of snow.

At 2.0 miles (2,500 ft. elev.), a rocky promontory juts out into the river. To the right of the rocks, there's a small swimming hole; you can work your way down into the pool. Soon after, you'll pass the intersection with Poundingmill Trail [#349], heading right to Poundingstone Mountain. Keep paralleling the river, which becomes shallow as you go upstream. Here it's easy to get down to the bank of the river to cool your feet off. This point is about halfway to the lodge site.

At 2.7 miles, a mysterious brown carsonite sign, with longitude and latitude numbers, points into a field. When the Forest Service replaced the bridges that were wiped out by the 2004 hurricanes, they

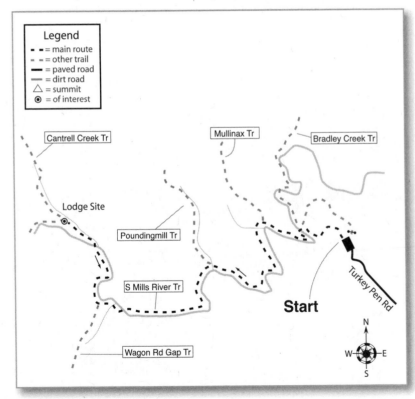

brought in equipment and supplies by helicopter and the flat field on the right was their landing pad. Some remnants of the old bridges are still sitting on the side of the trail.

You can see far into the distance on this flat and straight section. In another 0.3 mile, turn left to continue on a new wooden suspension bridge. A sign overhead says "one person" at a time on the bridge—a good guideline to follow on any backcountry trail bridge. Turn right on the other side of the river; the short trails going into the river are for horse crossings.

Pass the junction with Wagon Road Gap Trail [#134], a short trail on the left which connects with Turkey Pen Gap Trail [#322]. As the trail moves away from the river, it becomes wider and even flatter, if that's possible. It's more open to the sky, with fewer rhododendrons blocking the views.

At 3.7 miles continue left, avoiding the horse crossing, and cross the third bridge on your right, also a wood plank suspension bridge. The trail continues left, passing a wide, flat area with American holly. At 3.9 miles, turn left to cross the river on a small log bridge over Cantrell Creek—this turn is easy to miss. At the horse crossing, after the last bridge, there's another brown carsonite sign pointing to a flat field.

The huge chimney is all that's left here of Cantrell Creek Lodge. South Mills River Trail continues to the left of the chimney and eventually goes to the Cradle of Forestry. A large wooden sign explains the site's

Stopping for a photo at the South Mills River.

historical importance. Here is another attractive place to camp by Cantrell Creek, which flows into South Mills River. Cantrell Creek Trail [#148] intersects South Mills River Trail just north of the chimney.

Return the way you came. On the way back, after you cross the big first bridge, take a right. Go to a split in the trail, then take the right turn which will take you to the information board and your car to end the hike.

The original Cantrell Creek Lodge chimney.

Cantrell Creek Lodge

Cantrell Creek Lodge was built in the "Black Forest" style in the late 1890s. At that time, Schenck's forest rangers managed what was then George Vanderbilt's Biltmore Forest. Unfortunately, the lodge had to be moved because of vandalism. In 1979, the Young Adult Conservation Corps took the building apart at the site and flew the pieces by helicopter to the Cradle of Forestry site, where it was reassembled. You can see it at the edge of the Cradle of Forestry parking area.

Cantrell Creek Lodge today.

Pink Beds is as easy a hike as you'll find in the Pisgah District. This clockwise loop encircles a high mountain bog with little elevation gain; it's a popular hike with a well-marked trail. Because sections of this loop have been flooded by beaver work, several bridges and boardwalks have been installed along the route. At the trailhead, there's an open meadow with picnic tables, barbecue grills, and restrooms.

Type of hike: Loop

Distance: 5.4 miles

Total ascent: 400 ft.

Starting elevation: 3,300 ft.

Highlights: Pink flowers, high mountain bog, beaver work

USGS map: Shining Rock

Trail map: Pisgah Ranger District, Pisgah National Forest, National Geographic Trails Illustrated Map #780

Land managed by: Pisgah National Forest, Pisgah District

Getting to the trailhead: From NC 280 in the community of Pisgah Forest, go north on US 276 to enter Pisgah National Forest. Drive 11.6 miles and turn right at the Pink Beds Picnic Area. The turn is just

Trailhead GPS Coordinates: N 35° 21.20 W 82° 46.75

after you pass the Cradle of Forestry, also on your right.

The Hike
Facing the information board in the lower level parking area, go right for a few feet and make a right on an old road now blocked by a metal bar. You'll pass a faded board with a map showing the Pink Beds Loop. Walk on the closed-off road for a couple of hundred feet to the start of Pink Beds Loop Trail [#118 – orange blazes]. Cross a wooden bridge over Pigeon Branch in an area filled with rhododendron, mountain laurel, and galax.

When the trails forks, take the left branch; you'll come back on the trail to the right. On the right is a "wildlife opening," field created and maintained to attract wildlife. In this section of trail, you'll pass several more glades, alternating with a narrow woods trail. One meadow has perfectly symmetrical hemlocks. Usually hemlocks are hemmed in by woods and must compete for light, but here they're out in the open and get all the light they need. This land has been overworked but is bounding back.

At 1.0 mile, there's an apparent fork to the right. Continue left, paralleling Bearwallow Brook Branch which you'll cross on a bridge. Side streams meander slowly; on this hike, you're always close to water.

At 1.5 miles, Barnett Branch Trail [#618] crosses Pink Beds Loop Trail. Until it was decommissioned several years ago, this was also the Alternate Mountains-to-Sea Trail. Continue straight. There may be some misleading blazes facing the creek that that seem to indicate that you should cross there. But on this hike there's no need to cross a stream without a bridge, unless it is very shallow and you want to just hop across.

Soon a red arrow points right but the trail stays straight. You'll cross Barnett Branch at a tiny spillway created by a log. The trail starts gently downhill as it passes a bowl-like area on your left with small pine trees under a canopy of oak and maple.

At 2.5 miles, the trail turns sharply right, marked by an incongruous plastic blue blaze. In the woods, an old metal barrel lies on its side as you turn the corner. In another 0.2 mile, you'll reach a T-intersection. A left would

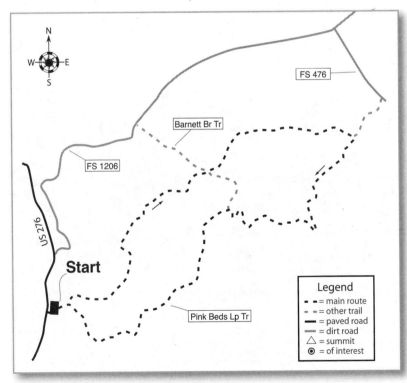

take you to the Wolf Ford Gauging Station, which used to measure the water flow on the South Fork Mills River, near its headwaters. Turn right to continue the loop and follow the river downstream. The water is still because beavers have built dams a little downstream to create a lake. Cross on a new wooden bridge, placed after beaver activities destroyed the old one. You'll walk on a short stretch of gravel and start climbing gently on a new piece of trail that meanders up another sidehill, leaving the creek for a while.

At 3.6 miles, on the left of the trail, you'll pass a downed tree which had been growing on almost pure rock and must have had very thin roots. At the second intersection with Barnett Branch Trail, which goes off to the left, stay right. This area had been flooded by beaver work, but now the right end of Barnett Branch Trail has an impressive new boardwalk. It's 5 ft. wide so Pisgah Forest rangers can drive their vehicle over it for search and rescue or fire fighting, if needed. Cross a bridge and go under a latticework of blowdown branches about 6 ft. over your head; this blowdown is too big and complex to be moved. Cross a right-angle bridge. The first section is on a sawed-off log; the second section was built with a flat deck. The trail narrows and crosses more bridges. You'll enter a cathedral-like area of hemlocks where there's a wide opening on the left. The trail

This right-angle bridge on the Pink Beds Loop is built partly on a fallen tree trunk.

Wet sections of trail are easily crossed by a boardwalk.

goes straight and right and is well marked. At 5.2 miles, you'll close the circle. Make a left to retrace your steps back to the car and end the hike.

Variation: Pink Beds Loop Trail, right to Barnett Branch Trail, and right again to continue the loop—3.3 miles with minimal altitude gain.

Afterwards, visit the Cradle of Forestry, just south of the trailhead, to learn about the beginnings of scientific forestry in the United States.

Heritage

Blooms and Beavers: The Pink Beds

Pink Beds Valley was named by settlers who first cleared the land in this mountain bog. From the surrounding mountains you could see an ocean of azalea and mountain laurel blooms in spring with rhododendron and wild phlox continuing the pink theme in summer. These days you can get a good view from Pink Beds Overlook on the Blue Ridge Parkway at milepost 410.3, although since trees are filling in the area, the pink is not as visible. Swamp pink, a native wetland perennial with pink flowers in a tight cluster that blooms in April and May, is registered as threatened on the endangered species list.

Beavers complicate the work of Forest Service personnel in this area. Several years ago, beavers flooded the trail in places and dislocated a low-lying bridge. After repairing the old bridge several times, the Forest Service gave up and built a higher bridge. Beavers are persistent creatures; they moved downstream and worked on another section of the trail. In 2008, the Carolina Mountain Club maintenance crew built a new 245-ft. boardwalk to replace a 1990 bridge that had collapsed. A plaque honoring the volunteers on both bridges had been placed at the end of the bridge.

Twin Falls Loop

This loop incorporates waterfalls, lush coves, and many creek crossings. The trail follows old railroad beds much of the time, a constant reminder of Pisgah Forest's long logging history. On this easy hike, you'll go to Twin Falls, a popular family destination. But whereas most tourists return on the same trail, you'll continue on a Forest Service access road to Clawhammer Cove, a small green jewel of a trail. The hike ends with a walk around a large beaver pond.

Type of hike: Loop

Distance: 5.7 miles

Total ascent: 750 ft.

Starting elevation: 2,600 ft.

Highlights: Twin Falls, creeks, beaver pond, railroad artifacts

USGS map: Shining Rock

Trail map: Pisgah Ranger District, Pisgah National Forest, National Geographic Trails Illustrated Map #780

Land managed by: Pisgah National Forest, Pisgah District

Getting to the trailhead: From NC 280 in the community of Pisgah Forest, go north on US 276 to enter Pisgah National Forest. Drive 2.3 miles and turn right at the horse rental sign

Trailhead GPS Coordinates: N 35° 19.33 W 82° 45.46

(FS 477). Drive 2.4 miles, passing the Avery Creek Trailhead, and then another 0.3 mile to Buckhorn Gap Trailhead.

The Hike

Buckhorn Gap Trail [#103 – orange blazes] goes down through a tunnel of rosebay rhododendron and mountain laurel. The wide railroad-grade trail flattens out and enters a hemlock grove. At 0.6 mile, watch for an unnamed cascade on your right. This cascade is seen more clearly on Avery Creek Trail, though you'll have to diverge off this hike to find it.

At 0.9 mile, Avery Creek Trail [#327 – blue blazes] comes in from the right and both trails run together for a short while. You could have come in from Avery Creek Trail and that's the way you'll end the hike. Ignore the horse water crossing and stay left on the trail, which parallels Avery Creek (Avery and Henry Creeks converged farther up). Go up steps on a narrow trail and cross on a three-log bridge.

The trail turns right and crosses the creek twice

more, with a wooden sign for Buckhorn Gap Trail pointing the way. Avery Creek Trail now heads left; stay right on Buckhorn Gap Trail.

You'll cross Henry Creek

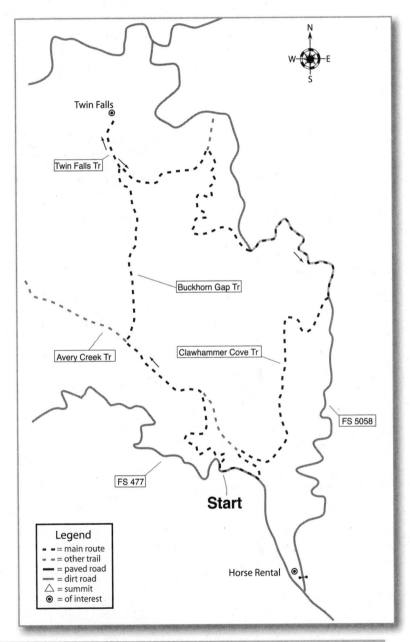

Twin Falls

Twin Falls Tr

Buckhorn Gap Tr

Avery Creek Tr

Clawhammer Cove Tr

FS 5058

FS 477

Start

Legend
- ▪ ▪ = main route
- ▪ ▪ = other trail
- ▬ = paved road
- ▬ = dirt road
- △ = summit
- ◉ = of interest

Horse Rental ◉

several times on log bridges, though when the water is low, it may be simpler to go through the creek. Look for a huge hemlock with roots growing out and over a rock. The trail goes down a short, steep incline on rocks so even that the path almost feels paved. Horse tie-ups have been placed on the right. In between two more bridges, the soil of the trail is so dark that it looks like the ground is lined with coal. Doghobble, bee balm, violets, and poison ivy grow in profusion.

At 1.5 miles, turn left on Twin Falls Trail [#604 – yellow blazes]. As you get closer to Twin Falls, before you reach a flat spot with a fire ring, look up to the left. In the distance you'll see the bare, steep rocks of an intermittent waterfall, an unnamed child of Twin Falls. You'll reach the first of the Twin Falls, about 80 ft. high, at 1.8 miles. The trail crosses at the base of the waterfall—a good place to take a photo. Continue on a narrow trail to the second Twin Falls. From the bottom, this second waterfall looks like a cascade, but from the top you can see that airy wisps of water fall about 60 ft.

Retrace your steps to the fire ring and make an immediate left turn downhill toward a tributary of Henry Branch. On this steep and muddy side trail, you'll pass the huge root system of a blown-down tree. When you get to a large flat area with several

At the first of the Twin Falls, the trail crosses at the base of the waterfall.

horse tie-ups, make a left to get back on Buckhorn Gap Trail.

At 2.5 miles, reach a T-junction and turn right, heading south on an old forest road. Look for cable on the ground, left over from the trail's railroad origins. At 3.4 miles (3,200 ft. elev.), where the trail converges with FS 5058, take a right. A trail wand indicates that a left would take you to Buckhorn Gap. Along the road blackberries abound, tart even when ripe and black at the end of July. Stands of jewelweed, a folk antidote for poison ivy, flourish here along with lots of Virginia creeper. It's a pleasant, gentle downhill walk; stay alert and look for the turn onto Clawhammer Cove Trail on the right.

At 4.1 miles, make a right on Clawhammer Cove Trail [#342 – blue blazes] where several tuliptrees stand tall and straight. The trail, narrow and green, is in a charming cove with dense fields of ferns, a welcome contrast from the wide, old railroad trails you've been walking on. Cross Clawhammer Creek at 4.5 miles on a good bridge. The trail now parallels the creek as it passes several huge boulders, hugged tightly by hemlock tree roots. Take a side path around a permanent blowdown of a huge tree that came down roots and all. With a blowdown this immense, maintenance crews often feel it's easier to route hikers around it than to take out the tree.

Suddenly the trail becomes bare under a dark stand of hemlocks. Toward the end of Clawhammer Cove Trail, on your left, beavers have created a large marsh. The trail goes around the swamp and ends at 5.2 miles. Make a left on Avery Creek Trail and cross Avery Creek on a wide three-log bridge. If you want to get a closer look at the waterfall mentioned at the beginning of the hike, you'll need to make a right here.

On this section of Avery Creek Trail the beaver work is more extensive; fallen trees and bare soil islands lie in sluggish water. You'll leave the creek and beaver work behind as you climb up steeply. At 5.4 miles, you'll be back on the gravel road. Turn right to walk to your car and end the hike.

Variation: To Twin Falls and back—3.7 miles with 400 ft. ascent.

On Buckhorn Gap Trail, a huge hemlock seems to grow straight out of the rock.

Art Loeb

Heritage

Who was Art Loeb?

It is proposed that a scenic foot trail to be known as the "Arthur J. Loeb Trail" be established in the Pisgah Ranger District of the National Forest in N.C. beginning at U.S. Highway 276 and 64 immediately south ... to the summit of Cold Mountain (elevation 6,030 ft.) in the Shining Rock Wild Area.

This is from a carbon copy of the original proposal to the Forest Service from the Carolina Mountain Club (CMC). Someone had crossed out "Arthur J. Loeb" and replaced it with "Art Loeb."

The proposal is dated June 7, 1969. Four months after it was filed, the Art Loeb Trail became official.

Art Loeb wasn't always a hiker. Like many present-day CMC members, he came late to the hiking life. Born into a Jewish-German family in Philadelphia in 1914, Loeb moved to Brevard in 1936 to work for his cousin, Harry Strauss, who founded the Ecusta paper mill.

Strauss was originally from Germany and he'd brought with him a process for making fine papers, suitable for bibles and cigarettes, from flax. Loeb traveled all over the United States buying up flax for the business. After serving in the military during World War II, Loeb and his wife Kitty settled in Brevard where he worked his way up to vice-president and general manager of the Ecusta Paper Division of Olin Mathieson Chemical Corporation.

When he was in his forties, Loeb suffered a heart attack. Doctors encouraged him to walk as a means of rehabilitation and he took their advice. He began by walking around Strauss Lake but eventually ranged farther afield, climbing a fire road near his house to a mountaintop in Pisgah National Forest. He joined the CMC, where he found a congenial group of hiking partners.

"He lived to hike," Loeb's youngest daughter, Katie Loeb-Schwab, recalls. Loeb carried a stick and hiked in shorts well before either became popular on the trail. Back then, hiking in western North Carolina involved a lot of bushwhacking, map reading, and getting lost. During vacations and school holidays, Loeb was joined on the trail by his middle daughter, Joan Loeb Dickson, and her husband John. "There were maps, but they didn't help much," John Dickson recalls.

Gerry McNabb, a recent CMC president, describes Loeb as "tall, serious yet friendly, slender, nice looking" with "powerful legs." He adds, "He was a leader who could inspire confidence and was a real asset to the club with his business skills."

Sadly, the benefit of those skills turned out to be short-lived. Loeb was diagnosed with a brain tumor when he was 54 and he died in 1968. Almost immediately, the club went to work on a fitting memorial.

Art Loeb Trail

Loeb always liked the plaque on Tennent Mountain honoring Dr. Gaillard Tennent, who in 1923 became CMC's first president. By the 1960s, the Forest Service was no longer willing to change the names of mountains; instead, the CMC proposed a memorial trail made up of old roads, trails, and herd paths, many explored by Loeb. The trail would be a high ridgeline path through the area the late hiker had loved and cared for. Three entities led the effort to build the trail: the CMC, the Forest Service, and longtime western North Carolina Congressman

Roy Taylor, who'd known Loeb as a community business leader.

On November 9, 1969, hundreds of people attended the dedication of Art Loeb Trail. A large wooden plaque was placed at the trailhead (it was later vandalized and removed). At 30.1 miles, Art Loeb Trail is the longest in the Pisgah Ranger District. Starting at Davidson River, it goes west toward Butter Gap, offering winter views of three massive plutons: Cedar Rock, Looking Glass Rock, and John Rock. Then it heads north toward Gloucester Gap, crosses Pilot Mountain, and reaches the Blue Ridge Parkway, where it joins the Mountains-to-Sea Trail for a short while before veering off toward Black Balsam Knob. The latter is the most popular section of the trail because of outstanding views from the mountain balds. The trail continues into the Shining Rock Wilderness, past Shining Rock itself and then through The Narrows to Deep Gap, below the summit of Cold Mountain. A steep descent ends at Camp Daniel Boone on the Little East Fork of the Pigeon River.

The official trail blaze for Art Loeb Trail is white. But if you hike from its beginning along Davidson River, you'll also see the trail's original markings: intermittent faded yellow paint stencils of the silhouette of a hiker holding a staff. With a little imagination, you can see Art Loeb still walking the mountains he loved so well.

The hike starts at the Pisgah Center for Wildlife Education on the Cat Gap Loop Trail and travels south, diverting shortly to two lovely waterfalls. At Cat Gap you'll turn east on Art Loeb Trail and hike the Shut-In Ridge until you reach Davidson River. During much of the hike, three rocks, John Rock, Cedar Rock, and Looking Glass Rock, are visible. As you descend, you'll see the Ecusta plant, where Art Loeb spent his entire career.

Type of hike: Shuttle

Distance: 8.8 miles

Total ascent/descent: 2,300 ft. /2,500 ft.

Starting elevation: 2,350 ft.

Highlights: Waterfalls, views of rock formations and mountain ridges

USGS map: Shining Rock and Pisgah Forest

Trail map: Pisgah Ranger District, Pisgah National Forest, National Geographic Trails Illustrated Map #780

Land managed by: Pisgah National Forest, Pisgah District

Getting to the trailhead: From NC 280 in the community of Pisgah Forest, go north on US 276 to enter Pisgah

★ =Start
★ =End

Blue Ridge Pkwy
US 276
FS 475
Pisgah Ctr Wildlife Edu ★
NC 280
US 64
Pisgah Forest
Brevard

Trailhead GPS Coordinates: N 35° 17.05 W 82° 47.47

National Forest. Drive another 1.1 miles and turn left at a sign pointing to the Schenck Civilian Conservation Center and the English Chapel. Make another quick left to the Art Loeb trailhead. Leave one car there.

Get back on US 276 and continue north for 4.4 miles. Turn left on FS 475, drive 1.4 miles, and turn left into the Pisgah Center for Wildlife Education parking lot where the hike begins.

The Hike
The hike starts at the back of the parking lot for the Pisgah Center for Wildlife Education on Horse Cove Rd. (FS 475C). Cross a bridge and turn right on Cat Gap Loop Trail [#120 – orange blazes], which you'll take counterclockwise. Parallel a chain-link fence on the right, the boundary of the Wildlife Education Center. Cross a little stream and continue on a manicured trail, paralleling Cedar Rock Creek North on the right (There are two Cedar Rock Creeks in the Pisgah District; according to a long-time Forest Service volunteer and hiker, this stream should be referred to as Cedar Rock Creek North).

At 0.3 mile, cross the creek on Roberts Bridge, named for Dick Roberts, a maintenance trail crew leader whose team members called themselves Roberts Rangers. Pass a Fish Hatchery sign and continue climbing. At 0.7 mile, take a herd path left and down to Cedar Rock Creek Falls. Before reaching the waterfall, you'll pass a huge rock cave with constantly dripping water. The waterfall is not high but it's very photogenic, with a rainforest feel. You can go back to the main trail by following a steeper but shorter trail from the cave or return to Cat Gap Loop Trail on the herd path you came in on.

A few hundred feet after your return from Cedar Rock Creek Falls, take a second herd path on your left and go down to Grogan Creek Falls. The falls are on your right after a campsite. This multilevel cascade is a lovely destination, but the view will never win a photo competition because a tree trunk lies sideways in front of the falls.

Back on Cat Gap Loop Trail, cross Butter Gap Trail [#123] which goes off to the right, leading to the top of Grogan Creek Falls. Cross a bridge at the confluence of Cedar Rock Creek North (left) and Grogan Creek (right). You'll enter Picklesimer Fields on your right, though it may be difficult to recognize it as a field because bushes are filling it in. After a second bridge crossing, the trail passes through a cathedral of white pine with a groundcover of club moss.

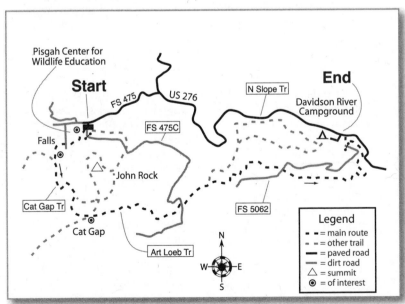

Cross Cedar Rock Creek at 1.3 miles on flat rocks. The trail veers to the right and starts climbing. At 1.7 miles, pass Cat Gap Bypass Trail [#120A] on your left. As you climb, turn around for a view of Pilot Mountain, the most prominent mountain in the area (see Pilot Mountain hike, p. 256). Go down to Cat Pen Gap and climb back up. The views of Looking Glass Rock get better as you continue climbing. You'll pass several Carolina hemlocks on the right. Carolina hemlocks differ from the more prolific Eastern hemlocks in that their needles are notched at the tip, not toothed, and they have narrower cones.

At 2.3 miles (3,400 ft. elev.) at Cat Gap, you'll reach the intersection of several trails. The first right is Art Loeb Trail, going north toward the Blue Ridge Parkway. The next right is an unmaintained trail to Kings Creek toward Brevard. Take Art Loeb Trail [#146 – white blazes], going straight and a little to the right, with both blue and white blazes. The blue blazes mark the now decommissioned Alternate Mountains-to-Sea Trail, used before the MST was completed through this area. Cat Gap Loop Trail continues left and leads back to the parking lot you came from.

Go through Cat Pen Gap; you'll reach the top of Chestnut Knob at 3.1 miles (3,850 ft. elev.) where downed logs on top of the mountain make a good lunch spot. As you come down from Chestnut Knob, look right for a view of Cedar Rock. At 4.1 miles, go down a few wooden steps with a wobbly handrail to reach FS 475C. Turn left on the road and then make a quick right back into the woods on Art Loeb Trail. Looking down to the right (southeast) you'll start to see Brevard and the community of Pisgah Forest.

At 4.6 miles, the trail turns sharply left. If you went straight, you'd find a campfire ring and a dead-end under Stony Knob. After the turn, the trail continues down toward Neil Gap and meets the North Slope Connector [#359A], which comes in from the left, connecting Art Loeb Trail to the North Slope Ridge. Follow Art Loeb Trail, which narrows and stays right. Looking to the left (northeast), Black Mountain is the tallest peak, with Hickory Knob on the right and Clawhammer on the left.

You'll reach Neil Gap at 5.3 miles (2,900 ft. elev.). The trail climbs to the Shut-In Ridge—don't confuse this section of trail with the Shut-In Trail, part of the MST which goes from the North Carolina Arboretum to Mt. Pisgah. Shut-In Ridge, enclosed by mountain laurel and rhododendron, undulates up and down until the end of the hike. As you descend, look to your right (southeast) to see the Ecusta plant with its several water towers. The site will be redeveloped for residential and commercial use.

At 6.3 miles, make a right on FS 5062 and then a quick left to stay on Art Loeb Trail. You might hear but not see Joel Branch Cascade below you while crossing the road. As you go down the steep, switchbacked trail through a rhododendron tunnel, you have a good look at the Ecusta plant site on the right. The dominant mountain in front of you is Johnson Mountain.

At 8.0 miles, you'll cross the mouth of Joel Branch on a good bridge. The trail is flat as it parallels Davidson River on your right. Sycamore Flats Picnic Area is on the other side of the river. As you approach the bridge, the buildings to your left are at the edge of the Schenck Civilian Conservation Center. Turn right on a steel and wooden bridge and then left to continue on Art Loeb Trail. Walk another five minutes, paralleling US 276 as you head back to your car to end the hike.

A waterfall doesn't have to be high to be photogenic, as evidenced by Cedar Rock Creek Falls.

Pilot Mountain is a landmark which can be seen from several highpoints in Pisgah District. On this hike, you'll climb Pilot Mountain for great views into both Pisgah and Nantahala National Forests. These views make it a favorite any time of the year. If you go in May, the area is covered with pinkshell azalea, a rare flower native to only a few mountain counties in North Carolina.

Type of hike: Loop

Distance: 7.6 miles

Total ascent: 1,950 ft.

Starting elevation: 3,200 ft.

Highlights: Views, flowers, pinkshell azalea

USGS map: Shining Rock

Trail map: Pisgah Ranger District, Pisgah National Forest, National Geographic Trails Illustrated Map #780

Land managed by: Pisgah National Forest, Pisgah District

Getting to the trailhead: From NC 280 in the community of Pisgah Forest, go north on US 276 to enter Pisgah National Forest. Drive 5.5 miles and turn left on Fish Hatchery Rd. (FS 475). Continue 6.4 miles to Gloucester Gap, a four-way

★=Start

Blue Ridge Pkwy

US 276

★ Gloucester Gap

FS 475

● Pisgah Ctr Wildlife Edu

NC 280

Pisgah Forest

US 64

Brevard

Trailhead GPS Coordinates: N 35° 15.96 W 82° 50.81

intersection; the road turns to gravel after the turnoff to the Cove Creek Group Camp.

The Hike
Art Loeb Trail [#146 – white blazes] starts on wooden steps on the northwest side of the Gap. Walking through mountain laurel and rhododendron, pass a boulder to your left with obstructed views—hints of better things to come. The trail switchbacks gently uphill under a maple and oak canopy through a full array of wildflowers. In early fall, white and purple asters, goldenrod, yellow mandarin, and coneflowers line the trail. You'll cross Pilot Mountain Rd. [FS 229] at 0.5 mile. In spring, roadside and trail alike explode with blooming flame azalea. Cross the road again in another 0.1 mile and go up steps into the woods. A brown carsonite sign which reads "Art Loeb" guides you back on the trail.

Soon you'll pass a flat spot on the left—a possible campsite, though there's no water around; this is a dry area. Occasional blue circles are left over from the old Alternate Mountains-to-Sea Trail, now decommissioned.

When the trail climbs a little more steeply, be on the lookout for a rocky spot on the left at 1.1 miles (4,200 ft. elev.). Walk out a few feet on a slanted overlook for stunning views of the southeastern mountain ridges and maybe a snack break.

In May, you'll see pinkshell azalea here, a tall shrub which produces flowers before

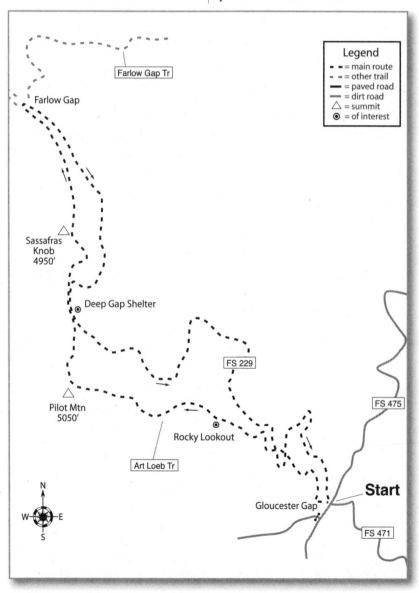

Legend
- = main route
- = other trail
— = paved road
— = dirt road
△ = summit
◉ = of interest

Farlow Gap Tr

Farlow Gap

Sassafras Knob 4950'

Deep Gap Shelter

FS 229

Pilot Mtn 5050'

Rocky Lookout

Art Loeb Tr

FS 475

Start

Gloucester Gap

FS 471

N
W E
S

Waves of mountain ridges make up the view from Pilot Mountain.

its leaves unfold. In this flat section they line the trail, making it look like a church aisle decorated for a wedding procession. The trail narrows, with banks of mountain laurel and rhododendron encroaching on either side. You'll go down a little to cross an unnamed gap at 1.4 miles. Continue straight and up, following white blazes. In the spring, as you cross the dirt road, this small area is full of wildflowers, a lush spot on a generally dry mountain climb. You know you're getting close to the top of the mountain when you start seeing obstructed views to your left. You'll reach the top of Pilot Mountain at 1.7 miles (5,050 ft. elev.). The rocky top with an almost 360-degree panorama has the remains of a fire tower. To the west, most of the views look out into Nantahala National Forest.

From here, Mt. Hardy, a tall, imposing mountain, stands out on your far right (see Mt. Hardy hike, p. 265). To the east there are several tiers of mountain ranges. Looking at the closest range from left to right, you'll see Looking Glass Rock, John Rock, and Cedar Rock. Clawhammer and Black Mountain are farther back. In the distance, all the way left, you might be able to make out Mt. Pisgah with its distinctive tower. Think about where you're standing now—you may at some point have seen Pilot Mountain from Devils Courthouse, Black Mountain, Silvermine Bald, or Black Balsam Knob (see Sam Knob/ Black Balsam hike, p. 260).

The trail, enclosed with azaleas and rhododendrons, switchbacks downhill nicely. You'll pass a long metal pipe, some of it in the ground, some loose on a steep downhill, as you approach Deep Gap. At a fork in the trail where the pipe goes to the right, continue left on Art Loeb Trail. You'll reach Deep Gap at 2.3 miles. There are several good, flat camping spots here, though there's no dependable water. Stay to the left; the shelter bypass trail goes right. You may hear a creek below to your left but you can't see it. The trail continues around the back of the A-frame shelter and quickly veers right and then left to rejoin the main trail.

The trail climbs easily to Sassafras Knob with its flattish, tree-covered top at 2.8 miles (4,950 ft. elev.). Coming down, you'll pass a rhododendron tree on your right, surrounded by rocks. The setting almost looks artificial, as if the rhododendron was pruned into a tree and placed in a rock garden. In another 0.5 mile you'll cross FS 229, the road you'll return on, but continue straight on Art Loeb Trail. Yellow trout lilies cover the ground in mid-spring. You'll pass a campsite area on the right and a huge rock informally dubbed Bruce Rock on the left.

At 3.5 miles (4,600 ft. elev.), you'll reach Farlow Gap. Farlow Gap Trail [#106] goes east toward Davidson River. Art Loeb Trail continues on your left and goes up to the Blue Ridge Parkway. Note a metal cable hanging down from a tree like a long snake. This is your turnaround point.

Return to the road crossing and take FS 229 on the left; Art Loeb Trail takes off to the right. Here the forest road, closed to vehicles, looks more like a gentle, well-maintained trail. Wildflowers line the trail and a piped spring lies on the left. Soon an unofficial trail comes in from the right, but stay on the road. You'll reach your first intersection with Art Loeb Trail.

At 5.0 miles, the rough road widens and is open to traffic, but you shouldn't expect more than an occasional truck. In summer the road is lined with blackberries, asters, ironweed, filmy angelica, and azalea. At 6.0 miles, there's a good view of Cedar Rock on the left. As blackberries and other vegetation keep growing, this spot may soon revert to a winter view only. The trail leads through shade with rocky ledges on the right and obstructed views to the left. The road intersects Art Loeb Trail twice more and reaches Gloucester Gap and your car at 7.6 miles to end the hike.

Variation: To Pilot Mountain and back—3.4 miles with 1,550 ft. ascent.

This hike offers views that rival those of the Swiss countryside and will have you singing "the hills are alive with the sound of music." Since you start above 5,600 ft. and won't get below 5,000 ft., you'll be walking in cool, high-mountain terrain the whole day. You'll visit the two summits of Sam Knob and Devils Courthouse and end at Black Balsam Knob. Two shorter variations are also possible. This hike is located close to Shining Rock Wilderness but doesn't enter it.

Type of hike: Loop

Distance: 9.0 miles

Total ascent: 1,500 ft.

Starting elevation: 5,800 ft.

Highlights: Views, high-mountain meadows

USGS map: Sam Knob

Trail map: Pisgah Ranger District, Pisgah National Forest, National Geographic Trails Illustrated Map #780

Land managed by: Pisgah National Forest, Pisgah District

Facilities: The trailhead at the end of FS 816 has paved parking and a stone building with two privies. A three-part information board lists regulations for the Shining Rock Wilderness Area. However, the rules

Trailhead GPS Coordinates: N 35° 19.54 W 82° 52.92

don't apply to this hike since it's not in the Wilderness.

Getting to the trailhead: From Blue Ridge Parkway milepost 420.2, turn on FS 816 and drive 1.3 miles to the end of the road where you can park.

The Hike
The Sam Knob Summit Trail [#617A – blue] starts in the weeds to the right of the bathrooms where there's a wand which reads "To Sam Knob Summit." Facing the bathrooms, the Flat Laurel Creek Trail is on the left; it's where you'd come out if you chose a shorter option.

You'll be walking west in a high-elevation meadow dotted with fireweed in summer. This perennial with tall, pinkish-purple flowers gets its name from the open burned areas where it likes to grow. However, the plant is not common in the Southern Appalachians; it's more prevalent in the northern states, reaching as far as the Gaspé Peninsula in Canada. You'll head right toward Sam Knob, two bumps with a depression between them.

At 0.6 mile you'll reach a wand at the intersection of Sam Knob Trail on the left and the continuation of Sam Knob Summit Trail. Turn right to stay on Sam Knob Summit Trail. The trail turns left and soon climbs a ladder. As you go up and west through laurel and blueberry bushes, Devils Courthouse is in the distance to your left. This massive rock outcropping looks like the supine profile of a giant head. You'll be on top of Devils Courthouse in a couple of hours. To the right of Devils Courthouse, the highest mountain you see in the distance is Mt. Hardy, a trailless peak (see Mt. Hardy hike, p. 265).

Toward the top, at a split in the trail, take a left toward

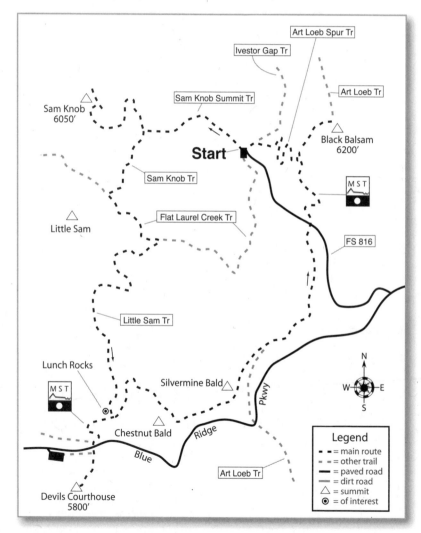

Sam Knob's northern peak. The field is filling in with flame azalea and blackberry and quartz rocks dot the landscape. You'll reach the northern peak of Sam Knob at 1.3 miles (6,050 ft. elev.), where you can see the ribbon-like Parkway. The Shining Rock Wilderness lies straight ahead to the north. Retrace your steps and at the junction make a left to take in the southern top of Sam Knob for another good view of Devils Courthouse. With two tops of Sam Knob and Little Sam to the west—you could say you're at Sam's Club.

After enjoying both summits, retrace your steps to the trail intersection at 2.1 miles. Continue straight where the wand says "To Flat Laurel Creek." You'll be on Sam Knob Trail [#617 – no blazes] going down on a rocky path and the open meadows will have disappeared from view.

At 2.5 miles, you'll cross Flat Laurel Creek. At a T-intersection, go left on Flat Laurel Creek Trail [#346 – orange blazes], a wide railroad-grade road at this point. Cross Flat Laurel Creek again on slippery rocks. Turn right on Little Sam Trail [#347 – yellow blazes] to go uphill and cross the creek with several tiny cascades at 3.4 miles. The trail goes gently up and away from the creek. Turn right to stay on Little Sam Trail at a T-junction after the creek crossing.

At 4.3 miles in a flat area, look right for a rock wall, locally

The Sam Knob Summit Trail crosses a high-elevation meadow.

known as Lunch Rocks. Lunch Rocks is a favorite name for rocky outcroppings from which to enjoy a picnic with a view. Soon you'll make a right on the Mountains-to-Sea Trail [#440 – white circle blazes], going west toward Devils Courthouse. Note the many uprooted trees lying on the side of the trail where the soil is thin. These large trees have shallow roots so that wind or ice storms can easily bring them down. Cross several small wooden bridges on the MST in a balsam-covered tunnel. When you hear the whine of motorcycles, you know you can't be too far from the Parkway.

When the MST goes sharply to the right, go straight on a blue-blazed side trail to

Devils Courthouse, crossing over the Parkway above a tunnel. You'll reach Devils Courthouse at 4.9 miles (5,800 ft. elev.). From here, on a clear day, you have 360-degree views encompassing four states: North and South Carolina, Georgia, and Tennessee. Small metal tables with compass-like plaques (these devices are known as "sight overcomes") point to peaks as far away as the Snowbird Mountains west in Tennessee and across the Georgia state line to the south.

Cherokee legend says that an evil spirit, *Judaculla*, translated as "slanting eyes," held court and passed judgment in a cave inside Devils Courthouse. Tourists walk up from the overlook at Parkway milepost 422.4. In the fall, this spot is a favorite place to watch migrating hawks.

Retrace your steps on the blue side trail. When you see a paved walkway going left, go straight and right on the MST. You'll be heading east on a gentle climb through thick balsams. When the MST junctions with Little Sam Trail, stay right on the MST. Here it's a mostly level and rocky trail, going due east, lined with blackberry bushes. Turk's-cap lilies, bright orange spotted flowers on tall stems, bloom profusely in midsummer.

On the MST at 6.1 miles, you'll pass the start of a short but difficult bushwhack to Chestnut Bald (6,040 ft.), a mountaintop with no views. Continue a little farther to a side trail on the right leading to rocks with one of the finest views available of the Pisgah District, including Pilot

Crossing Flat Laurel Creek.

Mountain in the southwest (see Pilot Mountain hike, p. 256) and the Parkway to the left. Clouds roll in and out often at this altitude.

Back on the MST as you climb Silvermine Bald, you may be lucky to see rare pinkshell azalea. Native to only to a few counties of western North Carolina, the delicate light pink flowers appear in late May.

At 6.4 miles, Art Loeb Trail comes in from the right and both trails run together where you enter several cathedral stands of balsam. The upper canopy has shaded out everything else; there's no undergrowth here. After the third major stand of balsam, the trail opens up to a peek at Black Balsam Knob, your next destination. You'll come out on FS 816 at 7.6 miles. If you made a left here on the road, you'd get back to your car in about a half-mile, but you'd miss Black Balsam Knob with its outstanding views.

Cross the road and continue on the MST and Art Loeb Trail. As soon as you get back in the woods, the MST peels off to the right. Stay left on Art Loeb Trail, which climbs steadily. If you reach this point in the middle of the afternoon, you may find this to be the most crowded part of your hike. Many tourists start from the road you've just crossed and walk up Black Balsam Knob.

The trail goes through the balsam grove from which it gets its name, but quickly opens up into a grassy meadow. A wooden sign on your left says "Art Loeb Trail," but stay on the trail you're on to get to the top of Black Balsam Knob.

The trail turns right and then quickly left. As it turns left, you'll see a group of rocks on your right with a plaque dedicating the trail to the memory of Art Loeb.

At 8.3 miles (6,200 ft.), you'll reach the benchmark at the top of Black Balsam Knob with its sweeping views and alpine meadows. Hiking couples have been married there, taking advantage of the scenery and the short walk from the road. Retrace your steps to go down from the Knob. After the first uphill bump, take a right on the Art Loeb Spur [#108 – no blazes]. This unmarked trail goes down into the woods where you'll reach the bottom just inside the barrier on the Ivestor Gap Trail. From here, it's a couple of hundred feet to the left to the parking lot.

Variations: Sam Knob and back—2.8 miles with 600 ft. ascent; omit Black Balsam Knob—8.1 miles with 1,200 ft. ascent.

Mount Hardy

50

This hike takes you on the Mountains-to-Sea Trail into both Nantahala and Pisgah National Forests, through beautiful balsam woods with a carpet of ferns and mosses. You'll stay high, above 5,000 ft. elev., through the whole hike and take a side trip to climb Mt. Hardy, a peak above 6,000 ft. Most of the hike is in the Middle Prong Wilderness, where your hiking group must be limited to 10 people. Country cousin to the Shining Rock Wilderness to the east, this wilderness area is not as heavily used and not as well maintained.

Type of hike: Shuttle

Distance: 9.4 miles

Total ascent/descent: 1,350 ft./1,650 ft.

Starting elevation: 5,600 ft.

Highlights: Forest, views, solitude

USGS map: Sam Knob

Trail map: Pisgah Ranger District, Pisgah National Forest, National Geographic Trails Illustrated Map #780

Land managed by: Pisgah National Forest, Pisgah District

Getting to the trailhead: To place a car at the end of the hike, drive on the Blue Ridge Parkway to milepost 423.2 at NC 215 (Beech Gap). Go north on NC 215 for 0.4 mile and

Trailhead GPS Coordinates: N 35° 19.29 W 82° 57.91

park on the left side of the road. Place the second car at Bearpen Gap (milepost 427.6 on the Blue Ridge Parkway) where the hike begins.

The Hike

At Bearpen Gap, go down a blue-blazed access trail through heavy tree cover with filmy angelica, white snakeroot, jewelweed, and coneflowers carpeting the ground. At 0.7 mile, the Mountains-to-Sea Trail [#440 – white circle blazes] rises from the right to meet you. Continue straight to stay on the MST, heading trail east. You'll pass a post for a gate meant to keep vehicles out, but the gate is on the ground now on the side of the trail, no longer doing its job. Climb up gently on a jeep road where the trail turns left, with obstructed views to your right.

When the MST makes a sharp left, continue straight for a few hundred feet to a beautiful flat, open meadow at 1.4 miles with several good campsites. In late summer, this short diversion in this high-mountain bog offers tons of

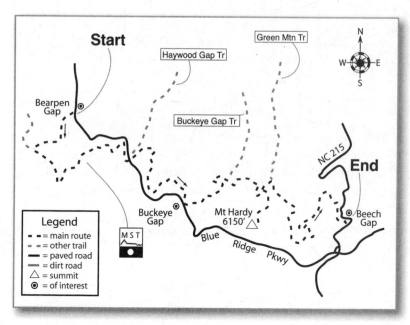

Start

Green Mtn Tr

Haywood Gap Tr

Bearpen
Gap

Buckeye Gap Tr

NC 215

End

Buckeye
Gap

Mt Hardy
6150'

Beech
Gap

Legend
- – = main route
- – = other trail
— = paved road
— = dirt road
△ = summit
◉ = of interest

M S T

Blue Ridge Pkwy

blueberries. An informal trail to the right leads to a spring. Retrace your steps to the MST (signposted) and turn right into the woods on a narrow trail that weaves up and down the side of a rocky ridge. The trail keeps switchbacking up with views to the south. Look for interesting fungus through a rhododendron and mountain laurel tunnel. Many balsams here have died from effects of the balsam woolly adelgid.

At 2.3 miles the blueberry- and blackberry-lined trail levels out, with soft pine needles underfoot. Go through a grove of balsams where you'll begin to hear sounds from the Blue Ridge Parkway.

Cross the Parkway at 3.1 miles (5,250 ft. elev.) at Haywood Gap and turn right to continue on the MST. Haywood Gap Trail [#142] comes in from the left. You'll now enter the Middle Prong Wilderness where the blazes disappear. The footpath takes you gently up and down through rhododendron and reaches a flat, grassy area under cover, giving you a little break.

After walking through a thick, dark cathedral of balsams, you'll reach a high mountain bog, a wet area with turtlehead flowers in early fall, and occasional birdhouses nailed high on trees. At 4.2 miles you'll reach Buckeye Gap, where an access trail to Rough Butt Bald Overlook takes off to the right. Make a sharp left to cross several small streams with a waterfall and cascade. At 5.1 miles, this section of trail is covered with logs laid perpendicular to the trail, meant to keep hikers out of the muck. However, they are slippery when wet, so watch your step—they are sometimes called "rollover," since the slickness can "roll you over" in wet weather. Roots grow straight out from the hillside, clasped around boulders. The rocks offer a good lunch spot.

Soon after you cross Buckeye Creek, Buckeye Gap Trail [#104] comes in from the left. Go straight and uphill to stay on the MST. To the right is a campsite as the trail climbs into a peaceful meadow which is filling in with brush. After you pass through an old orchard, now overgrown with ferns and heath family plants, including prolific high-bush blueberries, you'll head back into the woods as you skirt Mt. Hardy.

At 5.7 miles (5,800 ft. elev.), follow a side trail leading straight toward Mt. Hardy, a 6,000-footer. The MST goes left (signposted) in the mountain bog; you'll return to this spot. The trail to Mt. Hardy is obvious most of the way. Stay basically southwest, toward your right. The trail comes out to a meadow through a thick blackberry patch, then goes back into the woods. Avoid any trail which goes down steeply. You may note a USGS marker on a fallen tree.

You'll reach a larger meadow with excellent northeastern views at 6.1 miles (6,150 ft. elev.). From left to right, you'll see the two peaks of Sam Knob, Black Balsam Knob, Devils Courthouse, and the Parkway, including a tunnel. You're not quite at the top yet. Continue through a balsam grove and walk a few hundred feet to a wooded top. You'll know you're on top only when the trail starts to head down. Turn around and retrace your steps back to the MST. You'll see Black Balsam Knob and Sam Knob as you descend.

Back on the MST at 6.6 miles, make a right at the wooden sign. The trail here is flat and dark with lots of uprooted trees. Green Mountain Trail [#113] comes in from the left in another 0.1 mile. At 7.4 miles, cross a little creek—a

From Bearpen Gap, filmy angelica, white snakeroot, jewelweed, and coneflowers line the trail.

good place to wet your bandana. To your right, you're paralleling the Parkway through thick stands of snakeroot, goldenrod, and ironweed, but you won't meet the road here.

The trail leaves the Parkway and moves north in a quiet area through yellow birch, rhododendron, and mountain laurel slicks. Follow the switchbacks and pass a creek with several tributaries in a flat, rocky spot at 8.4 miles.

The trail is on a gentle railroad grade; you might even see some cables. To your left lie the depths of the wilderness as the trail enters a meadow of cow parsnip and goldenrod. The bare rock to your left is Devils Courthouse. When you reach an access trail coming in from the left at 9.1 miles, stay straight on the signposted MST. You're close to NC 215, and if you get off the trail here you'll have to walk the road. Bubbling Spring Branch comes down the mountain, paralleling NC 215. Cross the creek, turn left to reach NC 215, and then go right to the parking area to end the hike.

Pinnacle Park

51

Pinnacle Park is a 1,088-acre jewel set in the Fisher Creek section of the Plott Balsams, close to downtown Sylva. The main trail, which goes from Sylva to Waterrock Knob on the Blue Ridge Parkway at milepost 451.2, is well blazed with yellow and purple blazes, the school colors of nearby Western Carolina University. This clockwise loop with two tails incorporates amazing 360-degree views from two knobs: The Pinnacle and Black Rock. You'll go up the west fork of Fisher Creek and come down the east fork, primarily on old roads.

Type of hike: Loop

Distance: 10.1 miles

Total ascent: 3,300 ft.

Starting elevation: 3,150 ft.

Highlights: Views, solitude, wildflowers

USGS map: Sylva north

Trail map: None

Land managed by:
Little Tennessee Land Trust (www.ltlt.org)

Getting to the trailhead:
From the old Jackson County Courthouse, drive southeast on Main St. for 0.8 mile and make a left at a traffic light on Business 23N at its junction with NC 107. Drive 0.2 mile and turn left on Skyland Dr. (SR 1432). Continue 1.7 miles, turn left on Fisher Creek Rd., and drive 2.3 miles to the end of the road into a parking area.

The Hike
The hike starts behind a metal gate to the left and follows purple and yellow blazes up West Fork Trail on a jeep road. Disregard steps on the right that seem to go nowhere. You'll pass an old dam on the west fork of Fisher Creek on the right. On the other side of the creek, small water pipes are still visible.

The trail crosses Fisher Creek as it climbs on a rough, rocky road. Ignore a side trail coming from the right, but take a short path on the left to the creek and a picturesque cascade. At 0.4 mile (3,400 ft. elev.), you'll reach the split between the West Fork and East Fork trails. Stay left on West Fork Trail; new signage helps direct you. In the spring, wild geranium, trillium, bloodroot, violet, and star chickweed carpet the trail. Soon, on the left, another side trail leads to a campfire ring and a second defunct dam with a couple of wheels floating in the water.

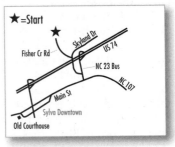

Trailhead GPS Coordinates:
N 35° 25.34 W 83° 11.47

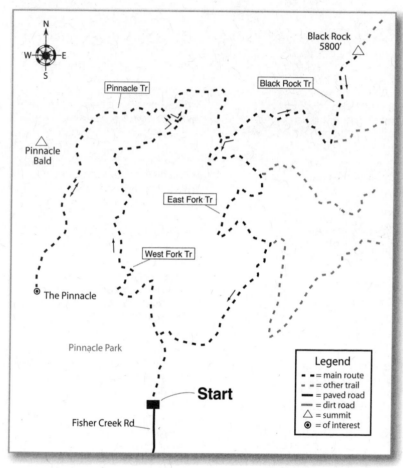

The climb on this rocky jeep road is broken up by the charming sound of the creek and innumerable wildflowers. A little farther on, a huge slit rock sits right of the trail. Cross Fisher Creek again and you'll be on a smoother trail, leaving the creek for a while. Zigzagging north, the trail alternates between rocky and just plain steep. At 1.9 miles on the left, another cascade tumbles down; its volume depends on recent rainfall. To your right, you'll get your first views toward Sylva.

At 2.0 miles (4,400 ft. elev.), at the well-marked intersection of Pinnacle Trail and Black Rock Trail, stay left on Pinnacle Trail [no blazes] and head toward The Pinnacle; a sign says 1.4 miles. The purple and yellow blazes, which mark the main trail toward Black Rock and eventually Waterrock Knob on the Parkway, have ended.

The trail turns flat and grassy through rhododendrons and doghobble. Close to the top you'll enter an open area with Pisgah National Forest on the left, Nantahala National Forest on the right, and beyond that the Great Smoky Mountains National Park; a campfire ring is straight ahead. Past the flat spot, turn left and head down through rhododendron—there really is a trail there. Stay left coming out of the tunnel on The Pinnacle, a rock outcrop filled with mountain laurel at 3.3 miles (4,850 ft. elev.). This top has outstanding views of ridge after mountain ridge. Look down (southwest) into downtown Sylva; the smokestack is at Jackson Paper Company, which manufactures recycled paper.

Retrace your steps to the intersection with the main trail toward Black Rock and turn left to continue on West Fork Trail. This uphill is gentler than at the start of the hike, but it might be a shock after the pleasant downhill from The Pinnacle. You'll pass an old metal gate where the trail then climbs moderately through rhododendron.

At a three-way intersection at 5.4 miles (5,000 ft. elev.), stay left toward Black Rock. It's a smooth, grassy trail, in some sections almost flat. At 6.0 miles (5,100 ft. elev.), you'll reach an intersection where the trail makes a sharp left toward Black Rock through a narrow rhododendron tunnel. You'll return to this point after you climb to Black Rock. A sign here reads "0.6 mile." Follow

The first of two old dams on Fisher Creek.

blazes on an extremely steep trail which may be dubbed a "half-mile of hell." A little piped spring is in a corner where the trail turns left. Orange blazes denote the boundary of the conservation area.

In a half-mile you'll reach a huge rock; this is not yet Black Rock. Turn left to go around the rock. A little farther on you'll reach a spot where the trail seems to encircle a hill, going both left and right. Take the trail to the right and continue up to Black Rock. The trail goes under a second huge boulder— watch that you don't bump your head as you go under it—then follow the trail left to the top of Black Rock. The main trail continues right and down.

The top of Black Rock, at 6.6 miles (5,800 ft. elev.), seems like the top of the world and better than The Pinnacle, if that's possible. Sylva is below you and Cullowhee lies beyond. Countless peaks in the Pisgah and Nantahala National Forests and the Great Smoky Mountains National Park extend out to the horizon.

Return by descending the steep slope off Black Rock. At 7.1 miles, make a right and continue to retrace your steps on the easy trail to the three-way intersection. Make a left on East Fork Trail; a sign says "East Fork Trail Fisher Creek Parking Lot 2.5." East Fork Trail is not as well manicured as West Fork Trail, but intermittent blazes will guide you. You'll reach a flat informal campsite

On top of Black Rock.

on the right at 7.9 miles (4,950 ft. elev.), but stay left to descend through birch and mountain laurel. Make a right turn in another 0.3 mile. The trail narrows—a nice change after all that road walking.

After a poorly maintained stretch, the trail makes a left turn back on a road and goes down gently, following the East Fork of Fisher Creek. The creek crosses the trail with a series of tiny, green cascades. At 9.1 miles (4,250 ft. elev.), turn right through rhododendrons; it's easy to overshoot this turn. Then the trail opens up and continues steeply down, following the East Fork on your left. Even with the creek by your side, this trail is drier than West Fork Trail. In winter, before the vegetation gets thick, a long, cascading waterfall is visible—altogether, a very pleasant downhill. At 9.8 miles, you'll close the loop. Make a left to walk down to your car and end the hike.

Variation: To The Pinnacle and back—6.6 miles with 2,200 ft. ascent.

The view from Black Rock with Sylva and Cullowhee below.

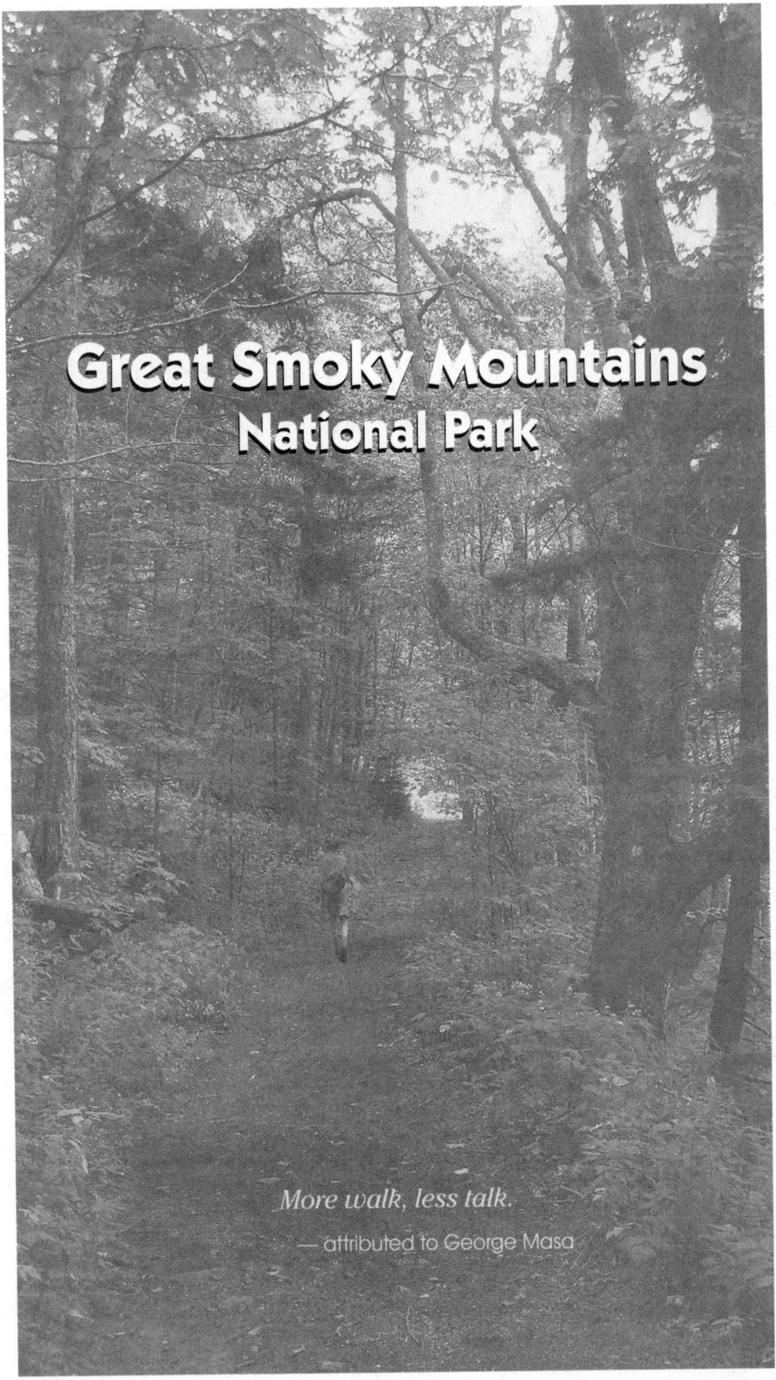

Great Smoky Mountains
National Park

More walk, less talk.

— attributed to George Masa

Great Smoky Mountains National Park

Essential Facts

Rules:
Dogs are not allowed on hiking trails

Facilities:
Backcountry campsites and shelters; car-camping. All shelters and some campsites require reservations; call (865) 436-1231 up to a month before your trip. All rules are spelled out on the Great Smoky Mountains Trail Map, available from park visitor centers or on the park website

Closest towns:
Bryson City, Cherokee, Maggie Valley, Robbinsville, Waynesville

Website:
www.nps.gov/grsm

Related books:
The Wild East: A Biography of the Great Smoky Mountains by Margaret Lynn Brown; *Cataloochee: A Novel* by Wayne Caldwell

There's something magical about entering the Great Smoky Mountains National Park (GSMNP). Yes, sometimes the main roads are crowded, but at the visitor center the folks behind the desk, whether rangers or volunteers, are friendly, knowledgeable, and so happy to see you. The trails are well-marked and maintained; you can feel that hikers are taken seriously here. You immediately know you're in a *national* park.

Because these mountains make their own weather, the Smokies are always wetter than the surrounding area and green is the dominant color. There's a tremendous variety of wildflowers, from the first bloodroot in March to the last

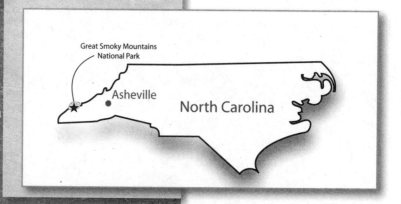

Great Smoky Mountains National Park

Asheville

North Carolina

aster in October. And you're almost always close to water—branch, brook, creek, fork, spring, stream—there are so many words for running water. In 1992 the GSMNP was designated an International Biosphere Reserve for its tremendous diversity of plants and animals.

The Cherokees inhabited the area for thousands of years but most of the changes to the land occurred when white settlers arrived at the end of the 18th century. The Cherokees moved out or were driven out by Federal troops in 1838; this forced removal is known as the Trail of Tears. The pioneers cleared the land for subsistence farming and later for commercial apple growing and cattle raising. Most people first settled in the rich bottomland by a stream because that's where farming was better. Later, people expanded into remote coves. To understand how families lived, you have to picture the forest cleared for a log cabin and a garden, fenced to keep hogs and cattle out of flower and vegetable beds.

In the 1880s logging companies moved in, attracted by the wealth and quality of timber. Having clearcut the Northeast and Midwest, they turned to the Southern Appalachians as their next destination. Almost every area in the North Carolina Smokies was affected except Cataloochee. Railroads made possible an increased rate of

Clouds hang over the Great Smoky Mountains National Park.

logging. Timber companies built roads and narrow-gauge tracks far into coves, creating paths we hike on today. Farmers went to work for the timber companies because a steady paycheck was more attractive than the economic ups and downs of farming. In many cases, families sold their land to the logging company and became tenants in a company town. They lost their independence but gained health care, education for their children, and more organized religion. They were able to replace their log cabins with frame houses.

A national park movement gathered momentum at the same time that loggers arrived and began cutting the woods with no thought of sustainable forestry. The first suggestion of turning the

Smokies into a national park was made in the early 1880s. Several national parks had already been created from land owned by the Federal Government out west, but here the logistics were more complicated because families and private companies held ownership.

Horace Kephart, with the help of George Masa's photographs, published articles in national magazines to promote the idea. Boosters in both North Carolina and Tennessee realized that a park would be good for tourism and improve the local economy. Once Congress approved the formation of the park, the two states had to raise the money to actually buy the land—6,600 private tracts in all. Though there were many contributions, including the legendary story of school children collecting pennies, the two states could only come up with about half the money. John D. Rockefeller, Jr., who had already contributed financially to help other parks, donated five million dollars in the memory of his mother. A plaque in her honor is located on stonework at Newfound Gap.

Most residents moved out when they sold their land. Folks were told they could live out their days in the park but they couldn't farm, hunt, graze animals, or cut timber, so only a few people with other sources of income stayed. Probably the most famous were the Walker sisters in the Little Greenbrier section on the Tennessee

Little Cataloochee Baptist Church is the site of an annual Decoration Day.

side, who sold souvenirs to tourists visiting their home.

The official birth date of the park is June 15, 1934, though it was not dedicated until 1940 when Franklin D. Roosevelt spoke at Newfound Gap. The GSMNP was created in the middle of the Depression at about the same time that the Civilian Conservation Corps was formed. The young men of the CCC built roads, trails, and shelters in the Smokies. Another major chapter in the story of the GSMNP was written during World War II when the Tennessee Valley Authority built Fontana Dam and land north of Fontana Lake was incorporated into the park.

The park is now protected from loggers, railroads, and extraneous road building, but is still under attack by forces harder to control. In the 1930s, the chestnut blight killed chestnut trees, a dominant canopy tree that provided high-quality lumber and food for people and animals. Balsam woolly adelgid, a non-native sucking insect, attacked Fraser firs, turning them into giant gray skeletons. Currently the hemlock woolly adelgid threatens the hemlocks, some over five hundred years old.

The GSMNP is the most visited national park in the nation, but most people keep to the roads and the visitor centers, never seeing most of the park's 521,455 acres. With almost eight hundred miles of trail, you can hike for weeks. More than 230 people have hiked every trail in the park and become members of the "900-Miler Club." Each section of the park has its own history and feeling. The hikes in this chapter offer a look into North Carolina's rich mountain heritage—a heritage that you can see, touch, and understand.

As the GSMNP celebrates its 75th anniversary, we can thank the visionaries and boosters who promoted the idea of a national park in the Southern Appalachians and the families who sold their land and changed their way of life to accommodate the park. We can also thank the Great Smoky Mountains Association and Friends of the Smokies, organizations that today support this park in ways not funded through the federal budget.

Most residents left their homes when the park was established. This photo shows the Steve Woody Place, a working farm, in the 1930s.

Big Cataloochee Drive 52

Directions to Cataloochee:
From I-40 exit 20 (US 276), make the first right onto Cove Creek Rd. Drive 6.0 miles to Cove Creek Gap at the park entrance and down into the valley.

Land managed by:
Great Smoky Mountains National Park

Related Book: *Cataloochee: A Novel* by Wayne Caldwell

Turn left into the Cataloochee Valley to visit several fascinating historical buildings and sites. From the four-way intersection, turn left where the road becomes paved again. After a couple of miles you'll pass an intersection with an information board where you can pick up a Cataloochee auto tour booklet. The gravel road heading right leads to the Palmer House, which has a small visitor information display.

Continuing on the main road you'll pass the Messer barn, built about 1902 and moved from Little Cataloochee, and the ranger station. After open fields, you'll reach the Palmer Chapel Methodist Church, across a grassy meadow on your left. The entrance to the plain white building faces Cataloochee Creek. Inside, a simple cross hangs on the wall and the pulpit usually holds an open bible.

On the right you'll see a sign for Palmer Chapel Cemetery.

You'll see the Woody House on the Caldwell Fork Loop.

Climb the steep, small hill to one of several Caldwell family cemeteries. The names on the graves recur often in the Cataloochee Valley: Caldwell, Palmer, Messer, Sutton.

Beech Grove School is next, tucked away on your right after the Pretty Hollow

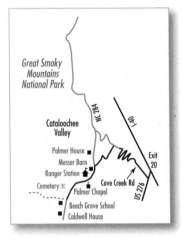

Gap Trailhead. The two-room schoolhouse was built in 1903 and used until the 1950s for children of park employees. The desks and blackboard are still there.

Then you'll come to the Caldwell House which replaced a log cabin in 1903. The framed clapboard house, painted white with blue-green trim, stands on a stone foundation. Daffodils still bloom on the lawn in spring. Cross the little bridge and go inside. It's a large house with four rooms upstairs and four downstairs, many with closets. The spring house is to your left as you face the house.

Heritage

Cataloochee

Located at the southeastern edge of the park, Cataloochee was first settled in 1836 by families living on the East Fork of the Pigeon River, near Waynesville. The Cherokee called the area Gadalutsi, which means "standing up in rows" or "wave after wave," which could refer to rows of trees or mountain ridges that extend far into the horizon. The Cataloochee area of the park is tucked away behind Cataloochee Divide; Nolan Divide separates Little Cataloochee from Big Cataloochee. In the 1850s, the next generation of settlers looking for their own land moved into Little Cataloochee and along Caldwell Fork. These three Cataloochee communities (Big Cataloochee, Little Cataloochee, and Caldwell Fork) thrived, becoming the largest in the area that later became the park.

In contrast to the rest of the Smokies, there was very little commercial logging in Cataloochee, so this might be the best place to see massive old-growth trees. Robert Palmer, known as "the Boogerman," in particular did not allow anyone to cut down trees on his property (see Boogerman Loop hike, p. 283). By the 1900s, well-to-do families expanded their houses so they could take in sightseers and fishermen as boarders.

But in the 1930s, everyone sold their land to make way for the GSMNP. They left not only their homes, schools, churches, and post offices, but also their cemeteries—over two hundred of them in the park, according to Tom Robbins, an interpretive ranger. Little Cataloochee and Big Cataloochee each hold community gatherings, called Decoration Days, which still attract hundreds of people.

Decoration Days, also known as reunions or visitations, differ in size and details. Rather than family visits, most are recognized as community affairs, partly because of tradition, partly because of logistics. Since Little Cataloochee Baptist Church is a two-mile walk from the road, rangers open the gates once a year to let people drive on Little Cataloochee Trail and bring in picnic coolers.

Descendants, families, friends, and sometimes hikers gather to decorate cemeteries, renew friendships, hear stories, and, of course, eat. A silk flower is placed at every headstone. Graves of families who no longer live nearby are cared for by the rest of the community. The Park Service maintains the cemeteries and does extra sprucing up just before Decoration Day. If you see a cemetery devoid of flowers, it's probably because you've come just before a Decoration Day and the old flowers have been removed.

During the casual memorial service, the names of those who died since the last reunion are called out and the chapel bell is rung. Once the service is over, it's time to eat. Former residents and their descendants have been returning here to decorate graves since moving out of their homes. At some point

someone suggested, "Well, if we're all bringing a lunch, why don't we have it the same time?" Harold Hannah, the son of Mark Hannah, the first ranger in Cataloochee, grew up in the park and went to Beech Grove School. He explains how Little Cataloochee reunions started. "We used to have a proper service with a guest pastor. But people decided they didn't want a regular preaching service. They would rather talk to people they hadn't seen all year. For that one day, they could skip church."

Cataloochee was once considered a remote part of the park because the roads there don't connect to the rest of it. But when elk were reintroduced in 2001, more visitors began to discover this section of the Smokies. Elk are native to the area but disappeared by 1790 because they were overhunted. As an experiment, the park brought in 25 of these large animals, plus another 27 the following year, from the Land Between the Lakes National Recreation Area along the Tennessee-Kentucky border. Each elk is tagged with a radio collar and is carefully monitored and studied. From the periodic elk reports posted on the park website, you can learn that #47 is a reclusive female and that #3 is one of two dominant males during the rutting (mating) season.

Elk may look placid, but they are wild animals that can be dangerous. The best time to see them is early morning or at dusk. When you spot an elk, be sure to stay on the road and enjoy them at a distance through binoculars.

Boogerman Loop

53

Boogerman Loop is the quintessential Cataloochee hike, with gentle trails, winter views, and many historical artifacts. You'll start on the Caldwell Fork Trail and turn on Boogerman Trail at its second intersection, taking the loop counterclockwise. On the Boogerman property you'll see several stone walls which enclosed the house and family garden and protected them from roaming farm animals, springs which provided families with water, and an old wheel leaning against a tree. You'll return via Caldwell Fork Trail. This low-altitude hike is suitable any time of the year.

Type of hike: Loop

Distance: 7.5 miles

Total ascent: 1,150 ft.

Starting elevation: 2,700 ft.

Highlights: Creek, stone walls, historical artifacts

USGS map: Dellwood

Trail map: Great Smoky Mountains National Park, National Geographic Trails Illustrated Map #229

Land managed by: Great Smoky Mountains National Park

Getting to the trailhead: From I-40 exit 20 (US 276), make the first right onto Cove Creek Rd. Drive 6.0 miles to Cove Creek Gap at the park entrance and down into the Cataloochee Valley. At the

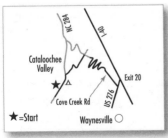

Trailhead GPS Coordinates: N 35° 37.89 W 83° 05.32

four-way intersection, turn left. Drive 3.4 miles, passing a campground on the left, and park on the left, just beyond the Caldwell Fork trailhead.

The Hike

From the parking area, walk back to the Caldwell Fork Trailhead and cross Cataloochee Creek on the longest wooden bridge in the park. As Caldwell Fork Trail starts up, trees are perched precariously on top of broken rocks. It's a muddy trail at times because of horse traffic, but wooden planks have been placed over the worst of the muck. You'll cross two bridges before reaching the first intersection with Boogerman Trail at 0.8 mile. Continue on Caldwell Fork Trail.

As the trail goes down briefly, look to your right for a cascade over a horizontal log. Between its first and second junction with Boogerman Trail, Caldwell Fork Trail crosses eight more bridges across Caldwell Fork. Each bridge has its own character: concrete, wooden, plank, new,

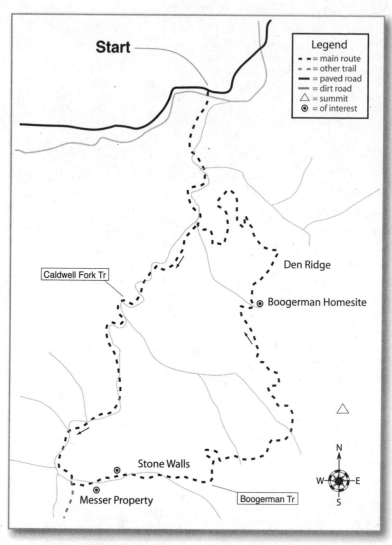

Start

Legend
- **= =** main route
- **= =** other trail
- ━━ = paved road
- ━ = dirt road
- △ = summit
- ◉ = of interest

Den Ridge

Caldwell Fork Tr

◉ Boogerman Homesite

△

N

W ✳ E

Stone Walls ◉

◉
Messer Property

Boogerman Tr

S

old, sturdy, rickety. The trail is lined with doghobble, rosebay rhododendron, and galax. After crossing the ninth bridge, the rocky trail goes up gently. Stay to the right; the muddy trail on your left is for horses. Huge old-growth hemlocks stand on the right, some infected with hemlock woolly adelgid. The trail climbs up gently as Caldwell Fork narrows. Yellow violets, bloodroot, and trailing arbutus bloom here in spring.

At 2.8 miles, make a left on Boogerman Trail. Soon after, look right for two pieces of timber in a depression in the ground lined with rocks. A piece of metal sheeting lies nearby. This may have been a root cellar on the Carson Messer homesite. Climb gently among old-growth hemlock and cross Snake Branch, a small creek.

Reach the first wall on the left, which makes a right angle to enclose a flat area. Before reaching the second wall, you'll see a short side trail on your left which leads to another homesite on a hill. These dry-laid stone walls, about 3 ft. high, were built without mortar. Come back and continue on Boogerman Trail, paralleling another long wall on the left. Cross the creek twice more.

You can get a better idea of the size of the huge trees by looking at the cut logs on the ground, some over 3 ft. in diameter. Note a tuliptree with a hollow trunk, which looks burned; hikers here often want their pictures taken inside the trunk, framed by the opening. Another wall juts out perpendicular to the trail. The trail goes left and then right, continuing gently uphill. There's a broken fence post on the right, possibly denoting another property boundary.

The trail climbs more steeply, reaching drier ground with white pine and fewer rhododendron; large trees are keeping down the undergrowth. You'll reach a local top at 3,700 ft. elev. and soon wander downhill among white pine and hemlock.

Cross a creek with a partially enclosed spring on the left, a good sign of a nearby farmhouse site. At a huge tree on the right, see how many people you can get to hold hands around the trunk. This is the Boogerman (Robert Palmer) property. Palmer held out against logging companies and didn't allow anyone to cut trees on his land. We now enjoy the benefit of his decision. Notice an old wheel on the left leaning against a tree.

As you go down Den Ridge, look to your right (east) for winter mountain views. It's a lovely gentle downhill among huge hemlocks; you can hear Caldwell Fork at the bottom. At 6.7 miles, make a right at the junction with Caldwell Fork Trail. Before you cross the last bridge, look for a water gauge on the left which measures water level. Return to the parking area to end your hike.

A log bridge crosses Caldwell Fork.

Caldwell Fork Loop

54

This hike takes you on a clockwise loop into the heart of Caldwell Fork country, one of three Cataloochee communities. It blends the old—homesites, graves, and the Steve Woody House—with the new, the return of the elk and the unfortunate assault on hemlocks by the hemlock woolly adelgid. But dead trees cannot mask the beauty and serenity of an area returned to wilderness after decades of human inhabitation.

Type of hike: Loop

Distance: 9.4 miles

Total ascent: 1,650 ft.

Starting elevation: 2,850 ft.

Highlights: Gravesite, historic house, big poplars

USGS map: Dellwood

Trail map: Great Smoky Mountains National Park, National Geographic Trails Illustrated Map #229

Land managed by: Great Smoky Mountains National Park

Getting to the trailhead: From I-40 exit 20 (US 276), make the first right on Cove Creek Rd. Drive 6.0 miles to Cove Creek Gap at the park entrance and down into the Cataloochee Valley. At the four-way intersection, turn left. Continue 6.1 miles to the end of the road and park.

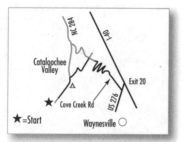

Trailhead GPS Coordinates: N 35° 36.99 W 83° 07.25

The Hike

From the end of the road, walk back about 500 ft. to the Big Fork Ridge Trailhead, which will now be on your right, opposite a large meadow. Head into the woods, cross Rough Fork on a bridge, and start a steady climb. This trail was used by Caldwell Fork residents to get to Big Cataloochee Valley.

At 0.3 mile, you'll see an elk pen, a large wooden enclosure, on your right. This structure was used to familiarize the newly imported elk with their surroundings. Climb the steps and note the narrow chute, designed so that only one elk can squeeze through at a time and elk movement can be controlled. When the elk were first brought in, they were kept here until the Park Service felt they were ready to be released. The first group was here about two months.

Continue climbing Big Fork Ridge in a forest of red maple, hemlock, and white pine. Christmas fern, Bowman's root, goldenrod, and aster carpet the forest floor. Many hemlocks here are dead; unfortunately, you'll see the same problem throughout the hike. Huge ones have turned gray and feathery and are now ghosts of their former selves—awe-inspiring in a macabre way.

The trail moderates as it continues up gently among tuliptrees. At 1.1 miles, reach a plateau with a field of dead hemlocks to the right. The trail narrows and may be eroded because of heavy horse use.

At 1.6 miles (3,700 ft. elev.), you'll reach the top of Big Fork Ridge. As you go down gently into this idyllic forest, you might flush a grouse, a bird not usually seen. You'll reach a flat area on your right at 2.9 miles; it doesn't have posts or bear poles, so you know it's not a legal campsite. Cross Caldwell Fork on a long footbridge.

At 3.1 miles (3,100 ft. elev.), make a right on Caldwell Fork Trail to continue the loop, going southwest. A left turn would take you toward Boogerman Trail (see Boogerman Loop

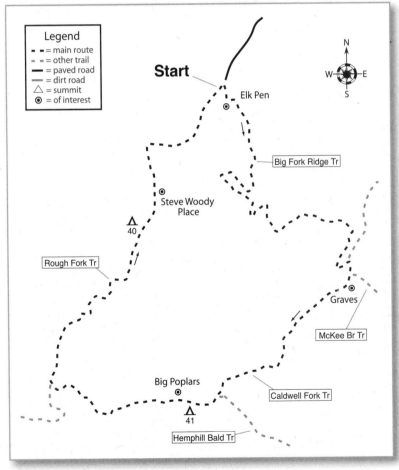

hike, p. 283). In 0.1 mile, McKee Branch Trail takes off on your left. This was the site of the Caldwell community school, where now there are several horse tie-ups. In another 0.1 mile, you'll see a "No Horses" sign on your left and an obvious steep trail. Take this short diversion, about 100 ft., to visit a gravesite with two stone stumps marking the graves of three Union soldiers. An old, frayed American flag hangs on a barbed wire fence. Return the same way and turn left to continue on Caldwell Fork Trail where the trail is flat and wide. At 3.7 miles, cross Clontz Branch which flows into Caldwell Fork. As the trail narrows and becomes muddy in places from seepages and horse traffic, continue to climb up among majestic trees. Looking at the hills and skyline, you may feel as if you're in a bowl; the stream gets louder and wider down below. You'll pass huge blowdowns, some 3 ft. in diameter, cleared from the trail.

This flat area to the left is jam-packed with wildflowers, including lilies, bloodroot, and asters. The trail here feels like a promenade, a straight, flat section lined by tall trees, where you can see a couple of hundred feet ahead. At 4.5 miles you'll cross Double Gap Branch, a wide, flat stream with a little cascade toward the end of the crossing. In another 0.1 mile, Hemphill Bald Trail goes off to the left to eventually meet Cataloochee Divide Trail.

Cross Caldwell Fork, a wide stream, on a split-log bridge, and pass Campsite #41 with bear poles on both sides of the trail. At 5.0 miles (3,500 ft. elev.), make a right at the "Big Poplars" sign. Pass several horse tie-ups and continue for a few hundred feet to a huge tuliptree. (Often known as tulip poplars, these trees are related to magnolias and are not true poplars.) It takes eight adults to encircle this tree, which at its widest is 25 ft. in diameter. Settlers used these large, straight trees to build houses and barns. There are a few more big tuliptrees further back. This flat, wide area makes an attractive lunch stop.

Return to Caldwell Fork Trail and make a right to continue climbing, sometimes in a ditch, with an undergrowth of ferns and winterberries, around enormous blowdowns. The trail zigzags up to its intersection with Rough Fork Trail at 6.3 miles (4,050 ft. elev.). Make a right on Rough Fork Trail; a left would take you to Polls Gap.

Here the trail is on a drier slope and goes down the whole way to the Woody Place, a pleasant downhill stretch. You'll reach a T-junction at 7.8 miles where a left turn leads to Campsite #40, encircled by rhododendrons. Make a right turn; you'll cross Rough Fork Creek and walk on a flat road, a reminder that families lived here. Cross the creek which was the Woody water supply. Through the trees on your right, you'll get your first look at the Steve Woody Place. Pass the small springhouse to reach the house at 8.3 miles (3,050 ft. elev.).

The white frame house, with its gingerbread scallop trim, faces Rough Fork. You're free to explore the house with its three rooms downstairs, a couple of fireplaces, a kitchen, and three large bedrooms upstairs. A juniper tree in the front yard may be part of the original landscaping. The property is kept mowed around the house to keep the feel of the historic landscape.

After leaving the house, follow Rough Fork on an old, wide roadbed. The trail crosses the creek three times on sturdy log bridges. This mile attracts tourists who make the house their destination, so you can expect to see visitors, especially during fall elk rutting season, as you return to your car and end the hike.

Variation: From the parking area, take Rough Fork Trail to the Woody House; round trip the walk is 2.0 flat miles.

Tuliptrees, often known as tulip poplars, grow large in the Great Smoky Mountains National Park. This tree is 25 ft. in diameter.

A *walk on Little Cataloochee Trail offers a glimpse into life in this remote mountain community before it became part of the Great Smoky Mountains National Park. This out-and-back hike takes you to two cabins, two cemeteries, and a chapel. But these are only the main attractions. If you look carefully, you'll find many other signs of the past. The drive on NC 284 is also part of the adventure; it's a well-maintained dirt road, typical of roads in the area about 80 years ago.*

Type of hike: Out and back

Distance: 6.1 miles

Total ascent: 1,100 ft.

Starting elevation: 3,000 ft.

Highlights: Chapel, cabins, other artifacts

USGS map: Cove Creek Gap

Trail map: Great Smoky Mountains National Park, National Geographic Trails Illustrated Map #229

Land managed by: Great Smoky Mountains National Park

Getting to the trailhead: From I-40 exit 20 (US 276), make the first right on Cove Creek Rd. Drive 6.0 miles to Cove Creek Gap at the park entrance and down into the Cataloochee Valley. At the four-way intersection, continue

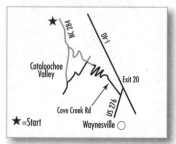

★=Start

Trailhead GPS Coordinates: N 35° 40.56 W 83° 05.25

straight on NC 284, following the sign for Big Creek and Cosby. Drive the dirt road for 6.0 miles, passing a gauging site to a gate on the left and signs to Little Cataloochee Trail. Park at a wide spot on the roadside just before the gate.

The Hike
Little Cataloochee Trail is a wide jeep road which starts downhill at the gate. You might see deer, generally an unusual sight at higher elevations. The wide road is lined with mountain laurel and Robin's-plantain, also known as daisy fleabane (the flower was used to get rid of fleas in mattresses).

At 1.1 miles, turn on Long Bunk Trail, where in late spring you'll see an abundance of yellow star grass and toothwort under a tunnel of mountain laurel. You'll reach Hannah Cemetery in another 0.2 mile. Yucca plants cover the sidehill in front of the cemetery, which is surrounded by a tall chain-link fence. You can go in, but remember to close the gate behind you. You'll see old graves, some with elaborate headstones and some marked only with rock stumps. Visitors always note children's graves, particularly with the same birth and death date. People have been buried here recently. If a person can prove descent from a former resident and the cemetery still has room, he or she can be buried in the Great Smoky Mountains National Park.

Return to Little Cataloochee Trail. At 1.6 miles, turn right to Hannah Cabin. This cabin is typical of many that stood in the Cataloochee community. Built in 1864, two generations of Hannahs lived here before it was turned over to the park. Blackberry canes crowd the trail to the cabin and a small cleared garden area remains. You can walk in and go up the stairs to the sleeping area. Go out the back door to see the creek.

Again walk back to Little Cataloochee Trail. At 2.1 miles, on the right you'll pass a spring enclosed by rocks with two poles marking it. A half-mile later, you'll reach Little Cataloochee Baptist Church, built in 1889. The bell tower—the bell can still be

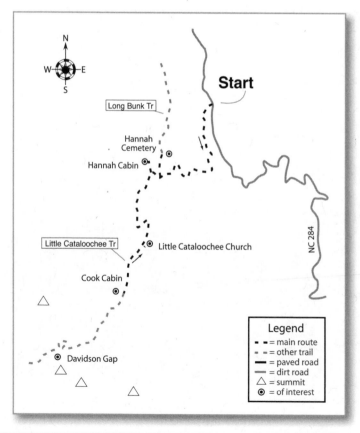

rung—was added 25 years later. The small, plain, white chapel sits up on a little hill, its scalloped trim along the roofline providing a touch of decoration. The inside is plain and painted white just like the outside, without even a cross or picture on the wall. The room is furnished with benches and a potbellied stove. It's a picture-perfect mountain chapel.

The well-maintained cemetery rolls downhill in front of the church. Look for J.V. Woody's grave; he was a community leader born on February 14, and the V stands for Valentine.

The trail parallels the creek on the way to the Cook Cabin. At 3.3 miles you'll reach the restored cabin, enclosed by split-rail fencing. Across the trail, the stone enclosure is all that remains of a storage area for apples. Apples were an important crop in Cataloochee; they provided residents with cash to purchase store-bought goods. For the Messer family, apples also brought wealth. The site of the Messer holdings is farther up on Little Cataloochee Trail, but their apple house was relocated to the Mountain Farm Museum at Oconaluftee Visitor Center and their barn was moved to Big Cataloochee. The trail continues up Davidson Gap and eventually down into Big Cataloochee via Pretty Hollow Trail. However, Cook Cabin is the turnaround point for this hike. Retrace your steps to return to the trailhead.

The restored Cook Cabin is the turnaround point for the Little Cataloochee hike.

This hike takes you to Charlies Bunion on the Appalachian Trail. It's one of the most popular hikes in the park, and with good reason. From the Bunion, a huge bare rock, you can see into the heart of the Smokies. Then the hike leaves the A.T. (and most hikers) behind and leads into a remote section, down to Kephart Prong and an old Civilian Conservation Corps camp. Much of this portion of the hike is downhill.

Related book: *Our Southern Highlanders* by Horace Kephart

Type of hike: Shuttle

Distance: 10.0 miles

Total ascent/descent: 1,200 ft./3,100 ft.

Starting elevation: 5,050 ft.

Highlights: Views, flowers, shelters, rocky knobs

USGS map: Mt. LeConte

Trail map: Great Smoky Mountains National Park, National Geographic Trails Illustrated Map #229

Land managed by: Great Smoky Mountains National Park

Getting to the trailhead: Place a car at Kephart Prong trailhead, the end point, 7.2 miles north of Oconaluftee

Trailhead GPS Coordinates: N 35° 36.64 W 83° 25.53

Visitor Center. Drive north on Newfound Gap Rd. to Newfound Gap where the hike starts. There are restrooms to the right of the A.T. trailhead.

The Hike

From Newfound Gap, the highest point on US 441, the Appalachian Trail passes the observation platform where, in 1940, President Franklin D. Roosevelt dedicated the Great Smoky Mountains National Park.

Spring arrives late and fall comes early on this ridge. Under a light canopy of balsam, the ground here is covered with bluets in spring and white snakeroot, filmy angelica, and goldenrod in late summer. As you walk along, views offer a good look at Mt. LeConte, the highest mountain you can see in the foreground. At 1.3 miles, on your right, a rock wall is covered with spotty yellow lichen patches.

At 1.7 miles, the trail intersects with Sweat Heifer Creek Trail, an alternate route down to Kephart Prong Trail. Continue on the A.T. and soon you'll get a good view of the

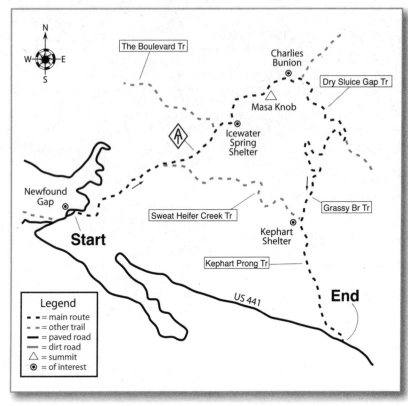

southern mountain ranges and US 441. In another mile, make a right to stay on the A.T. The Boulevard Trail continues straight to Mt. LeConte (see Mt. LeConte hike, p. 298).

Take a side trail on the right at 3.1 miles to Icewater Spring Shelter. There's no sign but because of its location and outstanding eastern views, the shelter is a very popular destination for a short backpack. The roof overhang on the renovated stone shelter covers benches and a long wooden counter for preparing and eating meals. As you face the shelter, a short trail leads to a composting privy on the left. Continue on a side trail to your right which leads back up to the A.T. and soon to a pipe from Icewater Spring, providing water for the shelter. Even at a high altitude you need to treat your drinking water.

Descend on a rocky, balsam-covered trail with lots of roots. The A.T. passes heavily forested Masa Knob on your right. As you come around Masa Knob, the bare rock to your left is Charlies Bunion.

When the trail splits, take the left branch, following

the signs, to reach the rocky outcropping of Charlies Bunion at 4.0 miles. The A.T. continues right. This bare slate was created by a combination of unfortunate events. Loggers clearcutting the upper mountain slopes left piles of brush in place. In 1925 a fire stripped the area clean of vegetation. In 1929, a heavy downpour washed away what little soil remained on the exposed slopes.

Looking northwest, Mt. LeConte is the high point. If you stop to eat here, you may notice curious juncos flitting around and coming very close to your lunch. Continue around Charlies Bunion on a rocky and exposed trail back to the A.T. and make a left turn. The A.T. descends and then levels out through a canopy of rhododendron, mountain laurel, and high-bush blueberries. You'll reach an open view, looking south into the Kephart Prong area, then go through a stand of blackberries and back into the woods.

At 4.4 miles you'll leave the A.T. and turn right on Dry Sluice Gap Trail. The trail climbs gently southeast under balsams. Look for Rugel's ragwort, a rare flower found only at high altitudes in the Smokies. The yellow nodding flower heads are abundant here, though not particularly attractive, and wouldn't warrant a second look if they were more common.

This narrow trail through blueberry bushes and black cherry trees is not used much. When you reach the intersection with Grassy Branch Trail at 5.7 miles, you've done all the climbing for the day. Make a right on the wide Grassy Branch Trail, which starts in a trench created by horse traffic. This also is an inner trail, deep in the forest, where you won't see much traffic.

Then the trail changes character completely. It widens and curves gently, looks better maintained, and is more open and softer underfoot. After the 1925 fire, Champion Lumber Company planted Norway spruce here to replace trees that were burned, but the area became part of the national park where logging is prohibited, and the new trees were never harvested. At 7.2 miles, Grassy Branch, a tributary of Kephart Prong, crosses the trail. The creek, below

The rocky outcrop of Charlies Bunion was created by fire and erosion.

and to your right, parallels the trail. It becomes bigger, louder, and more powerful as it descends gently through a thick area of hardwood trees and rhododendron.

You'll reach Kephart Shelter at 8.1 miles (3,700 ft. elev.) on your right. This area was a logging camp. The shelter is similar to Icewater Spring Shelter, with a skylight overhang and covered eating area.

Leaving the shelter, stay left at a point of possible confusion. The trail going right is Sweat Heifer Creek Trail. Though the sign says you're continuing on Grassy Branch Trail, the trail soon leads into Kephart Prong Trail without a sign. From here, it's mostly a wide, gentle road built by Champion Lumber Company.

The wide creek cascades over boulders. The first crossing of Kephart Prong is on a narrow split-log bridge with a handrail, built to support only one or two hikers at a time. At subsequent crossings of Kephart Prong, the quality of the bridges improves. After another split-log bridge, you'll pass metal rails from a ruined bridge which once spanned the Prong. The third bridge is sturdier. The fourth bridge is wide and made of wooden two-by-fours. The trail widens out, and you can hear traffic from Newfound Gap Rd.

You'll pass a chimney on the left and a homesite in an old Civilian Conservation Corps camp where boxwoods still flourish. A large rock wall in front of a huge oak tree once held a plaque for the entrance to the camp. Cross the last, wide bridge over the Oconaluftee River to return to Newfound Gap Rd. and your car at hike's end.

Variation: To Charlies Bunion and back—8.2 miles with 1,650 ft. ascent.

Heritage

Horace Kephart: Champion of the Great Smoky Mountains National Park

It seems ironic that there are several places named Kephart on this hike, when in fact Horace Kephart spent much more time on Hazel Creek in the Fontana section of the park.

Kephart came to the Southern Appalachians from St. Louis in 1904 when he was 42. At the time he was a university librarian, a husband, and a father of six children, which he described as being "in a blessed rut." His growing interest in the outdoors finally impelled him to leave his family, career, and the Midwest behind.

Kephart said he chose the Smoky Mountains because he sought "the nearest wilderness in any direction." In *Our Southern Highlanders*, he writes, "When I went south into the mountains, I was seeking a Back of Beyond.... I yearned for a strange land and a people that had the charm of originality." He certainly found it on Hazel Creek (see Hazel Creek hike, p.307). After a few years, he moved to Bryson City and supported himself modestly by writing magazine articles. When he returned to Hazel Creek for a visit, he was shocked by the devastated landscape left by loggers. Kephart became one of the most vocal advocates of the establishment of the Great Smoky Mountains National Park.

In 1906, Kephart published *Camping and Woodcraft,* a how-to book on camping and backpacking. It was followed in 1913 by *Our Southern Highlanders,* stories of the mountain culture he found on Hazel Creek, often in the local vernacular. According to George Ellison, who wrote an introduction to the 1976 reissue of the book by the University of Tennessee Press, "*Our Southern Highlanders* is at once adventurous, anecdotal, and realistic writing."

Kephart's articles on the Smokies were illustrated with photographs taken by his friend George Masa. Other than the fact that Masa was originally from Osaka, Japan, nothing is known about how or why he came to the United States; there seems to be no record of his entry into the country. Masa arrived in Asheville in 1915. At the Grove Park Inn, where the rich and famous vacationed, he worked his way up to head porter. Interesting and deferential, he mingled easily with famous guests. Later, he started several photographic businesses, but he spent more time taking pictures in the Smokies than in his studio; some called him

the Ansel Adams of the Southern Appalachians in the way he waited for the right light before shooting.

Kephart and Masa (who also assisted in scouting the North Carolina portion of the Appalachian Trail) shared a desire to save the Smokies from loggers, and became hiking friends. Realizing that timber sales were a one-time windfall, but tourists would bring in money forever, they promoted the idea of making the Smokies a national park. Kephart was instrumental in naming features of the Smokies, including Charlies Bunion, now one of the most popular destinations in the park. Michael Frome, author of *Strangers in High Places*, interviewed Charlie Conner, a local guide for whom the site was named. Kephart, Masa, and Conner had gone on an expedition to inspect the erosion damage caused by a storm in 1929. Conner, possibly because of a foot problem, had removed his shoe. Looking at the craggy peak, Kephart told Conner, "I'm going to get this put on a Government map for you," and the name stuck.

In 1931, a peak on The Boulevard Trail was renamed Mt. Kephart, an unusual honor for a living person. A couple of months later, Kephart was killed in a car crash and buried in Bryson City. Two years later, George Masa died penniless in a county sanitarium from complications of influenza. In 1961, a small, rounded hill located close to Mt. Kephart on the way to Charlies Bunion was named Masa Knob.

Mount LeConte

Mt. LeConte, the third highest mountain in the Smokies, rises a mile from its base and can be reached by five different trails. The mountain dominates the view from Gatlinburg.

This varied hike starts at Newfound Gap on the Appalachian Trail and then takes The Boulevard Trail, which offers outstanding views, around the back of Mt. LeConte. The lodge area has sunrise and sunset views; both are worth a visit even at midday. Hiking down on Alum Cave Trail you'll look into Huggins Hell, pass Alum Cave Bluffs, and end on a pleasant river walk.

Type of hike: Shuttle

Distance: 13.1 miles

Total ascent/descent: 2,500 ft./3,500 ft.

Starting elevation: 5,050 ft.

Highlights: Lodge, views, rock formations

USGS map: Mt. LeConte

Trail map: Great Smoky Mountains National Park, National Geographic Trails Illustrated Map #229

Land managed by: Great Smoky Mountains National Park

Getting to the trailhead: From Oconaluftee Visitor Center, drive north 20 miles

Trailhead GPS Coordinates: N 35° 36.64 W 83° 25.53

on Newfound Gap Rd. and place a car at Alum Cave trailhead. Then drive 4.6 miles south to Newfound Gap, where the hike starts.

The Hike

The hike starts on the Appalachian Trail at Newfound Gap (5,050 ft. elev.). Go up wooden steps among white snakeroot, goldenrod, hobblebush, and blackberry cane. Scramble over rocks at 0.4 mile then continue on good log steps with obstructed northern views toward Mt. LeConte. The mountain looks far away on the left; it's the highest mountain you can see in the foreground.

The rocky trail climbs among balsams. At 1.3 miles you'll pass a rock wall on the right, spottily covered with yellow lichens. Soon a short side trail comes in from the right, offering a good view. The A.T. intersects with Sweat Heifer Creek Trail on the right at 1.7 miles (5,850 ft. elev.).

Sweat Heifer Creek Trail leads eventually to Kephart

Prong Trail. If you take Sweat Heifer Creek Trail for a hundred feet or so, you'll have panoramic southern ridge views. Continuing on the A.T., you'll reach an open view to your right, created by a rock slide. At 2.7 miles (6,050 ft. elev.), the A.T. turns right toward Charlies Bunion (see Charlies Bunion/Kephart Prong hike, p. 293). Go straight on The Boulevard Trail where, at the intersection, a wooden

sign says "Jumpoff 0.3 mile." A few hundred feet past the intersection, a sign points right to the Jumpoff, a sheer 1,000-ft. vertical cliff—it's a diversion on a rough trail which adds an extra mile round trip. If it's a clear day, from the Jumpoff you'll get amazing eastern views of Charlies Bunion and beyond. Along the way, you'll traverse the top of Mt. Kephart, a flat-topped mountain without a view.

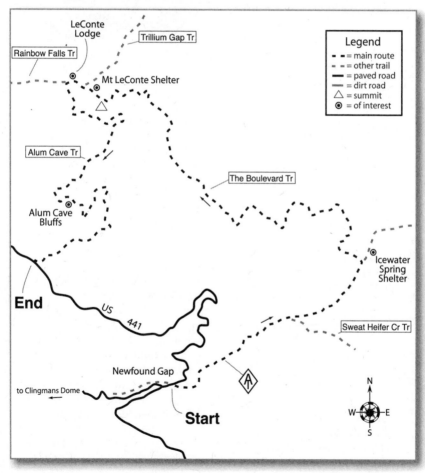

The Boulevard Trail goes up for a short while under a balsam canopy and then starts down seriously. You'll pass several impressive blowdowns, trees with upended, house-sized root systems. Flat rocks have been placed to reduce erosion. The trail continues to descend over mossy sidehills from which ferns and blue bead lilies peek up—it looks like hobbit land.

At 5.2 miles (5,900 ft. elev.) you'll reach Anakeesta Knob, a rocky knob where the trail goes sharply right and down to Alum Gap. Anakeesta is also the name for a hard, slate-like rock which, when exposed to oxygen and water, forms sulfuric acid. Enjoy this short, flat section of trail, with obstructed views and maybe a breeze, before you start the inevitable climb.

The trail comes around to the northwest to climb the back of the mountain (the lodge side is thought of as the "front" of the mountain). The trail winds in tighter and tighter spirals with outstanding views to your right. In the damper environment, you might see mountain St. John's wort hugging the trail along with clumps of grass-of-Parnassus, a gem of a flower with delicate green veins on its white petals.

At 7.2 miles, you'll reach a landslide area with cables that have been bolted into rocks. The stark forms of dead trees in front of you are victims of the balsam woolly adelgid, a small

Pack llamas carry supplies up Mt. LeConte three times a week.

exotic insect that decimated Fraser firs. At 7.5 miles (6,500 ft. elev.), Myrtle Point Trail takes off to the left for 0.2 mile to a rocky outcropping where you can take in the classic sunrise view. The Boulevard Trail continues right.

Since guests walk this section from the lodge in the dark to get to Myrtle Point at sunrise, the trail is well maintained with loose stones to prevent erosion. At 7.7 miles (6,600 ft. elev.), you'll reach High Point on your left; it's the top of Mt. LeConte, marked with a rock pile. LeConte groupies add a rock to the pile each time they come so that eventually the mountain will be higher than Clingmans Dome. (They have a long way to go.)

The trail goes down, turns west, and heads past the newly refurbished Mt. LeConte shelter. At 8.1 miles (6,400 ft. elev.), The Boulevard Trail ends. Make a left on Rainbow Falls Trail, which takes you to the lodge and connects with Alum Cave Trail. Go down a long set of steps leading to the lodge dining hall. Just beyond, there's a path on the left to Cliff Top, the sunset view.

LeConte Lodge consists of a set of sleeping cabins, a dining hall, and a building housing the office and library. Make a left to follow signs to the office, where you check in if you're staying overnight. If you're there for the day, spend a few minutes looking at the collection of historical news clippings about LeConte Lodge. In front of the office, you can refill your water bottles at the water pump; privies are a little farther on.

Continuing on from the office, go past the privies and take a side trail left and uphill. At the bridge, make a right on Rainbow Falls Trail and then a quick left on Alum Cave Trail. This trail, though rugged and rocky, is well-maintained with cables, rock

LeConte Lodge has rustic cabins, a dining hall, and a commons building.

steps, bridges, and wooden steps. For daytrippers and many overnighters, it's the most popular way to Mt. LeConte.

Alum Cave Trail starts out flat and rocky then soon descends, first gently, then steeply. The cables bolted to the rock are useful whether or not it's icy. Slow down to take in the views because you'll soon lose them, along with the altitude. This is a sociable trail; you'll be going down while most everyone else goes up, and they'll want to know how far it is to the top.

The trail is damp, with large areas of gentian and grass-of-Parnassus. At 9.2 miles, the trail turns sharply left around a big crag and continues down to a good set of steps with a handrail, followed by a steep section—a real knee buster.

Farther down, you'll leave the balsams and enter a hardwood cove forest with rhododendron. After descending a set of steps cut into a split log, at 10.5 miles (5,300 ft. elev.) you'll reach Gracies Pulpit, a rock promontory on the right where a tall tree has rooted itself. The rock was named for Gracie McNichol, who climbed Mt. LeConte many times, including on her 92nd birthday.

Pass huge rock folds that rise above you steeply on your left. You can see Alum Cave Bluffs before you get there at 10.8 miles (5,000 ft. elev.). You can also smell sulfur. Alum

Cave Bluffs is a bone-dry island of huge bluffs in one of the wettest places in the United States. The soil contains Epsom salt and other minerals; this site was the source of the raw materials for the Epsom Salt Company between 1838 and 1854. During the Civil War, William Holland Thomas and his band of Cherokees built a road to the bluffs to collect saltpeter, used in making gunpowder, which was mined from the Bluffs.

Use the handrail to continue down. You'll see more yellow lichen on bare rocks as you go down the steps. On a summer weekend, the trail below the bluffs teems with hikers, many asking how far it is to their destination, some heading to Mt. LeConte, others just to Alum Cave. Look out into the wilderness on your right to see the Eye of the Needle, a hole in a wall of bare rock. Cross Styx Branch and go through Arch Rock at 11.6 miles, a natural arch caused by water erosion. Hold on to the cable as you go down rock steps. This is a one-lane system—you don't want to meet someone coming up.

The trail parallels cascading Alum Cave Creek on your left then widens into a road as it crosses the creek several times on bridges. Huge hemlock trees guard the trail as you gently descend. After the last bridge you'll reach a T-intersection. Make a left if you parked on the road, or a right if you parked a little in from the road, to end your hike.

Variation: Alum Cave Trail to LeConte Lodge and back—10 miles with 2,600 ft. ascent.

Alum Cave Bluffs

LeConte Lodge

The lodge predates the park. In 1924, David Chapman, a national park advocate, guided VIPs on a trail ride to convince them to create a national park there. The next year, the Great Smoky Mountains Conservation Association established a tent camp and built the lodge. Jack Huff took over the lodge and 10 years later, he and his fiancée, Pauline, chose Myrtle Point for their mountaintop wedding. Jack Huff built a special chair to carry his mother up to the lodge. You can see that picture at the library/office on the mountain. The office is also the only place you can buy LeConte t-shirts. LeConte Lodge is now operated as a concession under the supervision of the National Park Service.

Once on top of Mt. LeConte, you can stay at the newly refurbished backcountry shelter or at the comfortable lodge. The lodge provides sheets and three blankets so there's no need for a sleeping bag, but there is also no electricity or running water. If you feel the need to wash up before dinner, take a washbasin from your cabin and fill it with warm water from a faucet outside the dining hall.

A hearty dinner and breakfast are both included in a lodge stay, so all you need in addition to your day-hiking gear is a toothbrush, small towel, and flashlight. After dinner, guests gather for the outstanding sunset at Cliff Top, a wide expanse of rocks a quarter-mile from the lodge. In the morning, be prepared to quietly creep out of your cabin in the dark with your flashlight and walk to Myrtle Point (0.75 mile) to watch the sunrise, an unforgettable (and usually more solitary) experience.

Supplies are brought up to the lodge by helicopter once a year and by llamas three times a week. Llamas are much easier on the trail than horses, which used to make the trip. The llamas generally pack on Monday, Wednesday, and Friday using Trillium Gap Trail, north of Gatlinburg. If you're at the lodge on a llama day, you may see these gentle animals from the dining room porch, being saddled with dirty linens and trash to take down from the top.

Lodge reservations open up on October 1 for the next season, which runs from the end of March to the end of November. The lodge is well above 6,000 ft.; in November, that makes for full winter conditions.

To get a reservation, you have to either plan ahead or be flexible with your dates. Write a postal letter and give several preferred dates and the number of people in your group. Follow it with an email, all before the first workday after October 1. Reservations are given out on a lottery system. Trying to telephone is a hopeless exercise; the phones are busy constantly for a couple of weeks after October 1, and then the lodge is filled. See www.leconte-lodge.com for complete reservation information.

If you can't commit so far in advance, call in the spring. If your group is only a couple of people, can go in the middle of the week, and is flexible with dates, you might get in. The list doesn't carry over from year to year; everyone has an equal chance. Plan ahead and good luck.

Gregory Bald is a legendary destination. In late June into early July, flame azalea blankets the top in a blaze of color. In August, you can eat your fill of blueberries. But the hike is more than its destination. The trail to the top climbs gently and steadily, as Smokies trails are known to do. Campsite #12 is a pleasant spot on the way up, perfect for a short backpacking overnight.

Don't let the slow drive through Cades Cove deter you from doing this hike. If you start early, you'll miss most of the tourist traffic. Though you'll be in a line of cars on your way out at the end of the day, the satisfaction of this outstanding hike will carry you through. Note that from early May through September, Cades Cove is closed to cars until 10 am on Wednesdays and Saturdays, so those two days may not be a good time to plan this hike.

Type of hike: Out and back

Distance: 11.2 miles

Total ascent: 3,000 ft.

Starting elevation: 2,000 ft.

Highlights: High-meadow bald, wonderful views, good campsite

USGS map: Cades Cove

Trail map: Great Smoky Mountains National Park, National Geographic Trails Illustrated Map #229

Land managed by: Great Smoky Mountains National Park

Trailhead GPS Coordinates: N 35° 33.75 W 83° 50.75

Getting to the trailhead: Take the Cades Cove Loop Rd. to just past the Visitor Center (about halfway around). Instead of continuing on the loop, go straight on gravel Forge Creek Rd. Drive 2.2 miles to the end of the road and park at a small circular parking area on the left.

The Hike

Gregory Ridge Trail starts at the end of Forge Creek Rd. with a short and steep initial climb. The trail then levels off through rhododendron and pine as Forge Creek meanders below on your right. Any downhill may seem disconcerting because you know you have a lot of climbing to do, but after you cross Forge Creek on a bridge, the trail starts up gently. As you climb, look up at the straight tuliptrees, the signature trees in this section.

Cross the creek again at 1.9 miles and then a third time. You'll reach Campsite #12 at 2.0 miles (2,600 ft. elev.), a lovely small site by the creek. This is the last water you'll find on this hike.

The trail turns away from the water as it switchbacks uphill above the campsite, and you'll soon start climbing seriously up the ridge in a northwesterly direction. Ferns dot the mostly bare and dry soil. At 2.3 miles you'll come out to an open area for the first time, where you look toward the western mountain ridges. The burned area is the result of a prescribed burn, the purpose of which was to perpetuate pine and oak communities, which require open areas and bare soil for their seeds to germinate.

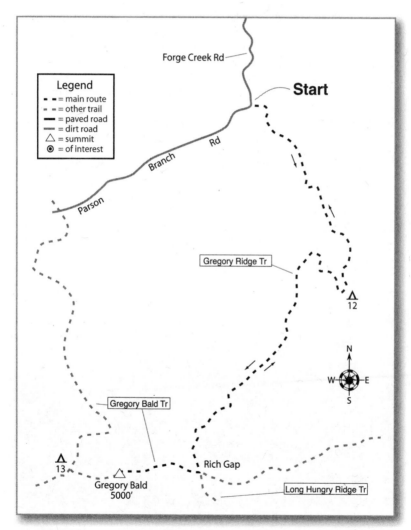

In May or June, mountain laurel blooms at this altitude. As you walk, the open area closes in. You'll pass a car-sized boulder as you go back into the woods. At 3.1 miles (3,400 ft. elev.), you'll reach a flat area in a laurel tunnel. In early June, galax is in bloom; the flower resembles the long spiky bloom of the foam flower. Farther up, you might find fields of trillium blooming in early May. At 3.8 miles, the trail flattens out a little, but you know it can't last long. At 4.6 miles, you'll pass a tree trunk sawed off at tabletop height, its flat surface showing beautiful knots in the grain.

At 5.0 miles (4,600 ft. elev.), you've reached the end of Gregory Ridge Trail at Rich Gap, in an open stand of oak trees. Turn right on Gregory Bald Trail. A left turn here would put you on the Long Hungry Ridge Trail, a remote trail that goes down into North Carolina in one direction and to the A.T. in the other. Turn right, as most hikers do, and climb about 400 ft. in 0.6 mile to Gregory Bald.

The bald covers a large area. Hikers spread out to picnic, photograph the azaleas and the views, or just stretch out on the ground for a midday nap. Gregory Bald is a popular destination despite the long climb, but you won't feel crowded. Relax on top, then retrace your steps and enjoy the long downhill back to your car to end the hike. Gregory Bald Trail continues to Parson Branch Rd., a one-way gravel road which ends at US 129, north of Twentymile Ranger Station.

Valleys and ridges spread out below Gregory Bald.

The walk up Hazel Creek is one of the most pleasant and relaxing hikes available in the Smokies. It starts at the historic abandoned community of Proctor, which still appears in the news today. The many artifacts left in Proctor allow you to appreciate the region's complex and varied history. As described here, the excursion includes a boat ride across Fontana Lake. Fontana Village Marina offers both boat rentals and shuttles. You can also hike in from Fontana Dam for a three-day backpacking trip.

Type of hike: Out and back

Distance: 11.0 miles

Total ascent: 750 ft.

Starting elevation: 1,700 ft.

Highlights: Hazel Creek, cemetery, house sites, lumber company artifacts

USGS map: Tuskeegee

Trail map: Great Smoky Mountains National Park, National Geographic Trails Illustrated Map #229

Land managed by: Great Smoky Mountains National Park

Related books and movie: *Our Southern Highlanders* by Horace Kephart; *Fontana: A Pocket History of Appalachia* by Lance Holland; *Nell* (1999) with Jodie Foster

Trailhead GPS Coordinates: N 35° 28.28 W 83° 43.52

Getting to the trailhead:
Take a boat from Fontana Marina to Hazel Creek. To get to Fontana Marina from the center of Robbinsville, take NC 143 east for 9.1 miles. Turn left on NC 28 north. Drive for 10.3 miles and turn right at the Fontana Village sign. Turn right again at the Marina sign. Parking and restrooms are available at the top of the hill before the road goes down to Fontana Marina.

The Hike
Once your boat lands at Hazel Creek, walk from the boat landing about 0.4 mile to Campsite #86. This campsite, which accommodates both hikers and horses, sits right at the shoreline when the lake is full.

At the bridge you'll intersect Lake Shore Trail, which heads east for 24 miles toward Bryson City and the tunnel at the end of the Road to Nowhere. In Proctor's heyday, it was also known as Struttin' Street, where Ritter Lumber Company executives lived in the best houses in the community.

Cross the bridge over Hazel Creek and turn right

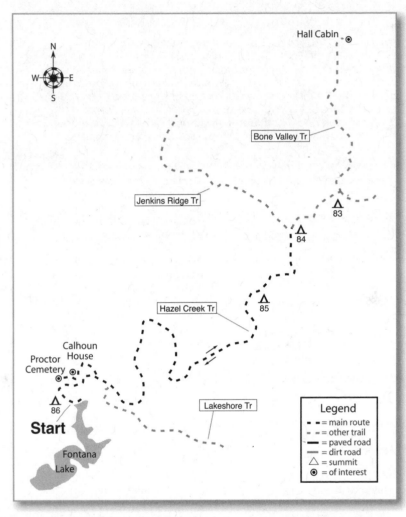

on Hazel Creek Trail to follow the creek upstream. This was once called Calico Street, and was a more modest part of town. Continuing up the trail, on the left are the remains of Ritter Lumber Company, where a busy and productive sawmill once stood. Poison ivy covers stone and concrete pump houses.

In 1.0 mile, you'll pass a concrete water gauge on the banks of Hazel Creek. The wide trail is lined with rosebay rhododendron, mountain laurel, and iris. You'll cross two sturdy bridges maintained by the Park Service so vehicles can transport people visiting Bone Valley Cemetery and the Hall Cabin farther north. At 3.0

miles, you'll reach Campsite #85 by the creek. Huge boulders are pockmarked with potholes created by swirling water and sand. Various narrow trails take off to old homesites. In spring, daffodils still bloom here. Poison ivy prevails at the edges of the trail.

At 4.5 miles, after crossing another bridge, you'll reach the intersection with Jenkins Ridge Trail, a steep trail that eventually leads to the Appalachian Trail on the North Carolina-Tennessee border. Bear right, heading to Campsite #84 at the confluence of Hazel Creek and Sugar Fork. This is a beautiful campsite with easy access to water and several downed logs where you can sit and enjoy lunch. You could continue on Hazel Creek Trail for 0.8 mile to Bone Valley Trail and in another 1.8 miles to Hall Cabin and the cemetery.

Retrace your steps to the center of Proctor. At the first bridge, continue on Lake Shore Trail straight ahead and pass a horse barn and the Calhoun House, which is open to visitors. Continue another half-mile on Lake Shore Trail, going west toward Fontana Dam to Proctor Cemetery. Go up the steps to the largest cemetery on the North Shore; Proctor Cemetery holds over 190 graves. Return to Hazel Creek Bridge and cross it, then turn right toward Fontana Lake and the boat landing to end the hike.

Variation: Extend the hike to Hall Cabin and back—add 5.2 miles and 400 ft. ascent.

Most hikers get to Hazel Creek by crossing Fontana Lake.

Great Smoky Mountains National Park: The North Shore, Tennessee Valley Authority, and the Road to Nowhere

The first settlers, Moses and Patience Proctor, arrived on Hazel Creek in the early 1830s from Cades Cove; even then Cades Cove must have been too crowded for them. They built a cabin on the site that is now the Proctor Cemetery, where they lie under a modern gravestone.

By the turn of the 20th century, logging companies were well established in the Southern Appalachians. Ritter Lumber Company arrived in 1902 and prepared to log the Hazel Creek watershed, building a railroad to bring timber down from high up the cove. Proctor had electricity by 1907. At its height, the town of Proctor was home to over a thousand people, with pool halls, barber shops, cafés, and a movie theater.

Proctor Gravestone

Ritter clearcut the woods as quickly as possible; there was no attempt to manage the forest in a sustainable manner. By 1928 the area had been stripped of all valuable timber. When Ritter moved on to the Pacific Northwest, many workers went with them. The families who stayed had become used to regular wages and modern amenities. After Ritter left, they built their own generator to create electricity, but their attempt to continue maintaining the telephone system proved unsuccessful.

The only building left standing in Proctor is the restored white frame Calhoun House, which has a broad covered porch across the front. Granville Calhoun bought the house just as Ritter Lumber was leaving. Calhoun was a larger-than-life entrepreneur who took in visitors who wanted to fish and hike. A side room with no access to the main house was kept for tourists, a visiting preacher, or a teacher. By the time Proctor was abandoned, Calhoun owned 17 houses; he was the last to leave, in 1944. For many years, the Calhoun House was used as a ranger station. From the outside the house appears to be in poor condition but a new roof was put on a few years ago; a roof is crucial to the preservation of a building. Visitors can walk through the house.

When the Great Smoky Mountains National Park was created in 1934, the Fontana area was not part of it, so residents did not have to leave the area at that time. When World War II was declared, the demand for electricity to produce aluminum skyrocketed. Alcoa had already bought land along the Little Tennessee and it transferred that acreage to the Tennessee Valley Authority (TVA) for the Fontana Project in exchange for future electric power.

When TVA built a dam to create electricity, five communities and NC 288, the only road into the area, were flooded. TVA then turned over the remaining land to enlarge the Great Smoky Mountains National Park. Families who moved out often took their log cabins with them because lumber was in short supply. Many stayed in the area to work on Fontana Dam and lived in cabins and cottages which are now part of Fontana Village, a family resort.

In 1943, the Federal Government promised to build a road on the North Shore of Fontana Lake to go from the dam to Bryson City, if Congress appropriated the money. For many years this promise lay dormant; in the meantime, a modern highway, NC 28, was constructed outside the park. From Fontana Dam, less than a mile of the promised road was built. From the eastern boundary of the park in Bryson City, the National Park Service built about six miles, ending abruptly in a tunnel and dubbed the "Road to Nowhere." In 1971, acid-bearing anakeesta rock was uncovered there, and the park stopped construction, due to the known environmental effects of such acid leaching into streams.

The issue was revived again in 2001 when former Congressman Charles Taylor obtained $16 million for further construction of the road. This initiated a study of the environmental impact of a 35-mile road. The National Park Service held public input forums in various locations around the Smokies and accepted comments from anyone in the United States on how to resolve the problem of the unfulfilled 1943 agreement. Thousands of pages were generated, reviewed, and discussed. Descendants of the original settlers were the only ones who wanted a road in the park. Almost all comments were against the road and for a financial settlement with Swain County, where Fontana Dam is located. Swain County is one of the four parties to the original agreement.

In December 2007, the Department of the Interior made a decision that officially called for a monetary settlement to Swain County in lieu of a road through one of the most pristine and untouched areas in the East. Though the park is now protected and the North Shore Rd. will never be built, Congress still has to approve the funds to close out the 1943 agreement, currently the longest running open item on its agenda.

Hall Cabin in Bone Valley

Highlands Plateau

....We began to descend the mountain
on the other side, which exhibited
the same order of gradations
of ridges and vales as on our
ascent, and at length rested on a
very expansive, fertile plain...

—William Bartram,
The Travels of William Bartram, 1791

The Canebrake Trail in the eastern section of Gorges State Park goes down steadily to Lake Jocassee on the North Carolina-South Carolina border. You'll be walking on old, wide roads, with a beautiful lunch spot at a picnic table where the Toxaway River flows into Lake Jocassee. The 1,150-ft. descent provides a good opportunity to see early spring flowers or late autumn foliage. Gorges State Park is a popular jumping-off point for the Foothills Trail, a 76-mile trail that traverses the Blue Ridge escarpment along the South Carolina border from Oconee State Park to Table Rock State Park.

Rules: Pets must be on a leash.

Closest town: Rosman

Website: www.ncparks.gov

Related book: *One Foot in Eden* by Ron Rash

Type of hike: Out and back

Distance: 11.0 miles

Total ascent: 1,900 ft.

Starting elevation: 2,200 ft.

Highlights: Lake Jocassee, solitude, early spring flowers

USGS map: Reid

Trail map: Available on the web

Land managed by: Gorges State Park

Trailhead GPS Coordinates: N 35° 06.52 W 82° 53.02

Getting to the trailhead:
From Brevard, travel west on US 64 toward Rosman. About 1.5 miles past the intersection with NC 178, turn left on Frozen Creek Rd. The Frozen Creek entrance to Gorges State Park is 2.8 miles on the right.

The Hike
The start of the trail is to the left of the information board, following an arrow on a wooden post. Canebrake Trail [yellow square blazes] runs concurrently with Auger Hole trail [red square blazes] for a while, where hiking, biking, and horses are all permitted. You'll cross Frozen Creek on a wooden bridge and walk on an old road lined with doghobble, hemlock, and holly. The trail intersects an unpaved road open to cars then turns right onto an old, wide, rocky road through logged land. The skeleton of an old car on the left is probably considered an artifact by now. Pass a fenced-off road to your right where the trail turns left. A minor creek passes under the trail, which starts climbing.

At 0.9 mile (2,350 ft. elev.), the two trails split. Turn left to stay on Canebrake Trail, a smooth, hiking-only trail covered with soft pine needles. At a second split make a well-marked left, continuing south on the state park boundary.

There are obstructed western views through Virginia pines to your right. The descent on this old road is effortless as the wind whistles through pine trees. At 3.6 miles (1,650 ft. elev.), there's a short diversion to the right

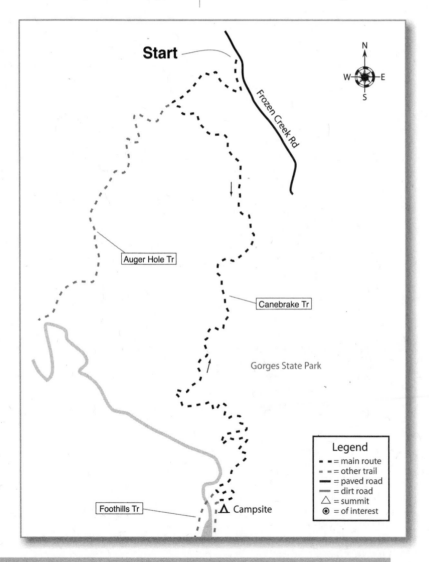

at a boulder where you can look deep into the cove.

In early spring you can see many wildflowers, including blue violet, halberd-leaved violet, foam flower, and Robin's-plantain, which look like blue daisies. At 4.4 miles, a little rise on the left allows for the first sighting of Lake Jocassee. Bell Morgan Branch crosses under the trail and soon after, you'll cross a minor creek with a small cascade. The trail goes up and around the cove, making a well-signposted right turn, then continues down more steeply. You'll hear the river and see the placid lake in the distance. The sounds of water and wind mingle as you start the steep descent. Rhododendron grow along the rocky sides of the trail. When you start seeing litter on the ground, you'll know you're getting close to the lake.

At 5.4 miles (1,150 ft. elev.), Canebrake Trail ends at the state park boundary. Make a left on Foothills Trail [white blazes] and cross a suspension bridge over Toxaway Creek, which flows into the Toxaway River below. Another quick left takes you to picnic tables at a backcountry campsite at 5.5 miles (1,150 ft. elev.).

From here you can take Foothills Trail through the campsite for good views of Lake Jocassee. How close you get to the lake will depend on the water level.

Near the boundary of Gorges State Park, the Foothills Trail crosses Toxaway Creek on a suspension bridge.

The lake views are better on the return, which is good since it will be a steep climb up as you retrace your steps to the trailhead and end the hike.

Gorges State Park: A Plan for Muliti-Use

Gorges State Park is North Carolina's westernmost state park. It lies on the Blue Ridge Escarpment, a rocky dividing line between the mountains and the foothills of the Piedmont. Gorges State Park was created in 1999 from 10,000 acres acquired from Duke Energy (formerly Duke Power Company). The initial plan was to convert the whole purchase into a state park, but many local residents wanted to continue to hunt and fish on the property as they had when it was privately owned. After extensive negotiations, a combination of land uses was agreed on. About 3,000 acres of the acquired land was set aside to be managed by the North Carolina Wildlife Resources Commission, and hunting is allowed there.

The master plan for the park is very ambitious, calling for new roads, a visitor center, and campgrounds, but most of that construction will happen on the western end of the Park at Grassy Creek Access. The Frozen Creek Access area will not be developed and will be devoted to hiking, biking, and horse riding.

The Highlands Plateau

The town of Highlands sits on a 4,000-ft. plateau at the point where North Carolina, South Carolina, and Georgia meet. It was founded in 1875 by Samuel Kelsey and Clinton Hutchinson, two developers from Kansas. According to legend, the men looked at a map and drew a line from New York to New Orleans and another line from Chicago to Savannah. They predicted these lines would become major trade routes in the future, and where they crossed, present-day Highlands would some day be a great population center. It turned out that

dragging cargo up and down mountains for long-haul travel was not practical. Instead, the Highlands plateau developed as an upscale summer resort.

Kelsey and Hutchinson actively promoted the area as early as 1876, mailing pamphlets all over the country proclaiming that Highlands's high altitude would cure consumption, malaria, yellow fever, and other diseases of the lowlands. Their pamphlet included a long letter from Thomas Clingman extolling the virtues of the Blue Ridge. Highlands became the highest incorporated town east of the Rockies, attracting both northern and southern settlers.

The railroad never reached Highlands. The area's remoteness may be its greatest asset. You really have to want to get there because you don't pass through it on the way to somewhere else. But the landscape that hindered business in the 19th century made Highlands perfect for the lifestyle business that has thrived there ever since.

Highlands Plateau

Asheville

North Carolina

The Chattooga River and Cullasaja River have their headwaters near Highlands. The Cullasaja tumbles through the gorge, paralleling US 64 and creating several outstanding waterfalls. Realtors praise "the majestic appeal of the Cashiers-Highlands Plateau as an unparalleled draw for vacationers and homeowners alike." It attracts many weekenders from Atlanta, less than two and a half hours away. The 3,200 year-round population of the Highlands Plateau explodes to over 18,000 in the summer. There are no fast food restaurants or chain stores in Highlands and the plateau is very quiet in the winter, when some merchants take their businesses to Florida.

Highlands receives 90 inches of rain annually, the highest rainfall in the Continental United States outside of the Pacific Northwest. The moisture and abundant sunshine create a lush, green microclimate which has long fascinated those interested in the vegetation of the Southern Appalachians. Botanical gardens there feature an unusual variety of plants. The Highlands Biological Station started as a museum in 1927 to preserve natural history collections of early settlers—pressed plants, mineral specimens, and mounted animals. Today it conducts research in the ecology and conservation of the Southern Appalachians and attracts students from all over the world.

Though the mountains and the cool weather may have been the original attraction for lowlanders, now Cashiers and Highlands offer sophisticated urban pursuits with great shopping, restaurants, and galleries. But the mountains are always a powerful presence.

Whiteside Mountain

The history of the Highlands plateau is intimately tied to the history of Whiteside Mountain. The Cowee range forms an arc around the eastern rim of the Highlands Plateau and many consider Whiteside Mountain to be the defining feature in the area. Its sheer cliffs rise 2,000 ft. above the Chattooga River valley.

Numerous adventurers and botanists visited the area in the 19th century and were amazed by the size and shape of Whiteside Mountain, though it's not clear how many of them actually climbed it. André Michaux, the first botanist to name and describe flame azalea and Catawba rhododendron, reached Whiteside Mountain in 1787 and may have shipped specimens of those plants back to France from the Highland Plateau. In 1849, explorer and historian Charles Lanman described the mountain as "one of the most remarkable curiosities in the mountain-land."

Samuel Kelsey realized that the spectacle of Whiteside Mountain would draw visitors and residents to the new town and he built a carriage road to view the mountain. For a long time, the Kelsey Trail, which started in Highlands, was the only way up to it.

In 1873, 10 years before the Kelsey Trail was built, Edward King, author of *The Great South*, predicted that "in a few years, its wildness will be tamed; a summer hotel will doubtless stand on the site of Wright's farm house, and the lovely forest will be penetrated by carriage roads; steps will be cut along the ribs of Whiteside; and a shelter will be erected on the very summit." His prediction was not far wrong.

Ten years later, Margaretta Ravenel, the wife of Capt. Samuel Prioleau Ravenel, Sr., a Civil War hero, bought a piece of Whiteside Mountain. The couple's names are carved on a memorial on top of Sunset Rock. Though they were summer residents, they felt very protective about their forest, which they called Ravenel Woods.

Many mountains surrounding Highlands, including Scaly Mountain, were sold to the Forest Service in 1920 when Nantahala National Forest was created, but Whiteside Mountain remained in the Ravenel family. The Ravenels' son and heir died in 1940, and Beatrice, his second wife, did not have the same feelings for Highlands as her husband had. That was before land conservancies could

After World War II, Whiteside was turned into a commercial operation.

have protected the mountain, and Beatrice soon sold the land to timber and development interests. Champion Paper logged the forest and that was the end of the Kelsey Trail.

After World War II, a group of businessmen turned Whiteside Mountain into a commercial operation. They built a gravel toll road and a parking lot so people could drive almost to the top of the mountain. From there a narrow road was bulldozed through the forest on which a tram, pulled by a jeep, could take sightseers to the very top. Attendants at a toll house on US 64 collected a dollar per person and another 25 cents for the tram. A concession stand sold hot dogs and cold drinks. This was the mood of the times—motorists could also drive to the top of Mt. Mitchell, Clingmans Dome, and Wayah Bald.

But the Whiteside Mountain road venture was not profitable and the owners wanted to sell the land. Congressman Roy Taylor, an environmentally sensitive legislator representing western North Carolina, worked to provide funds for the Forest Service to buy Whiteside Mountain. The mountain finally became part of Nantahala National Forest in 1975.

The old toll road to the summit became not only a foot trail but a National Recreation Trail as well, which meant increased visibility, and the Forest Service created a pamphlet for Whiteside Mountain. Some old-timers, like Robert Zahner in *The Mountain at the End of the Trail*, resent that the mountain has been "packaged by the U.S. Forest Service and marketed by the Highlands Chamber of Commerce." Even with its handrails and crowds of visitors, Whiteside Mountain should not be missed.

This view of Whiteside Mountain was taken by photographer George Masa in 1929.

This drive takes you from Cashiers to Highlands the long way. As you go, you'll see several outstanding waterfalls, go up Sunset Rocks for a great view of Highlands and the surrounding mountains, and stop at the old Grimshaws Post Office, once the smallest post office in the country.

The Drive

Starting at the intersection of US 64 and NC 107 in Cashiers, set your odometer to zero. The mileages from here are cumulative.

Take NC 107 south for 4.2 miles and park at a pulloff on the left.

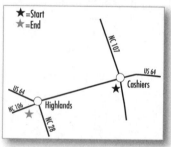

★ =Start
★ =End

NC 107
US 64
Cashiers
US 64
NC 106
Highlands
NC 28

Drive Start GPS Coordinates:
N 35° 06.83 W 83° 06.04

4.2 miles on the left—
Silver Run Falls

In a few minutes' walk, a gravel trail leads to the bottom of the waterfall. You can hear the rushing water as soon as you get on the trail. Cross a bridge and take a short path on the right. The falls are almost too perfect to be natural. The pool at the bottom looks very inviting on a hot summer day.

Back on NC 107, drive north for 2.5 miles. At 6.5 miles, turn left on Whiteside Cove Rd. (SR 1107). You'll follow the magnificent granite face of Whiteside Mountain as you head toward Highlands on this back road, passing Holly Berry Lake, a private lake, on the right.

10.6 miles on the right—
Grimshaws Post Office

This tiny wooden cabin was once the smallest post office in the United States, measuring 5 ft. by 6 ft. It was built by Thomas Grimshaws, Sr., the first postmaster, and was open from 1909 to 1953. The next year, the Eisenhower administration closed all third-class post offices. The building was then moved to the parking lot on Whiteside Mountain and used as a ticket office. Now it stands in Whiteside Cove, flanked by two junipers, with Whiteside Mountain looming above.

11.4 miles on the left—
Barak Norton family church

Barak Norton (1817-1869) was the first white settler in Whiteside Cove. The small chapel served as a church, school, and community center. Barak Norton's descendants have been holding reunions there since 1872.

12.6 miles—Road turns to gravel.

14.4 miles—Turn right on Horse Cove Rd.

16.5 miles—Turn left onto Rich Gap Rd., a gravel road. Parking for the Bob Padgett Tulip Poplar tree is a few hundred yards down the road on the left at the Nantahala Forest information board.

16.6 miles—
Bob Padgett Tulip Poplar

It's less than five minutes' walk on a trail to the right to a large tree over four hundred years old. The trail goes up a few steps with a wooden banister. At the fork in the trail, make a right and go down to a small corral fenced in by wooden planks. The huge tree is next to the creek, with a plaque on a nearby rock. Bob Padgett, a U.S. Forest Ranger, worked to preserve

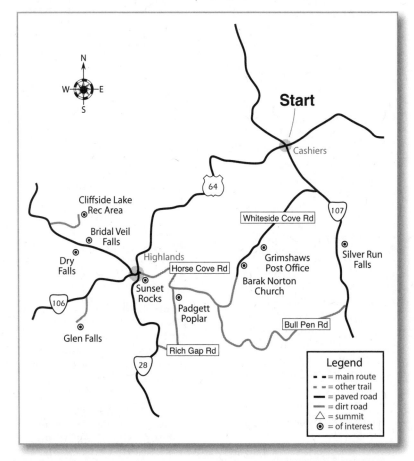

the natural environment of the Highlands plateau and this tree.

Return to Horse Cove Rd. and continue left.

18.8 miles on the left—
Sunset Rocks

The walk up to Sunset Rocks and back is 1.5 miles with a 200-ft. ascent. Park at a pulloff on the left side of the street and walk up unpaved Sunset Park Rd. Stay on the main road, which turns right and goes up gently through rhododendrons. You'll reach a large, flat circle. A stone commemorates Margaretta and S. Prioleau Ravenel, who owned the land. Go right between two small boulders to a flat granite overlook. The town of Highlands is below with private houses dotting the hills.

Return the way you came. Across the street you can visit the Nature Center, closed in winter, and walk through the Botanical Gardens, open all year; both are free.

At 19.4 miles, go through the second traffic light and onto US 64W through downtown Highlands.

US 64 enters Cullasaja Gorge, paralleling the Cullasaja River, from Highlands to Franklin. This road was carved into the side of a cliff and is a challenge to drive. The dropping river creates dramatic waterfalls, cascades, ripples, and pools.

On Sunset Rocks

22.1 miles on the right—
Bridal Veil Falls

There's a pulloff on the side of the road with a Forest Service sign. As its name implies, the falls are delicate, with a low volume of water. The classic picture includes someone behind the falls. You can even drive behind the falling water when it's not icy.

22.9 miles on the left—
Dry Falls

Dry Falls is so named because you can walk on a paved path behind its sheet of falling water without getting soaked. There's a wheel chair accessible area and pit toilets.

24.1 miles on the right—
Cliffside Lake Recreation Area

Drive about a mile to the

entrance gate where you'll pay a $4 parking fee. Here you can fish, picnic, swim, and hike. Turn right toward the fishing/swimming sign and park at the lake. For an easy, flat hike, take the 0.75-mile Cliffside Loop Trail. Go down the paved path and turn right at the trail sign. The gravel trail has several wooden decks for fishing. The trail goes down to the right to avoid the spillway and crosses a bridge. Farther on the trail is unpaved but it is always well maintained.

26.4 miles—Turn left on US 64E to return to Highlands.

30.8 miles—Turn right on NC 106S.

32.6 miles—Turn left toward Glen Falls on an unpaved road at the National Forest sign.

33.8 miles—

Glen Falls Trailhead

The hike to Glen Falls, 1.5 miles and 400 ft. ascent, is a gem of a walk on the east fork of Overflow Creek, with four distinct vantage points for views. Start to the right of the information board and turn left to follow signs to Glen Falls. A right would take you up Chinquapin Mountain. Almost immediately you'll reach a bench with a southern view into Georgia. The first overlook, with a metal railing, has a view of the cascading creek. At the T-junction, make a right and follow the sounds of the river to a second lookout, also with a railing, at the top of the first major waterfall.

Return to the split and take the left fork heading downhill. The trail turns away from the water but soon switchbacks to the right. The third lookout, without a barrier, should not be missed. Most times the water comes down in two streams like twin falls, but when the water is high, the twins merge. The water hits a flat rock and continues plummeting down.

The trail zigzags in wide switchbacks but always comes back to the river. At the last overlook, water tumbles down a gentle rocky slope. Retrace your steps to the trailhead.

35.0 miles—Turn right on NC 106 north.

36.8 miles—Turn right on US 64E in the center of Highlands. US 64E turns left at the next light and will get you back to Cashiers in about 11 miles.

Glen Falls on Overflow Creek.

The summit of Whiteside Mountain reaches an elevation of over 4,900 ft., rising more than 2,000 ft. above Whiteside Cove to the south. The southern side of the granite dome is white because of weathering due to wintertime freezing and thawing. Take this short loop clockwise to climb gently on an old roadbed and come down quickly on a steep trail, with numerous panoramic views from rock outcrops and cliffs. The Forest Service has placed cable railings along the trail to protect visitors from falling into the valley. This is a National Recreation Trail, so you can expect more visitors and more amenities than the average forest trail. For a longer hiking day, add the Scaly Mountain hike (see p. 333) on the western side of Highlands.

Type of hike: Loop

Distance: 2.1 miles

Total ascent: 600 ft.

Starting elevation: 4,400 ft.

Highlights: Magnificent views

USGS map: Highlands

Trail map:
Nantahala & Cullasaja Gorges, National Geographic Trails Illustrated Map #785

Land managed by:
Nantahala National Forest, Highlands Ranger District

Fee: $2 for parking

Getting to the trailhead: From Cashiers, drive west for

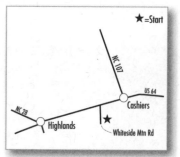

Trailhead GPS Coordinates:
N 35° 04.83 W 83° 08.64

4.8 miles on US 64 and make a left on Whiteside Mountain Rd. (SR 1690). Drive a mile to the parking area on the left.

The Hike

Whiteside Mountain Trail [#70 – no blazes] starts behind the information board to the right of the fee box. It soon turns left to go clockwise and continues on a wide, broken-up road through rhododendron and hemlock. Runoffs flow down the rocky walls and icicles remain on north-facing slopes after everything else has warmed up.

You'll be walking on the road that people drove in the 1950s. Look left down the valley to small ponds, golf courses, and lavish homes of the Highlands-Cashiers area. Soon the mountain slope becomes less rocky, with only an occasional boulder sticking out. The road also moderates. At 0.9 mile (4,800 ft. elev.), you'll reach the large, flat rocky outcropping where tourists parked when the mountain was a commercial attraction. Whiteside Mountain straddles the Eastern Continental Divide, with the Chattooga River ultimately flowing into the Atlantic and the Cullasaja River into the Mississippi River and the Gulf of Mexico. Straight ahead, you'll look south into the Chattahoochee National Forest in Georgia. The trail turns right and continues up on a narrow trail with outstanding southern views. An old roadbed to your right, paralleling the trail, was the "jeep road" that took people that last half-mile to the top for 25 cents.

Whiteside Cove Rd. is down below and you might be able to see Holly Berry Lake, close to the old Grimshaws Post Office. After the small wooden building was no longer a post office, it was moved to the old parking area on Whiteside Mountain and used as a ticket booth. Looking left, the Whiteside Mountain cliffs are visible, fringed with pines. Modern wooden post-and-cable fencing protects you from rolling down to Whiteside Cove Rd. This view gives you a good idea of how sheer and steep the rocky faces are. The views are tremendous from several vantage points, especially on the highest bluffs toward the top.

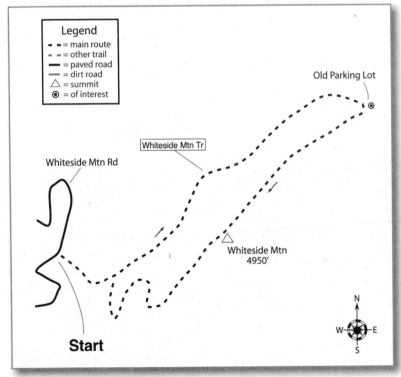

At 1.4 miles (4,950 ft. elev.), there are great southern and western views from the top of Whiteside Mountain. Red oaks have been twisted by wind and ice storms. In the spring, reintroduced peregrine falcons may be flying above you or resting on bare rock outcroppings. Unlike turkey vultures, which are common in these mountains, falcons don't soar.

The trail goes down on a rocky path. As you descend, look to the right for a set of rock steps where tourists got off the jeep to visit the top of Whiteside. The trail stays close to the cliff edge. Stay behind the railing for your final views.

Leaving the top, you'll go down quickly, first on rocks and then a dirt trail through a pleasant, cool forest of mixed hardwood trees with an understory of laurel and rhododendron. The trail switchbacks several times. A wooden and metal stairway takes you down around the back of the mountain below rocky cliffs. After you complete the circle, make a right down to the parking area to end the hike.

Dramatic mountain scenery rolls out below the slope of Whiteside.

Yellow Mountain

The Yellow Mountain Trail traverses a heavily forested area through the Cowee Mountains, climbing Cole Mountain and Shortoff Mountain and skirting the western side of Goat Knob. The last climb takes you to the top of Yellow Mountain and a historic fire tower with its tremendous 360-degree views. Though this hike starts on a side road between the two upscale tourist towns of Cashiers and Highlands, you won't see many people on Yellow Mountain Trail. It's a strenuous hike but a rewarding one.

Type of hike: Out and back

Distance: 10.0 miles

Total ascent: 2,850 ft.

Starting elevation: 4,300 ft.

Highlights: Outstanding views, solitude, fire tower

USGS map: Highlands, Glenville

Trail map:
Nantahala & Cullasaja Gorges, National Geographic Trails Illustrated Map #785

Land managed by:
Nantahala National Forest, Highlands Ranger District

Getting to the trailhead:
From Cashiers, drive west on US 64 for 7.9 miles and make a right on Buck Creek Rd. Drive for 2.2 miles to Cole Gap. There's a wide pulloff to the left for parking. The trailhead is on the right.

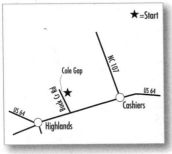

Trailhead GPS Coordinates:
N 35° 06.27 W 83° 12.25

The Hike

At the trailhead at Cole Gap, cross Buck Creek Rd. to a metal sign which reads "Leaving the Cullasaja River Watershed." Go up steps on Yellow Mountain Trail [#5 – no blazes] leading into a forest of oak, pine, and maple and a wooden forest information board. The hike starts gently with aster, phlox, gentian, and goldenrod alongside the trail. At 0.5 mile, a short side trail on the left leads to an overlook. From a flat, rocky lookout, you'll see layer upon layer of mountain ridges to the west. A camping area with a small house lies below. If you really look hard you can see a house here and there, but mostly it looks like untouched wilderness.

The trail flattens. A little barbed wire fence lining the trail is a reminder that you're passing through old pasture land. At 0.8 mile, the trail starts its first climb toward Cole Mountain, heads back downhill to an unnamed gap, and then climbs again steeply. To the left, due north, you'll recognize Yellow Mountain with its tower. The trail continues climbing

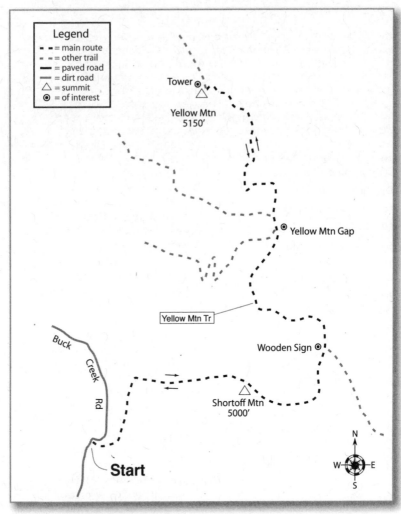

Legend
- **– –** = main route
- **· ·** = other trail
- **━** = paved road
- **─** = dirt road
- △ = summit
- ◉ = of interest

Tower ◉
△
Yellow Mtn
5150'

Yellow Mtn Gap ◉

Yellow Mtn Tr

Wooden Sign ◉

△
Shortoff Mtn
5000'

Buck Creek Rd

Start

N
W—◈—E
S

on a series of switchbacks through a rhododendron tunnel. Western views look out onto a sea of mountains and an occasional house. At 1.4 miles, take a side trail on the right and look southwest to see the valley below. In another 0.1 mile, you'll reach the Cole Mountain ridge at 4,900 ft. elev., with outstanding western views.

Shortoff Mountain lies ahead.

After a short downhill stretch, the trail goes straight up to Shortoff Mountain—no switchbacks here. The top of Shortoff Mountain at 1.8 miles (5,000 ft. elev.) is a flat ridge without much of a view. The trail goes straight down the same way it went up. Looking over your shoulder as you go down, you'll have gorgeous winter views of your hike so far.

At 2.4 miles (4,700 ft. elev.) you'll reach a wooden sign which reads "Yellow Mt. 2.4" and "Cole Mt. Gap 2.4." You'll be almost halfway to Yellow Mountain in distance but not in energy output. The trail continues down steeply, skirting Goat Knob on your right. You'll reach several flat spots; you may think you're at Yellow Mountain Gap, but then the trail continues in the same direction—down. You're going to have to climb back up and regain all that altitude.

Cross a tiny creek, surrounded by rhododendrons. Until now the trail has been dry and this little stream is the only water you'll see all day. A metal wand points you to Yellow Mountain as the trail becomes a road. Pass another old road shooting up steeply to your right at 3.3 miles. On the left, the flanks of Yellow Mountain are visible. The trail comes back to a narrow path and turns right, then left.

Finally you'll reach Yellow Mountain Gap at 3.6 miles (4,150 ft. elev.); this might be a point of confusion. At the gap, the trail turns right. On your left is an old road with a major blowdown. Don't get back on the road; stay on the trail which climbs gently north. From here, the trail will climb about 1,000 ft. to the summit of Yellow Mountain.

To the south through trees you'll see Shortoff Mountain, which looks high compared to where you are now. It's a long, steady uphill. Sometimes you may see an opening with a

The restored fire tower is a happy resting place at the top of Yellow Mountain.

view of Yellow Mountain, but then the trail goes back into the woods. Here at the edge of Nantahala National Forest, the footing is rocky and eroded in places. At 4.6 miles, the trail parallels a one-lane gravel road on the right. Decorative lot numbers signify a future housing development. A set of stairs to a wooden stand, which looks like the beginning of a treehouse, allows prospective land buyers to look at the views from the property.

Blue flagging tape keeps you on the trail in the forest, which is more pleasant than the road. The trail cuts to the left through mountain laurel back into the forest. Pass an old outhouse to your right at 5.0 miles then turn left toward the tower. On the right, a road goes downhill. You'll quickly reach the broad, rocky top of Yellow Mountain at 5,150 ft.

The tower, built by the Civilian Conservation Corps in 1934, was decommissioned in 1969. After the tower fell into disrepair, it was restored in 1992 and anchored by guy wires. A wooden stairway leads to a walkway below a dunce-cap roof. The views from here are amazing in every direction, especially south to Shortoff Mountain and farther on to Whiteside Mountain. On days with good visibility, you can see the high ridges in the Great Smoky Mountains National Park.

On top you may meet hikers who are casually strolling, some with dogs. How did they get up there? There is a maze of private roads and undocumented trails lying east of the top. As the area becomes more developed, these easier accesses will probably disappear. According to old-timers, until the late 1980s you could even drive up.

Retrace your steps to the trailhead. The ascents on the way back will seem longer and more strenuous, so be sure to leave yourself enough time for the return trip.

Views from Yellow Mountain are amazing in every direction.

On this hike you'll take the Bartram Trail, which crosses from Georgia into North Carolina on NC 106 and climbs gently to the top of Scaly Mountain. Once on top you'll explore several outstanding rocky outcroppings, looking into Georgia with the profile of Rabun Bald as your constant companion. This is a fine choice if you only have half a day but want a walk with good views. Alternatively, if you've done Whiteside Mountain and there's more time in your hiking day, this makes an excellent second outing.

Type of hike: Out and back

Distance: 4.0 miles

Total ascent: 1,100 ft.

Starting elevation: 3,700 ft.

Highlights: Great views

USGS map: Scaly Mountain

Trail map:
Nantahala & Cullasaja Gorges, National Geographic Trails Illustrated Map #785

Land managed by:
Nantahala National Forest, Highlands Ranger District

Getting to the trailhead:
From Highlands, take NC 106S for 6.0 miles to Osage Mountain Scenic Overlook on the left. The trailhead is across the road.

Trailhead GPS Coordinates:
N 35° 04.83 W 83° 08.64

The Hike

The Bartram Trail [#67 – yellow blazes] starts on the north side of NC 106 via a set of wooden steps. The trail goes basically north, crossing tiny creeks. Watch for shiny mica on the trail. Mica is an aluminum silicate mineral used in electrical equipment insulation; it looks like glass but splits into flexible sheets. There's one section of this trail that has so much mica, it looks at first as if someone has been smashing glass jars.

As you climb the switchbacked trail, you'll lose the highway noises to the sound of trickling water and pass a small cascade hidden in a rhododendron thicket. The trail offers obstructed views on the left. At 0.8 mile (4,250 ft. elev.), make a sharp right, turning away from a trail toward a private house. This area is second-home heaven and you may hear hammers and power tools. The dome-like mountain to the right is your destination.

The trail turns into a wide road and climbs moderately along the southern face of the mountain. In the distance, Rabun Mountain seems to follow you. In another 0.3 mile, a short side trail on the right leads to a small rocky ledge, a preview of the panorama to come. Farther up, the trail turns rocky and

if it has recently rained, you'll walk in a small stream.

At 1.4 miles (4,550 ft. elev.), make a sharp left to continue on the Bartram Trail. A spur trail coming in from the right allows for a shorter route but a more complicated drive

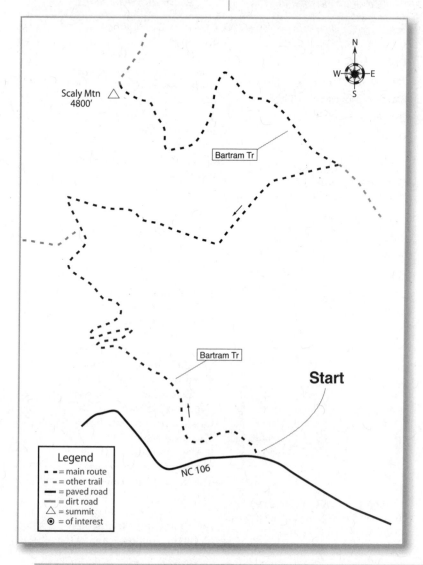

Scaly Mtn
4800′

Bartram Tr

Bartram Tr

Start

NC 106

Legend
▪ ▪ = main route
▪ ▪ = other trail
▬ = paved road
▬ = dirt road
△ = summit
◉ = of interest

to the trailhead. A brown carsonite sign labels the rest of this hike "most difficult."

The trail, lined with rhododendron and galax, is flat for a short while, then it starts climbing gently but persistently. You'll come out into the open on a rocky ledge, for the first of several outstanding views to the south, with Rabun Bald straight ahead of you. Green tunnels alternate with slightly higher outcroppings with windswept pitch pines. It may not be obvious that you've reached the top of Scaly Mountain (4,800 ft. elev.) until the trail starts sharply down. Retrace your steps to the trailhead to end the hike.

Rabun Bald is clearly visible to the south from the top of Scaly Mountain.

The Greenway is a pleasant, partially paved walk along the Little Tennessee River in Franklin. Its many amenities include benches, restrooms, and picnic tables. End to end it's four miles one way; round trip is a flat and easy eight-mile walk where you'll meet many friendly people. It's also a change of pace from the heavily wooded forest trails; here you'll see open sky, wetlands, historic bridges, and, yes, a little traffic. The mileage is posted every quarter-mile, starting from Suli Marsh.

Type of hike: Out and back

Distance: 8.0 miles

Total Ascent: 250 ft.

Starting elevation: 2,000 ft.

Highlights: River, birds, flat walking

USGS map: Franklin

Trail map: Available at several places on the Greenway

Land managed by: Macon County

Website: www.littletennessee.org

Getting to the trailhead: Entering Franklin on US 441 Business N, go over the bridge on E. Main St. and pass the second stop on the Greenway. In 0.3 mile, turn right on Depot St. Drive 1.2 miles and turn right into the Suli Marsh parking area; it's well-signed.

Trailhead GPS Coordinates: N 35° 11.81 W 83° 23.21

The Hike

The northern end of the Greenway starts at Suli Marsh and goes over a boardwalk above the marsh which is filled with cattails. *Suli* means buzzard in Cherokee, so it's appropriate that the volunteer crew that built the boardwalk calls itself Young Buzzard Construction Company. At the split, turn right. The river will be on your left with minor roads on either side and an occasional house and warehouse to remind you that you're in town. Pass a bench in memory of Charles O. Frazier, father of the famous author of *Cold Mountain*. Charles O. was a high school principal in Macon County.

After Big Bear Park, where you'll find a playground, restrooms, and picnic shelter, the path turns to dirt and goes under the East Main St. Bridge. When you come back to street level, you'll be facing the Friends of the Greenway (FROGs) headquarters, with a gift shop, coffee bar, and information.

Turn right, cross the bridge, and turn right again to parallel the river. You'll be walking behind the East Franklin Shopping Center, a strip mall, but not for long. Soon, the Greenway continues on a paved path where you'll pass a picnic pavilion (there are no other facilities) by the river and an exercise trail loop: chin-up, sit-up, and parallel bars. Stay right on the loop where a garden was planted to attract butterflies and hummingbirds. The Greenway maintainers leave the high brush to give birds and other wildlife some cover. You won't have a constant view of the river but if the vegetation along the riverbanks were cut low and tidy, you'd lose the cardinals, sparrows, and other birds flitting across the trail; to stay around they need to feel protected.

On the opposite side of the river you'll see the Zickgraf

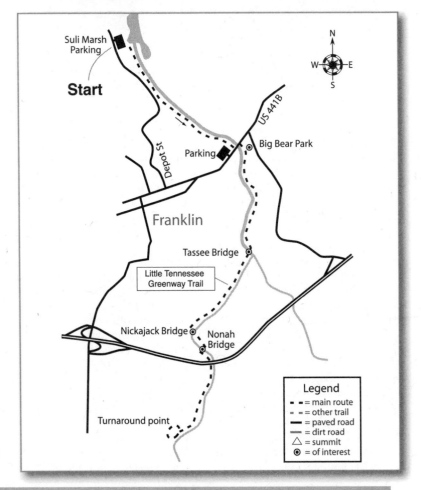

Nonah Bridge on the Little Tennessee Greenway.

plant, which manufactures hardwood flooring and is a major Greenway supporter. Benches here face away from the factory and the river. At 2.1 miles you'll cross Tassee Bridge, a charming wooden pedestrian bridge. Tassee was a Cherokee village located at the confluence of the Little Tennessee and the Cullasaja Rivers. After you walk under a highway bridge on Wayah St. you'll pass Tassee Park. This is another popular place to start walking the Greenway, and it has a picnic shelter, a fishing pier, and restrooms.

The trail moves farther into the woods, passing rocky boulders and an occasional house. Holly, doghobble, mountain laurel, juniper, and a few yucca plants line the trail. Tallulah Falls Railroad Trail starts here. The railroad, now abandoned, terminated at the Franklin depot. The falls themselves are in North Georgia, in Tallulah Gorge State Park. At 2.9 miles you'll cross Nickajack Bridge, a one-lane steel bridge which attracts anglers, and quickly after that the beautiful wooden covered Nonah Bridge. The trail goes under a highway bridge on US 64. When you leave the highway noises behind, the views open up and a dairy farm with pasture, cows, and barns stretches out on the other side of the river.

The trail narrows through another railroad cut, with high banks on both sides. Ignore the paved path to the right. The Little Tennessee, which you've been following in the upstream direction, merges with Cartoogechaye Creek. At the T-junction, take a right on the paved path. Future plans include a trail to the Macon County Library and Southwestern Community

College, where you'll be able to arrange for someone to pick you up. For now, go uphill and continue around the small loop. At the next intersection, turn left to head back the way you came to finish your hike.

Variation: If you want to walk the whole Greenway but minimize the amount of walking, place another car at Tassee Park—5.0 miles.

Heritage

Growing a Greenway

A greenway is an open space established for conservation, recreation, and even transportation along a natural corridor such as a river, stream, or rail-to-trail route. Greenways help preserve important natural landscapes, provide links between fragmented habitats, and protect wetlands. They can connect parks, nature preserves, cultural facilities, and historic sites with business and residential areas where people hike, run, bike, rollerblade, and walk their dogs. Greenways attract walkers who would not ordinarily go into the woods. One older couple walking their dog said that they probably do a thousand miles a year on the Little Tennessee River Greenway because they walk it every day.

The Little Tennessee River Greenway started when Franklin residents saw the potential of a long stretch of empty land along the Little Tennessee. At the same time Duke Power, through its local utility Nantahala Power & Light, needed a right-of-way for their transmission line through Franklin. The power company contributed the land in perpetuity as a greenway. To restore the riverbanks and build trails, the project received major grants which were matched by Zickgraf Industries, the largest employer in Franklin and a big financial supporter of the Greenway.

The Greenway is managed by Macon County with lots of help from its friends and volunteers. FROGs, Friends of the Greenway, continue to improve and extend it by helping to maintain trails, putting up bird boxes, and organizing walks and educational programs.

Cherohala Skyway

The Cherohala Skyway is an outstanding representation of a diverse, unique, and picturesque National Byway.

—From the Federal Highway Administration's 2003 Environmental Excellence Awards

Cherohala Skyway 66

Essential Facts

Rules/Facilities:
Picnic areas and restrooms at several stops on the Skyway. No gas stations or stores.

Closest town:
Robbinsville, NC, and Tellico Plains, TN

Website:
www.cherohala.org

Related movie:
Nell (1994) with Jody Foster

Highlights: Views, flowers, history

USGS map: Santeetlah Creek

Trail map: Available at the Visitor Center in Robbinsville, NC, and the Cherohala Skyway Visitor Center in Tellico Plains, TN

Land managed by:
Nantahala National Forest, NC, and Cherokee National Forest, TN. The Cherohala

Skyway itself is a state road, partly in North Carolina on NC 143, partly in Tennessee on TN 165.

Getting to the Skyway:
From Robbinsville at the intersection of NC 143 and NC 129, take NC 143 west for 12.2 miles and turn left on the Skyway at Santeetlah Gap. The driving mileages for all attractions are given from the North Carolina end of the Skyway at Santeetlah Gap.

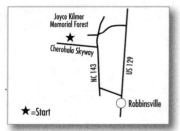

Drive Start GPS Coordinates:
N 35° 20.74 W 83° 53.66

The Cherohala Skyway, a 43-mile high-mountain road, connects Robbinsville, NC, with Tellico Plains, TN. You can experience the Skyway as a two-hour drive, stopping at occasional

lookouts with panoramic views, or you can hike the trails. Either way, it's a beautiful but little-used road with trails that see even less use. On the North Carolina side the hikes are short, all coming back to the Skyway. The road has been compared with the Blue Ridge Parkway, but it has much less traffic than the Parkway and its views are not obstructed by signs of civilization.

Spring arrives late on the Skyway and fall comes early. It's an exposed road which should be avoided in fog and ice. The Skyway is easy to get to; it just takes a long time from most population centers.

The Hikes
5.7 miles on the right—
Wright Creek Nature Trail

Type of hike: Loop
Distance: 0.5 mile
Total ascent: 200 ft.

To begin, go down steps on a well-maintained trail into a forest of hemlock, maple, and American beech. Cross an overgrown roadbed, which was once used to bring loggers here, and go straight, following signs to the Nature Trail. You'll be deep in the forest with an understory of fern and hobblebush; there are several benches along the way. The woods feel untouched but the area was logged as late as the 1970s.

8.7 miles on the left—
Spirit Ridge

Type of hike: Out and back
Distance: 0.7 mile
Total ascent: almost flat

This paved path through a hardwood cove forest is accessible to strollers and wheelchairs. The lookout faces northeast over the forest, where in the distance on the right you can see the Skyway; you can certainly hear it. Return the same way.

9.6 miles on the right—
Huckleberry Knob

Type of hike: Out and back
Distance: 2.5 miles
Total ascent: 310 ft.

Start at an old gated forest road lined with white snakeroot, jewelweed, and asters under beech and maple trees. The trail opens up into a meadow of grasses and thistle with huge blueberry and blackberry bushes. Bees and butterflies flit about through the wildflowers. The bald to your left is your destination. The trail goes back into the trees and climbs north into an open field.

Near the top, a cross on the left commemorates two lumberjacks who died there on December 11, 1899. Andy Sherman and Paul O'Neil, who worked at the Tellico Logging Camp, were walking from Tellico Plains to Robbinsville. They were trying to get home for Christmas but never made it. The next autumn a hunter

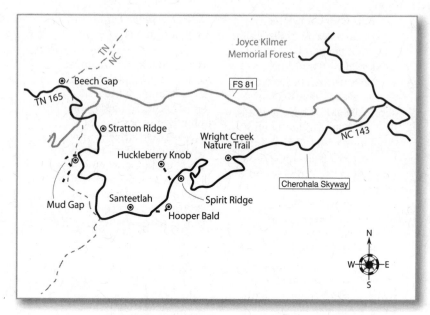

found their bodies, surrounded by whiskey bottles. They must have been cold and intoxicated, not a good combination. Only Andy Sherman is buried here; the body of Paul O'Neil was given to a doctor as a medical exhibit.

You'll reach the top of Huckleberry Knob at 5,550 ft. elev., with northern views into the Nantahala Mountains. The trail ends a little farther at an old campfire site.

Retrace yours steps to the trailhead. On your way back, you'll have a view of the Skyway.

10.8 miles on the left—
Hooper Bald Trail

Type of hike: Out and back
Distance: 1.0 mile
Total ascent: 150 ft.
This parking area is the starting point for a network of trails in the Snowbird Mountains. Hooper Bald can be seen to the left of the information board. The trail starts beyond the picnic table to the right; there are restrooms on the left.

The trail is lined with gravel. Continue straight after crossing a forest road. The trail ends in a grassy meadow, filled with blueberry bushes which are heavy with fruit in late summer. The trail continues right to a small rock outcropping with a view. Retrace your steps to get back to the parking lot.

1.4 miles on the right—
Santeetlah
At 5,377 ft. elev., there are a few picnic tables at this highest point on the Skyway.

14.9 miles on the left—
Mud Gap Trailhead

Type of hike: Out and back
Distance: 3.0 miles
Total ascent: 500 ft.

The Mud Gap Trail to Whigg Meadow is part of the Benton MacKaye Trail [white diamond blazes]. A 300-mile footpath, this trail starts at Springer Mountain, GA, the southern terminus of the Appalachian Trail, and travels to Davenport Gap at the northeast edge of the Smokies, where the A.T. leaves the park.

As you start the hike on an old road, Benton MacKaye Trail comes in from the right, paralleling the Skyway. The trail is lined with jewelweed, white snakeroot, and filmy angelica. You'll pass huge boulders on the left as it becomes rockier in spots. In about a mile, after you have climbed most of the 500-ft. ascent, the trail flattens out. Toward the end, it opens up to the sky and descends a little.

The trail ends at a large gravel parking area. On the right is Whigg Meadow, with awesome views. You can spend a lot of time exploring several side trails emanating, at a line of bird boxes, from the open bald. No wonder this field attracts serious birders. The Benton MacKaye Trail continues down the gravel road.

To see a Confederate grave off Mud Gap Trail, go to the next road on the left and walk past the metal gate. The grave stone, on the left and flat to the ground, reads, "Here lies an unknown man killed by the Kirkland bushwhackers."

Although the Cherohala Skyway is a favorite of motorcyclists, it sees little traffic.

The sky is big at Huckleberry Knob.

16.5 miles on right—
Stratton Ridge

Picnic tables and restrooms.

18.6 miles—
Beech Gap

Here the Skyway crosses the state line and continues through the Cherokee National Forest on TN 165 west for over 24 miles. It ends about 0.1 mile beyond the Cherohala Skyway Visitor Center in Tellico Plains, TN, on TN 68.

Heritage

The Cherohala Skyway and the Wagon Train

The Cherohala Skyway winds up and around for over 43 miles to almost 5,400 ft. elev. between Robbinsville, NC, and Tellico Plains, TN—18.6 miles in North Carolina and 24.5 miles in Tennessee. The idea of the Skyway started out almost as a joke at a Kiwanis Club meeting in 1958. At the time, the roads connecting Tellico Plains with the mountains in North Carolina could only be traveled by wagons. So a wagon train was formed to draw attention to a need for a road; this annual demonstration continued for years. The first wagon train traveled from Tellico Plains to Murphy, NC. In 1960, it was decided that a route to Robbinsville was more feasible, and two years later Congress made its first appropriation for the road.

The Skyway was completed in 1996 at a cost of 100 million dollars. It was a long project which was stalled by environmental concerns, since the road was cutting through two national forests. The name "Cherohala" comes from the two national forests the road goes through, the Cherokee and the Nantahala.

The Skyway is known as a motorcycle Mecca but in fact it's not used much by any type of vehicle. When it opened, the Forest Service estimated that five million cars a year would use the new road, which works out to 10 cars a minute year-round. The actual figure is more like 10 cars and 50 motorcycles a day.

The Cherohala Skyway is designated as a National Scenic Byway by the Federal Highway Administration because of its panoramic vistas and regional significance.

The Boars on Hooper Bald

Just below Hooper Bald was a hunting lodge where the first wild boars were imported from Europe. In 1908 the Whiting Manufacturing Company of England bought a large tract of land in Graham County's Snowbird Mountains. George Gordon Moore, an American advisor for the company, was allowed to establish a game reserve on the property for use by wealthy clients. He brought in buffalo, elk, mule deer, Russian brown bear, and boars.

Only the boars survive, having long ago escaped from the preserve, and they are still creating environmental havoc. Mature boars weighing over 400 pounds have spread north into the Smokies. They dig up the soil searching for roots and leave the ground looking as if it's been tilled. In the Great Smoky Mountains National Park, where hunting is not allowed, boar traps have been placed just off the trails. Hikers are more likely to see a bear in the woods than a boar. There are no remains of the lodge.

According to California's Monterey County Historical Society, Moore was not content simply to introduce boars and their problems into western North Carolina. He had boars shipped from Hooper Bald to the ranch he bought in the 1920s in Carmel Valley, where they are causing similar devastation.

Appendices

Appendix A: The Hikes

	Hike	Area
1	Hanging Rock Loop	Hanging Rock State Park
2	Moore's Wall Loop	Hanging Rock State Park
3	Pilot Mountain State Park	Pilot Mountain State Park
4	Chestnut Knob/Waterfall	South Mountains State Park
5	Jacob Fork Watershed	South Mountains State Park
6	Lake James State Park	Marion
7	Catawba River Greenway	Morganton
8	Stone Mountain Loop	Stone Mountain State Park
9	Wolf Rock Loop	Stone Mountain State Park
10	Basin Creek	Doughton Park
11	Bluff Mountain Trail	Doughton Park
12	Mt. Jefferson	Mt. Jefferson State Natural Area
13	Blowing Rock Drive	Blowing Rock
14	Rich Mountain Loop	Moses H. Cone Memorial Park
15	Bass Lake/The Maze	Moses H. Cone Memorial Park
16	Flat Top Tower	Moses H. Cone Memorial Park
17	Boone Fork Loop	Julian Price Memorial Park
18	Tanawha Trail	Grandfather Mountain
19	Grandfather Trail	Grandfather Mountain
20	Profile Trail	Grandfather Mountain
21	Lost Cove Loop	Wilson Creek
22	Linville Gorge Loop	Linville Gorge
23	Hawksbill	Linville Gorge
24	Table Rock/Chimneys	Linville Gorge
25	Linville Falls	Linville Gorge
26	Shortoff Mountain	Linville Gorge
27	Big Bald	Hot Springs
28	Roundtop Ridge	Hot Springs
29	Laurel Creek	Hot Springs
30	Max Patch Loop	Hot Springs
31	Pigeon River Gorge	Hot Springs
32	Hump Mountain	Pisgah/Appalachian District
33	Maple Camp Bald	The Blacks

Type of Hike	Mileage	Ascent (ft.)	Page
Loop	7.5	1,500	26
Loop	4.8	1,900	29
Loop	8.5	2,000	32
Loop	9.3	2,350	40
Loop	11.6	2,150	45
O & B	4.9	500	48
O & B	9.6	300	52
Loop	6.4	1,350	61
Loop	3.2	950	66
O & B	10.2	1,500	72
Shuttle	7.9	1,050	76
Loop	1.3	300	80
Drive	---	---	84
Loop	9.5	800	90
Loop	7.5	400	93
O & B	5.6	500	96
Loop	5.0	650	98
Shuttle	4.0	1,150	102
O & B	4.8	2,000	111
O & B	6.4	2,100	115
Loop	9.0	2,300	118
Loop	9.0	2,100	125
O & B	1.4	700	130
O & B	4.1	700	132
O & B	4.2	1,000	136
O & B	3.3	1,650	140
O & B	13.0	3,100	150
Loop	13.0	2,950	154
O & B	7.5	300	158
Loop	5.9	800	162
Loop	8.9	2,000	165
Loop	8.4	2,050	172
Loop	7.4	1,450	182

	Hike	Area
34	Big Butt Trail	The Blacks
35	Douglas Falls	The Blacks
36	Catawba Falls	Old Fort
37	Kitsuma Peak	Old Fort
38	Florence Preserve	Hickory Nut Gorge
39	Bat Cave	Hickory Nut Gorge
40	Chimney Rock	Chimney Rock State Park
41	Rumbling Bald	Chimney Rock State Park
42	Worlds Edge	Chimney Rock State Park
43	Coffee Pot Loop	Pisgah District
44	Cantrell Creek Lodge	Pisgah District
45	Pink Beds Loop	Pisgah District
46	Twin Falls Loop	Pisgah District
47	Cat Gap/Art Loeb	Pisgah District
48	Pilot Mountain	Pisgah District
49	Sam Knob/Black Balsam	Pisgah District
50	Mt. Hardy	Pisgah District
51	Pinnacle Park	Sylva
52	Big Cataloochee Drive	Great Smoky Mtns Nat'l Park
53	Boogerman Loop	Great Smoky Mtns Nat'l Park
54	Caldwell Fork Loop	Great Smoky Mtns Nat'l Park
55	Little Cataloochee	Great Smoky Mtns Nat'l Park
56	Charlies Bunion/Kephart Prong	Great Smoky Mtns Nat'l Park
57	Mt. LeConte	Great Smoky Mtns Nat'l Park
58	Gregory Bald	Great Smoky Mtns Nat'l Park
59	Hazel Creek	Great Smoky Mtns Nat'l Park
60	Canebrake Trail	Gorges State Park
61	Highlands Plateau Drive	Highlands
62	Whiteside Mountain	Highlands
63	Yellow Mountain	Highlands
64	Scaly Mountain	Highlands
65	Little Tennessee Greenway	Franklin
66	Cherohala Skyway	Robbinsville

Type of Hike	Mileage	Ascent (ft.)	Page
O & B	6.0	1,600	186
O & B	5.8	1,250	190
O & B	3.8	700	194
Loop	10.1	1,550	198
Loop	6.5	1,650	208
O & B	1.4	500	212
Loop	5.2	1,500	216
Shuttle	4.6	700	220
O & B	6.2	1,300	224
Loop	8.3	1,500	234
O & B	8.0	700	238
Loop	5.4	400	242
Loop	5.7	750	246
Shuttle	8.8	2,300	252
Loop	7.6	1,950	256
Loop	9.0	1,500	260
Shuttle	9.4	1,350	265
Loop	10.1	3,300	269
Drive	---	---	280
Loop	7.5	1,150	283
Loop	9.4	1,650	286
O & B	6.1	1,100	290
Shuttle	10.0	1,200	293
Shuttle	13.1	2,500	298
O & B	11.2	3,000	304
O & B	11.0	750	307
O & B	11.0	1,900	314
Drive	---	---	322
Loop	2.1	600	326
O & B	10.0	2,850	329
O & B	4.0	1,100	333
O & B	8.0	250	336
Drive	---	---	342

Appendix B: Hiking Safety and Skills

The most important safety tip is to remember that you're responsible for your own safety. Use common sense, know where you're going, have the proper gear, and start out early in the day.

Bears

Bears are always the first danger people mention when they talk about hiking in western North Carolina. In all my years of hiking I've seen fewer than 10 bears, and that's counting rumps dashing into the woods. Black bears are shy and don't want to be near people. But if you do see a bear on the trail coming toward you, the accepted advice is the following:

- Give the bear plenty of room and leave it alone.
- Don't try to feed the bear.
- Slowly back away. Don't run; you can't outrun a bear.
- Don't turn your back to the bear or crouch.
- Make yourself look and sound large by raising your arms and yelling.
- The bear will usually run away. If not, shout and throw rocks.

Snakes

Snakes are the other animal that new hikers worry about. In the Southern Appalachians, only timber rattlesnakes and copperheads are poisonous. Snakes will slither off the trail and into the grass very quickly. Like bears, they are typically afraid of humans. Stay on the

Safe hiking means being prepared.

trail and give the snake plenty of room to get away. Hiking boots which go over the ankle are also good protection against snakes.

Hornets and Yellow Jackets

These are much more dangerous than the potential bear or snake. At least with a bear, it's a one-on-one encounter; with hornets and yellow jackets, you may be up against a whole nestful. If you think you're allergic to stinging insects, ask your physician to prescribe an epinephrine pen. Carry it in your first aid kit along with an over-the-counter antihistamine, keep both current, and know how to use them.

Dogs

In most places, dogs are allowed but must be on a leash no longer than 6 ft. and always under the owner's control. A strange dog jumping on an oncoming hiker can be very intimidating and is not "friendly." Dogs are not allowed on trails in the Great Smoky Mountains National Park.

Poison Ivy

Poison ivy is prolific in the Southern Appalachians. It grows on disturbed land and not deep in the woods. Touching the leaves can give you a wicked rash, and the thick, fuzzy vines around trees are also poisonous. Poison ivy typically doesn't grow above 3,000 ft., but you may see it as high as 4,500 ft. Learn to identify it and stay away from it. If you think you've been in contact with poison ivy, scrub your skin with a strong soap, such as brown laundry soap, as soon as you get home. Some people have success using Dawn dish liquid.

Meeting Cyclists

You'll be sharing some trails with bikes. In general, the person traveling uphill has the right of way. Many cyclists like to climb a hill without stopping and on some hills, it is next to impossible to get going again once you're off your bike. However, if you're hiking up and cyclists come down fast, move to the side and let them through—they may not be able to stop. As they're zipping by, ask if there are any more bikers in their group.

Water

On a day hike, bring all your own water. You'll need at least two quarts, more on a long, strenuous hike. Treat any water you get on the trail. Some hikers carry water filters for that purpose. I carry iodine tablets which come in small bottles. Pop a tablet in a quart of water, wait 20 minutes, and you have potable water. If you don't like the iodine taste, after 20 minutes add some lemonade powder to make it more palatable.

Altitude, Rain, and Hypothermia

The mountainous nature of western North Carolina means you'll likely be changing climates as you hike. Climbing 3,000 ft. is the climatic equivalent of traveling 750 miles north.

In North Carolina's Blue Ridge, you'll likely be changing climates as you hike.

The temperature drops one degree with every 250 ft. above sea level, so it will be colder on top of a mountain than it is at the trailhead.

If you get wet and cold you're at risk for hypothermia, a condition when your body's control mechanism fails to maintain a normal temperature. It's more of a problem when it's 40 degrees and raining than when it's colder but dry. As with most problems, prevention is the best cure. Stay dry and don't wear cotton clothing, which stays cold when wet. Drink plenty of liquids, warm liquids, if possible.

No-Trace Hiking

Leave nothing in the woods—it's that simple. Of course, you wouldn't think of throwing your granola wrapper on the ground. But also pack out your apple cores, banana skins, and orange peels. According to the Leave No Trace Center for Outdoor Ethics, banana peel takes up to a year to disintegrate and orange peel up to two years.

Trail break, pit stop, bush break, bush stop—they're all euphemisms for going to the toilet in the woods. Go well off the trail and away from any water source. Bring a zip-lock bag to carry out your used toilet paper.

Otherwise, please stay on the trail. You'll protect wildflowers and other fragile plants, cut down on erosion, and be a lot safer. With thousands of miles of maintained trails at

Supervisory Ranger Lynda Doucette of Great Smoky Mountains National Park.

every challenge level, there's no need to bushwhack.

Leave artifacts, such as rusty buckets, old equipment, or pieces of railroad gizmos, where you find them.

Personal Safety

Before you go, leave your itinerary with someone at home. Write out the trailhead and trails you're taking or the hike number listed in this book. If you pass an open visitor center in the park or forest, it doesn't hurt to also give them a copy of your itinerary and your car license plate number. This also lets park personnel know that hikers are actually using the trails.

Lynda Doucette, supervisory park ranger in the Great Smoky

Mountains National Park, adds, "I'd also suggest that hikers—solo-hiking women in particular—be aware of their surroundings at all times. It's easy to get lost in thought on the trail. But if you are aware of your surroundings, it's harder for someone to sneak up on you. Hiking alone is relatively safe; more women are accosted at bars, parking lots, and other more populated areas than on a trail. You're more likely to have problems with a fall or other injury than to be kidnapped or killed. Common sense when alone or even with a group is always going to provide a level of safety that may be lifesaving."

Don't depend on a cell phone; it may not work on the trail. For more safety tips, see www.nps.gov/grsm/planyourvisit/hikingsafety.htm.

Hunting

It's illegal to hunt in national and state parks, so hunting season is only a concern in national forests during the bear and deer seasons, which occur between October and the beginning of January. This is when you'll see the bulk of the hunters in the woods. At this time, consider wearing an orange vest and/or hat if you are hiking in the national forest. During the other hunting seasons in September, January, February, April and May, there are far fewer hunters so you are less likely to run into any while on the trail.

Clothing and Gear

You need gear. You can borrow some gear, but the pack you carry and the boots you wear have to fit you. Make sure that you're comfortable with your equipment and it all fits into your daypack. Don't wrap a coat around your waist or hold anything in your hands. Carry your wallet and keys in your daypack or in your pocket at all times. Don't depend on anyone else to carry gear for you.

Dress in layers. Your first layer should be a short-sleeved t-shirt (synthetic, not cotton) even if it seems cool in the morning. You will warm up. Your next layer should be a long-sleeved shirt (also synthetic) followed by a fleece jacket and raingear. Shorts give you more mobility and keep you cooler; pants give you more protection from insects and brush. Don't wear jeans; they're heavy and they wick moisture, keeping you wet longer. For more on clothing, see the Day Hiking Gear checklist, p. 358.

For a simple lunch, start with a sandwich and a piece of fruit. Add snacks such as cookies, energy bars, and trail mix (nuts, chocolate, raisins, and other dried fruit).

Appendix C: Day Hiking Gear

Basic Gear

- Daypack
- Two quarts of water (minimum)
- Lunch and snacks
- Rain jacket (no matter what the forcast)
- Sunglasses
- Sun hat
- Insect repellent
- Sunscreen
- Tissues
- Personal first aid kit
- Small flashlight
- Plastic bag for trash
- Map (and know how to use it)
- Compass (and know how to use it)

You should be able to fit all your hiking gear into your daypack.

If it's not midsummer

- Warm fleece hiking sweater or jacket
- Woolen or fleece hat and gloves
- Rain pants

How to dress

- Shorts or light pants and a short-sleeved t-shirt as the bottom layer
- Hiking boots that are well broken in and that go over the ankles
- Good hiking socks (not sports socks)
- Sun hat with a wide brim
- Bandana (keep it handy)

Basic first aid kit

- Band-Aids
- Alcohol wipes
- Duct tape
- Gauze pads
- Moleskin
- Scissors
- Antibiotic ointment
- Latex gloves
- Clean bandana

Appendix D: Resources

National Parks

Great Smoky Mountains
National Park
107 Park Headquarters Rd.
Gatlinburg, TN 37738
(865) 436-1200
(865) 436-1231 for backcountry
information and permits
www.nps.gov/grsm

Blue Ridge Parkway
199 Hemphill Knob Rd.
Asheville, NC 28803
(828) 298-0398
www.nps.gov/blri

USDA Forest Service Ranger Stations

Nantahala National Forest
– Cheoah District
Route 1, Box 16A
Robbinsville, NC 28771
(828) 479-6431
www.cs.unca.edu/nfsnc

Nantahala National Forest
– Nantahala Ranger District
90 Sloan Rd.
Franklin, NC 28734
(828) 524-6441
www.cs.unca.edu/nfsnc

Pisgah National Forest
– Appalachian Ranger District
P.O. Box 128
Burnsville, NC 28741
(828) 622-3202
www.cs.unca.edu/nfsnc

Pisgah National Forest
– Grandfather Ranger District
109 East Lawing Dr.
Nebo, NC 28761

(828) 652-2144
www.cs.unca.edu/nfsnc

Pisgah National Forest
– Pisgah Ranger District
1001 Pisgah Hwy.
Pisgah Forest, NC 28768
(828) 877-3265
www.cs.unca.edu/nfsnc

North Carolina State Parks

Chimney Rock State Park
Hwy. 64/74A, P.O. Box 220
Chimney Rock, NC 28720
(800) 277-9611
www.chimneyrockpark.com

Gorges State Park
NC 281 South, P.O. Box 100
Sapphire, NC 28774-0100
(828) 966-9099
www.ncparks.gov

Grandfather Mountain State Park
US 221 & Blue Ridge Pkwy.
Linville, NC 28646
(800) 468-7325
www.grandfathermountain.com

Hanging Rock State Park
2015 Hanging Rock Park Rd.
Danbury, NC 27016
(336) 593-8480
www.ncparks.gov

Lake James State Park
P.O. Box 340
Nebo, NC 28761
(828) 652-5047
www.ncparks.gov

Mt. Jefferson State
Natural Area
P.O. Box 48
Jefferson, NC 28640
(336) 246-9653
www.ncparks.gov

Mt. Mitchell State Park
2388 State Hwy. 128
Burnsville, NC 28714
(828) 675-4611
www.ncparks.gov

Pilot Mountain State Park
1792 Pilot Knob Park Rd.
Pinnacle, NC 27043
(336) 325-2355
www.ncparks.gov

South Mountains State Park
3001 South Mountains
State Park Ave.
Connelly Springs, NC 28612
(828) 433-4772
www.ncparks.gov

Stone Mountain State Park
3042 Frank Pkwy.
Roaring Gap, NC 28668
(336) 957-8185
www.ncparks.gov

Scenic Highway

Cherohala Skyway Visitor Center
225 Cherohala Skwy.
Tellico Plains, TN 37385
(423) 253-8010
www.cherohala.org

Hiking Clubs

American Hiking Society
www.americanhiking.org

Appalachian Trail
Conservancy
www.appalachiantrail.org

Carolina Mountain
Club (Asheville)
www.carolinamtnclub.org

Carolina Berg Wanderers
(Charlotte)
hiking.meetup.com/323/

Chargers and Rechargers (Boone)
www.boonenc.org/hiking/

Friends of the
Mountains-to-Sea Trail (NC)
www.ncmst.org

Georgia Appalachian Trail
Club (Atlanta, GA)
www.georgia-atclub.org

High Country Hikers
(Hendersonville)
main.nc.us/highcountryhikers

Nantahala Hiking Club
(Franklin)
www.maconcommunity.org/nhc

Smoky Mountains Hiking
Club (Knoxville, TN)
www.smhclub.org

Tennessee Eastman Hiking
and Canoeing Club
(Kingsport, TN)
www.tehcc.org

Appendix E: Selected Hikes

Waterfall Hikes

- Chestnut Knob/Waterfall
  – South Mountains State Park
- Stone Mountain Loop
  – Stone Mountain State Park
- Lost Cove Loop – Wilson Creek
- Linville Falls – Linville Gorge
- Douglas Falls – The Blacks
- Catawba Falls – Old Fort
- Chimney Rock –
  Chimney Rock State Park
- Twin Falls Loop – Pisgah District
- Cat Gap/Art Loeb
  – Pisgah District
- Highlands Plateau
  Drive – Highlands

Mostly Flat Hikes

- Lake James – Marion
- Catawba River Greenway
  – Morganton
- Price Lake
  – Blowing Rock Drive
- Laurel Creek – Hot Springs
- Pink Beds – Pisgah District
- Little Tennessee
  Greenway – Franklin

Drives with Short Walks

- Blowing Rock Drive
- Big Cataloochee Drive
- Highlands Plateau Drive
- Cherohala Skyway

Challenging Hikes

- Tanawha Trail –
  Grandfather Mountain
- Grandfather Trail
  – Grandfather Mountain
- Linville Gorge Loop
  – Linville Gorge
- Roundtop Ridge – Hot Springs
- Hump Mountain – Pisgah/
  Appalachian District

- Gregory Bald – The Smokies
- Mt. LeConte – The Smokies
- Yellow Mountain
  – Highlands Plateau

Isolated Hikes

- Basin Creek – Doughton Park
- Linville Gorge Loop
  – Linville Gorge
- Shortoff Mountain – Linville
  Gorge Wilderness Area
- Pigeon River Gorge
  – Hot Springs
- Douglas Falls – The Blacks
- Canebrake Trail – Rosman
- Yellow Mountain – Highlands

Appalachian Trail Hikes

- Big Bald – Hot Springs
- Roundtop Ridge – Hot Springs
- Hump Mountain – Pisgah,
  Appalachian District

Appendix F: Hiking Glossary

Adelgid – Small, aphid-like sucking insects that feed on needles, stems, and through the bark of conifers. Since the 1950s the balsam woolly adelgid, originally from Central Europe, has been destroying fir and spruce trees. The resulting dead balsam trees can be clearly seen on the way to Mt. LeConte. The hemlock woolly adelgid from Asia now threatens hemlocks. The egg sacs, which look like cotton, are found along the stems of hemlock branches.

Bald – A bare mountaintop, characteristic of the Southern Appalachians. Most balds, if left alone, will fill in with shrubs and eventually with trees.

Basin – an area of land drained by a river and its branches.

Bear poles – A pulley-line arrangement set up in some backcountry campsites allowing campers to hang their food out of the reach of bears. There are bear poles (also called bear cables) in backcountry campsites in the Great Smoky Mountains National Park.

Blaze – A mark on a tree, rock, or post indicating the route of a trail.

Blowdown – A tree that has been toppled by wind. If a blowdown obstructing a trail is not cleared quickly, hikers tend to go off the trail and create a path around it.

Bushwhack – To make your way through the woods without an official trail.

Cairn – a pile of rocks serving as a landmark.

Carsonite sign – Brown vertical fiberglass sign stuck in the ground and labeled with a trail name to indicate the way, common in national forests. Also called a wand.

Civilian Conservation Corps (CCC) – A work relief program that recruited thousands of unemployed young men to rebuild the country's forests between 1933 and 1942. Nicknamed Roosevelt's tree army, these men planted billions of trees and built roads, trails, and picnic shelters in our national and state parks and forests and even on private land.

Contour line – A line on a topographic map which connects points of equal elevation.

Cove – A narrow draw or sheltered area between hills.

Divide – A ridge of land separating two valleys.

False summit – See *Local top.*

Ford – A shallow place to cross a stream.

Gap – An opening through mountains; a pass.

Gorge – A small canyon with steep, rocky walls. In the Southern Appalachians, a stream usually runs through a gorge.

GPS – Global Positioning System. A system that uses orbiting satellites to pinpoint locations on the globe and allows you to record your route by "dropping electronic bread crumbs." You can then download your trace on your computer and with proper software, lay it over a map. A GPS is not a substitute for a map and compass. However, it does allow you to keep a graphic record of your hike.

Grade – The degree of inclination of the slope of a trail. Percent grade is the relationship between horizontal distance and vertical gain.

Herd path – See *Social trail*.

Hiking challenge – A defined set of mountains or trails to be hiked. These include the Appalachian Trail, South Beyond 6000 (all the southern mountains above 6,000 ft.), and the heritage hikes in this book.

Local top – A minor summit, which looks like a peak as you hike. However, when you get to this top, you see a still higher top. Sometimes called false summit.

Monadnock – A mountain or rocky mass that has resisted erosion and stands isolated in an essentially level area. Examples

include Big and Little Pinnacles in Pilot Mountain State Park.

Pluton – A body of igneous rock formed beneath the surface of the earth when molten rocks consolidate, named for Pluto, ruler of the underworld. These become visible when softer layers above it erode away. Examples include Stone Mountain and Whiteside Mountain.

Quad map – Topographic map. Each map covers a quadrangle of 7.5 minutes of latitude and 7.5 minutes of longitude. See also *Topo map*.

Ridge – A long, narrow chain of hills or mountains. Also called a ridgeline.

Rock hop – To cross a stream by stepping from rock to rock to avoid getting your feet wet. Sometimes it's safer to get your boots wet instead of trying to balance on rocks.

Scree – A steep mass of loose rock on the slope of the mountain.

Shoal – A shallow place in a body of water, a sandbar.

Slope – An incline. The more vertical the slope, the harder the hike.

Social trail – An unofficial trail made by the passage of people. Sometimes referred to as a herd path or manway.

Appendix F: Hiking Glossary

Switchback – The zigzag course on a steep incline which allows the trail to maintain a reasonable grade. Switchbacks make the trail longer than if it went straight up the mountain, but they also makes it less strenuous.

Topo map – Topographic map. The best known USGS (U.S. Geological Survey) maps are the 1:24,000-scale "quad" maps based on 7.5-minute quadrangles. This is the only uniform map series that covers the entire area of the United States in considerable detail. Topo maps use contour lines to portray the shape and elevation of the land and show the three-dimensional ups and downs of the terrain on a two-dimensional surface.

Trail break – A euphemism for going to the toilet in the woods

Trailhead – Place where a hike begins.

Tuliptree – A large tree native to the Southern Appalachians. Also known as poplar, tulip poplar, or yellow poplar, it is not a true poplar, but a member of the magnolia family.

Watershed – The area drained by a river or river system.

Winter views – Views only available in winter, when the trees have shed their leaves.

Appendix G: Related Books & Movies

Books

Brown, Margaret Lynn. *The Wild East: A Biography of the Great Smoky Mountains.* University Press of Florida, 2000. A very readable history of the Smokies, concentrating on the natural history.
• Related hikes: Great Smoky Mountains National Park

Caldwell, Wayne. *Cataloochee: A Novel.* Random House Trade Paperbacks, 2008. A multigenerational family story set in Cataloochee before the area became a national park.
• Related hikes: Boogerman Loop, Caldwell Fork Loop, Little Cataloochee

Dykeman, Wilma. *The French Broad.* Wakestone Books, 1992. Dykeman uses this book, written in the 1950s, to explore the people and towns along the French Broad River.
• Related hikes: Roundtop Ridge, Laurel Creek

Ehle, John. *The Road.* University of Tennessee Press, 1998. A grand story of man against nature, this novel is about building the railroad through the Blue Ridge Mountains to Swannanoa Gap in the 1870s.
• Related hike: Kitsuma Peak

Holland, Lance. *Fontana: A Pocket History of Appalachia.* Appalachian History Series, 2001. A history of the Fontana area before and after TVA came in to build Fontana Dam.
• Related hike: Hazel Creek

Karon, Jan. *At Home in Mitford.* Penguin Books, 2005. The first of several successful novels about Father Tim, a small-town minister, and his friends in the small mountain town of Mitford, which is modeled on Blowing Rock.
• Related hikes: Blowing Rock Drive, Moses H. Cone Memorial Park

Kephart, Horace. *Our Southern Highlanders.* University of Tennessee Press, 1984. This book, first published in 1913, recalls stories of the land and people in what became the Great Smoky Mountains National Park.
• Related hikes: Charlies Bunion, Hazel Creek

McCrumb, Sharyn. *The Ballad of Frankie Silver.* Signet, 1999. In 1832, an 18-year-old girl, charged with murdering her husband, was tried and hanged in Morganton. More than a hundred years later, a Tennessee sheriff is determined to reveal the truth behind the crime.
• Related hike: Catawba River Greenway

Morgan, Robert. *Boone: A Biography.* Algonquin, 2007. An exciting modern biography of the legendary Daniel Boone.
• Related hikes: Blowing Rock Drive, Boone Fork Loop

Noblitt, Philip T. *A Mansion in the Mountains: The Story of*

Moses and Bertha Cone and their Blowing Rock Manor. Parkway Publishers, 1996. A biography of Moses Cone, concentrating on his work at Flat Top Manor.
• Related hikes: Moses H. Cone Memorial Park

Painter, Jacqueline Burgin. *The German Invasion of Western North Carolina: A Pictorial History.* Overmountain Press; 2nd edition, 1997. The book tells the history of Hot Springs with great pictures of old hotels and World War I German prisoners of war.
• Related hikes: Roundtop Ridge, Laurel Creek

Painter, Jacqueline Burgin. *The Stackhouses of Appalachia: Even to Our Own Time.* Grateful Steps, 2006. The story of Amos Stackhouse, a Pennsylvania Quaker, who settled on the banks of the French Broad, with photographs and maps.
• Related hikes: Roundtop Ridge, Laurel Creek

Rash, Ron. *One Foot in Eden.* Picador, 2003. A gripping novel set in the 1950s in the area that was later flooded to create Lake Jocassee.
• Related hike: Canebrake Trail

Silver, Timothy. *Mount Mitchell and the Black Mountains: An Environmental History of the Highest Peaks in Eastern America.* University of North Carolina Press, 2003. Silver's book is a fascinating natural and human history of the area, interspersed with his own exploration of the Blacks.
• Related hikes: Maple Camp Bald, Big Butt, Douglas Falls

Smith, Lee. *On Agate Hill.* Algonquin, 2006. An engrossing novel about an independent-minded woman growing up after the Civil War. Partly set in West Jefferson.
• Related hike: Mount Jefferson

Thompson, Neal. *Driving with the Devil: Southern Moonshine, Detroit Wheels, and the Birth of NASCAR.* Three Rivers Press, 2007. The title says it all; written in a lively, breathless style. A good read.
• Related hikes: Stone Mountain State Park

Whisnant, Anne Mitchell. *Super-Scenic Motorway: A Blue Ridge Parkway History.* University of North Carolina Press, 2006. A lively modern history of the most visited National Park unit in the United States.
• Related hikes: Tanawha Trail, Grandfather Trail, Profile Trail

Movies

A Breed Apart (1984) with Kathleen Turner. A rich egg collector hires a mountain climber to fetch rare bird eggs on top of a chimney rock.
• Related hikes: Hickory Nut Gorge

Dirty Dancing (1987) with Patrick Swayze and Jennifer Grey. Partly filmed at Lake

Lure, this coming-of-age story has become a cult classic.
- Related hikes: Chimney Rock, Rumbling Bald

The Green Mile (1999) with Tom Hanks. A story about a death-row prison in the 1930s, with scenes shot at Flat Top Manor.
- Related hikes: Moses H. Cone Memorial Park

The Hunt for Red October (1990) with Sean Connery. A techno-thriller set during the Cold War. The last scene, meant to be a river in Maine, was filmed at Lake James.
- Related hike: Lake James

The Last of the Mohicans (1992) with Daniel Day-Lewis. The movie, based on the James Fenimore Cooper classic, revolves around the battle between the English and the French for control of the North American colonies in the 18th century. Filmed in many locations in the Blue Ridge Mountains.
- Related hikes: Lake James, Linville Gorge and Falls, Chimney Rock Park

Nell (1994) with Jodie Foster. Nell, brought up in rural isolation and speaking a language only she understands, is discovered by outsiders. The movie was filmed at Fontana Lake and Robbinsville.
- Related hikes: Hazel Creek, Cherohala Skyway

Thunder Road (1958) with Robert Mitchum. A moonshiner hero,

trying to keep up the family tradition, fights both U.S. Treasury agents and outside racketeers.
- Related hike: Stone Mountain State Park

Winter People (1989) with Kelly McGillis. Much of this love story, set in the backwoods, was filmed in Barnardsville.
- Related hike: Douglas Falls

Appendix H: Heritage Hiking Challenge

This heritage hiking challenge consists of 30 hikes. Record the date of each hike that you complete. When you have finished them all, send this sheet (or a copy) to Milestone Press with your name, address, and email address. I will send you a certificate of achievement. Or, complete it online at www.hikertohiker.com.

#	Hike	Chapter	Date Hiked
3	Pilot Mountain State Park	1	
5	Jacob Fork Watershed	1	
8	Stone Mountain Loop	2	
10	Basin Creek	2	
16	Flat Top Tower	3	
18	Tanawha Trail	3	
19	Grandfather Trail	4	
24	Table Rock/Chimneys	4	
25	Linville Falls	4	
28	Roundtop Ridge	5	
29	Laurel Creek	5	
31	Pigeon River Gorge	5	
32	Hump Mountain	6	
33	Maple Camp Bald	6	
36	Catawba Falls	6	
37	Kitsuma Peak	6	
38	Florence Preserve	7	
39	Bat Cave	7	
40	Chimney Rock	7	
44	Cantrell Creek Lodge	8	
45	Pink Beds Loop	8	
48	Pilot Mountain	8	
49	Sam Knob/Black Balsam	8	
53	Boogerman Loop	9	
54	Caldwell Fork Loop	9	
56	Charlies Bunion/Kephart Prong	9	
59	Hazel Creek	9	
62	Whiteside Mountain	10	
65	Little Tennessee Greenway	10	
66	Cherohala Skyway	11	

Index

Index

Index

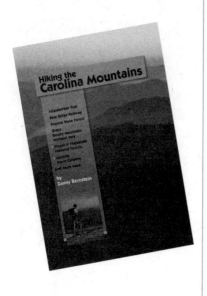

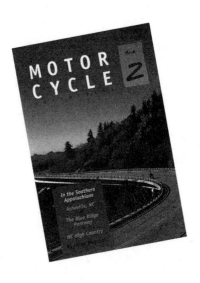

Motorcycle Adventure Series
by Hawk Hagebak

- 1–*Southern Appalachians*
  North GA, East TN,
  Western NC

- 2–*Southern Appalachians*
  Asheville, NC, Blue Ridge
  Parkway, NC Highcountry

- 3–*Central Appalachians*
  Virginia's Blue Ridge,
  Shenandoah Valley, West
  Virginia Highlands

Off the Beaten Track
Mountain Bike Series
by Jim Parham

- *Vol. 1: WNC–Smokies*
- *Vol. 2: WNC–Pisgah*
- *Vol. 3: N. Georgia*
- *Vol. 4: E. Tennessee*
- *Vol. 5: N. Virginia*

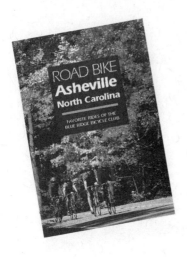

Road Bike Series

- *Road Bike Asheville, NC: Favorite Rides of the Blue Ridge Bicycle Club* by The Blue Ridge Bicycle Club

- *Road Bike the Smokies: 16 Great Rides in NC's Great Smoky Mountains* by Jim Parham

- *Road Bike North Georgia: 25 Great Rides in the Mountains and Valleys of North Georgia* by Jim Parham

Family Adventure

- *Family Hikes in Upstate South Carolina* by Scott Lynch

- *Natural Adventures in the Mountains of North Georgia* by Jim Parham & Mary Ellen Hammond

Playboating

- *Playboating the Nantahala River— An Entry Level Guide* by Kelly Fischer

Rockhounding

- *A Rockhounding Guide to North Carolina's Blue Ridge Mountains* by Michael Streeter

Can't find the Milestone Press book you want at a bookseller near you? Don't despair—you can order it directly from us. Call us at 828-488-6601 or shop online at www.milestonepress.com.